Jordan
Revealed

A comprehensive guide

by

Anthony King

BOXER
Publishing

Jordan Revealed, First edition 1996

Published by Boxer Publishing, London, UK
E-mail 100547.205@compuserve.com

Cover photographs:
Front: Wadi Rumm (Alan King)
Back: Petra Al-Deir (Tony Malac)

Maps and plans: Alan King

Layout, design and typesetting: Boxer Publishing

Printed by Redwood Books, Trowbridge, Wilts, UK

British Library Cataloguing in Publication Data.
A catalogue record for this book is available from
the British Library

ISBN 0-9525432-1-4

Behind every author is a someone whose encouragement and love makes the work possible. Ruth is such a one; and this book is dedicated to her.

ACKNOWLEDGEMENTS

No comprehensive guide book can be written without the help and advice of others. To all of them, especially Taari Basam, *'alf shukr,* thank you a thousand times!

Contents

Maps and Site Plans

INTRODUCTION

Although a small country that's about 90 per cent unihabitable desert, Jordan has within its borders, some of the most splendid and renowned sites of antiquity in the world. Yet until recently it has remained largely ignored by mainstream tourism, while some other destinations in the region have long been well travelled.

Now things have changed. More and more people are discovering that this proud Arab country is a place to visit, and so much so that it does not have to be "tacked on" to a visit to somewhere else.

No longer an out-of-the way location where a hardy and seasoned traveller would have to make his way over unpaved and unmarked desert tracks, Jordan is still far from being a destination that is ordinary. A tour of this history-steeped desert kingdom remains something of an adventure, where in the course of a few days you can take the same view Moses may have taken when he gazed across to the Promised Land, stand on the site where Salome enticed Herod with her seductive dance, visit one of the most outstanding of Roman provincial cities, journey deep into the desert to where the Caliphs "got away from it all", see the remains of Crusader castles, explore a fabulous rock city with an entrance passage like no other, descend to the lowest point on earth to float on the saltiest sea, and snorkel beneath—or relax besid —the crystal clear waters of the Red Sea.

Yet in spite of the growing popularity of this land, if you pick your season carefully you will not encounter the multitudes of visitors found at famous sites in the more well-trodden of tourist venues. And to make it even more attractive, Jordan is a country of moderate prices, and it will not cost you a King's Ransom to travel the King's Highway!

To all this there is the added pleasure of traditional Arab hospitality, which I have always found especially enhanced in Jordan.

This book is for the serious visitor, those who want to make the most of their stay in the country, not only seeing the sites, but delving deep into it's history and culture. Too often Jordan is thought of as only Petra, and although that wonderful and unique site of antiquity is indeed the jewel in the crown of Jordanian tourism, the Jordan experience is far more than that. For it was not only west of the river that events set out in the Bible were enacted; many, as readers of this guide will discover, took place in the area of the modern day Kingdom.

Never a tense land to visit, the peace accord with Israel has made the atmosphere even more relaxed, and opened the door to many further tourist possibilities.

For the convenience of the reader **"Jordan Revealed"** is divided into four parts as follows: Part I deals with the country, its history, geography and culture. Part II is a detailed guide to Jordan's sites, with itinerary recommendations. Part III provides all the practical information you will need to organise your trip and make it an experience to remember. At the end of the book, Part IV comprises an Arabic language guide and vocabulary, a glossary of terms used, bibliography of suggested reading and an index of biblical references as well as a comprehensive touring index.

If your mind has not already been made up to visit this unique country, I hope my book will be the catalyst that does!

Anthony King
January 1996

PART I
BACKGROUND

1. HISTORY

- Early History
- Modern History

2. GEOGRAPHY

- The Land
- Climate
- Flora and Fauna
- The Jordanian People
- Religion

3. JORDAN TODAY

- Government
- Economy
- Education
- Everyday Life
- Language

Jordan - its position in the Middle East

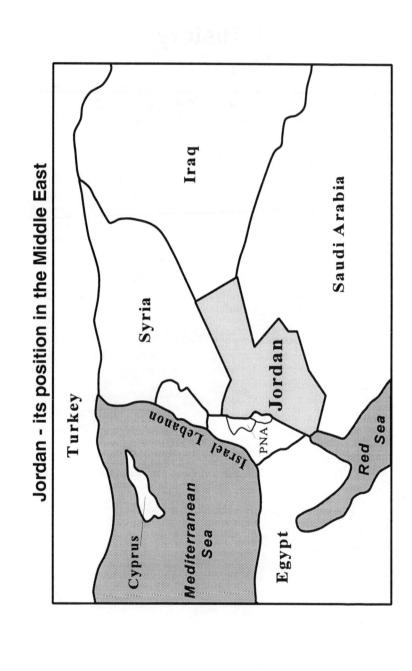

1. History

INTRODUCTION

This chapter on Jordan's history has been divided into two parts. The first is a chronological listing in abridged form of the major happenings from earliest times to the beginning of the twentieth century. The second part is a more detailed examination of the making of the modern kingdom. (The early history as it applies to the individual sites visited is covered in depth in the touring section of this book.)

Jordan is perhaps one of the most artificially created countries in the world, a product of British (and French) scheming during and after the First World War.

During the period when the whole area was under Ottoman rule, the countries which today comprise Syria, Lebanon and Jordan were all "Syria". Jordan itself was part of the *vilayet*, or administrative district, of Damascus. The subsequent carve-up was effected on the basis of political expediency only, as you can read later on in this chapter. Consequently, the history of Jordan is bound up almost entirely with the history of the region.

CHRONOLOGICAL OUTLINE OF JORDANIAN HISTORY TO THE OUTBREAK OF THE 1914 WAR

Palaeolithic era

Inhabitants lived largely as hunters and gatherers of wild grains etc. Flint tools and weapons from this era have been found.

9000 to 4500 BC

First villages emerge as well as the beginnings of agriculture. Settlements at Jericho (Tell al-Sultan) and Beidha (Seyl 'Aqlat) near Petra. Pottery unknown.

4500 to 3000 BC

Well-constructed villages with houses of mud bricks. At Telailat al-Ghassul, in the Jordan Valley, dwellings have painted plaster walls. Newcomers bring the art of making primitive pottery.

3000 to 2100 BC

Migrations from Arabia bring different peoples into the region. The more fertile areas become fairly well populated. Bab al-Dhra' on the Lisan (tongue) of the Dead Sea is a major settlement with defensive walls and Jericho, a flourishing city.

2100 to 1700 BC

Abraham begins his journey to Canaan? (2000).
Migration of Semitic nomadic tribes into TransJordan.
Jericho destroyed by these tribes penetrating west of the river Jordan (2000). Jericho rebuilt and surrounded by fortifications, which included a glacis of beaten earth and a 6 metre high stone wall (1700).
The Hyksos, a highly developed people from the north, invade the region and become rulers of Egypt. Area of Palestine and Jordan part of the Hyksos Empire.

1600-1500

The Hyksos driven out by Pharaoh Thutmose I, first pharaoh of the 18th dynasty (c1500).
Further migrations from the Syrian-Arabian desert of peoples known later as Edomites, in the south; Moabites, who settled between Wadi al-Mujib, the Arnon of the Bible, and the Dead Sea, and the Ammonites, who lived between Wadi al-Zarka, the Jabbok of the Bible, and the Dead Sea. (1800-1500)

1300-1000

Exodus of the Israelites from Egypt (c1250).
Israelites cross Jordan and settle in Canaan, as well as parts of the east bank (c1200-1150).
Beginning of the wars between Israel and peoples of TransJordan.
David, King of Israel (1000); subdues Moab and Edom, slaughtering much of the population. Later he takes Rabbath Ammon.

950-935

David dead, and Solomon becomes king of Israel. Port built on Red Sea, Ezion Geber. Israel controls most of TransJordan.

930-800

Death of Solomon (c930), and the nations on the east bank manage to partly free themselves.
King Mesha of Moab battles Israel and Judah, Mesha Stone (c850).
Edomites revolt against Jehoram, king of Judah.
Amaziah captures "Sela" and throws 10,000 Edomites to their death (800).

800-600

Rise of Assyrians in the east. Adad Ninari temporarily overruns TransJordan as far as Edom which is mentioned in Assyrian writings of the time (800).

Tiglath Pilesner III captures all of Jordan and the rulers become Assyrian vassals (745). Israel (northern kingdom) demolished by Sargon II, and inhabitants dispersed (c720).
Nineveh, Assyrian capital falls to the neo-Babylonians (612).

600-400
With the demise of the Assyrian empire the nations of Trans-Jordan try to assert themselves.
Nebuchadnezzar invades the area, and the Jews are taken to Babylon in captivity (590).
Ammon and Judah under Babylonian appointed governors.
Tribes of Nabaitu (Nabateans) from Arabia begin to move into Edom, and Edomites forced into Palestine (from c560).
Achaemenid Persians capture Babylon, end of the neo-Babylonian Empire (549).
TransJordan and Judah under Persian rule with appointed governors.
Cyrus, king of the Persians, allows Jews to return to Jerusalem (c500).
Tobias, first of a line that controlled Ammon for some centuries, governor of Ammon, opposes the rebuilding of the walls and Temple at Jerusalem.
Most of Middle East under Achaemenid Persians.

350-260
Alexander defeats Persians at Issus (333) and Mid-East comes under Greek control. Hellenisation begins.
Alexander dies (323).
Nabateans well established in the south with Petra their capital.
Seleucids rule Syria, northern Jordan, and Palestine.
Ptolemies control Egypt and southern Jordan including Ammon which is rebuilt and renamed Philadelphia (c260).

260-170
Philadelphia captured by Seleucid ruler Antiochus III (218).
Increase in Nabatean power.
Seleucid Antiochus IV makes edicts against Jews which cause a rebellion led by Judas Maccabeus, who defeated Seleucid armies sent against him (167-165).
Jewish kingdom re-established with Judas Maccabeus (House of the Hasmoneans) as ruler.
Death of Antiochus IV (164).
Judas attacks Ammon, and defeats them.

165-65 BC
Syrian army defeats the Hasmoneans in northern Jordan (163) but the country remains independent.
Constant conflict between Jews, Seleucids and the Nabateans.

Hasmonean Alexander Yannai controls Jordan with the exception of the Nabatean lands.

Nabatean king, Aretas III "Philhellene" extends his kingdom as far as Damascus (c85 BC).

64 BC-AD 70

Palestine and Jordan annexed for Rome by Pompey (64 BC).

Control over the Greek cities east of the Jordan returned to their inhabitants who were given a measure of autonomy under Roman rule. Decapolis league of 10 cities comes into being.

Herod the Great becomes king of Judea, which included a part of TransJordan (40 BC).

Herod pushes Nabateans from northern Jordan.

Death of Herod (4 BC).

District of Peraea, which stretched from Wadi Mujib in the south to Zarka in the north, and included Pella, but not Amman.

Herod's successor, Herod Antipater, marries daughter of the Nabatean king, Aretas IV.

Events at Machaerus in which Herod has John the Baptist beheaded (c AD 36).

Jews in Judea revolt against Roman rule, and Nabateans send an army to help the Romans quell it.

Romans destroy Jerusalem and expel the Jews (AD 70).

AD 98-324

Trajan Roman Emperor (98).

Nabatean lands annexed by Trajan, and *Provincia Arabia* created to include most of Jordan (106).

Road through Jordan, *Via Nova Traiana*, constructed.

Rise of Palmyra in the Syrian desert affects trade passing through Petra (c130).

Hadrian visits Jerash (130).

Zenobia becomes Queen and ruler of Palmyra (267) and seizes, amongst other places, most of Jordan (270).

Aurelian puts down the Palmyrenes and Jordan returns to Roman control (272-3).

Edict of Milan makes Christianity lawful in Roman Empire (313).

Christianity made the religion of the Empire (324).

395-614

Roman Empire splits and Byzantine Period begins (395).

Many churches built all over Jordan as Christianity flourishes.

Large parts of Jordan ruled by the Ghassanids, an Arab Christian sect who ruled under Byzantine suzerainty.

Byzantium and Sasanid Persians make agreement for a 'hundred year peace' (422).

Sasanid ruler, Chosroes II attacks Jordan, Syria and Palestine causing great destruction (611-614).

622-750

Muhammad flees Mecca for Medina, *the Hijra*, (622).
Byzantines under Heraclius launch offensive against Sasanians, reaching their capital, Ctesipphon (625-628).
First encounter between Muslims and Byzantines near Mu'ta, south of Kerak (629).
Death of Muhammad (632).
Battle of the Yarmouk, on the present Syrian-Jordanian border where the Muslims defeat the Byzantines (636). Muslims take Damascus soon after, and Islamic rule over entire area begins.
Muawiya, governor of Syria and Jordan (640).
Muawiya, first Omayyad Caliph. Damascus capital of Muslim world (661).
Omayyad rule in Jordan. Building of the Desert Palaces.
Jordan on the main *haj* route from Damascus.
Abbasids plot against Omayyads in the village of Humaimah in southern Jordan.
Overthrow of the Omayyad dynasty by the Abbasids (750).

750-1000

Abbasids transfer the Muslim capital to Baghdad, and Jordan enters a period of semi-obscurity as the country no longer lies on any route of importance.
Fatimids in control of Egypt and rest of the region (969).

1095-1500

Pope Urban calls for a crusade to liberate the Holyland from the Muslims (1095).
Crusaders land in Syria and capture Antioch after a long siege (1098).
Fall of Jerusalem to the Crusaders (1099).
Baldwin I creates Crusader Kingdom of Jerusalem.
Crusaders build the castles of Mont Real at Shobak (1115) and La Pierre du Desert at Kerak (1136).
Salah al-Din defeats combined Crusader armies at Hittin (1187) and takes Jerusalem.
Ayyubid rule.
Death of Salah al-Din and fragmentation of his empire (post 1193).
Mongols invade Syria.
Battle of Ain Jalud in which the Mongols are defeated by the Mamelukes from Egypt (1260).
Mamelukes control Syria (of which Jordan was a part).
Constantinople taken by Ottoman Turks (1453).

1510-1914

Ottomans capture Syria and extend their rule over the entire Middle East.
Jordan part of the *vilayet* (administrative district) of Damascus.

9

Under Ottoman rule Jordan stagnates and its primary significance is that it is on the *haj* route to Mecca.
Muhammad Ali usurps power in Egypt (1805). Ibrahim Pasha, his son, forces Ottomans to retreat from Syria (1831).
Ulrich Seetzen discovers ruins of Gerasa (1806).
Travels of J.L. Burckhardt and rediscovery of Petra (1812).
European powers force Muhammad Pasha's withdrawal (1841).
Opening of Suez Canal (1869).
Beginning of nationalist movement in Damascus (1890-).
Britain occupies Egypt (1882).
Abdul Hamid II, Ottoman Sultan (1876-1909).
Completion of the Hejaz railway connecting Damascus with Medina (1908).
Seizure of power by "Young Turk" nationalists encourages further nationalist sentiment in Arab lands.
Revolt by peasants in Shawbak (1905).
Serious uprising in al-Karak (1910).
Ottomans side with Germany on outbreak of World War (1914).

THE MAKING OF THE HASHEMITE KINGDOM OF JORDAN

THE BACKGROUND

Modern Jordan is a consolation prize! Given because those who promised something more substantial were not willing to stand by that promise. It is a product of British and French imperial double dealing during and after the First World War which saw the demise of the Ottoman Empire.

nineteenth century turmoil

The 19th century had been a period of turmoil in the Ottoman Empire. Muhammad Ali, the Sultan's ruler of Egypt had usurped power in that land, and had extended his rule so far that in 1832 he occupied all the land northwards into Syria. It was only with the help of Britain and France that he was ejected and the province returned to Ottoman rule.

sick man of Europe

So weak was the empire that the European powers were able to force on the Sultan all manner of capitulations, especially economic. It was the Russians who then coined the well-known phrase "the sick man of Europe" in reference to the crumbling empire.

In 1876 Abdul Hamid came to the throne as sultan. In an attempt to shore up his ailing domain and to pacify an increasingly restless population, he introduced a new constitution that allowed the election

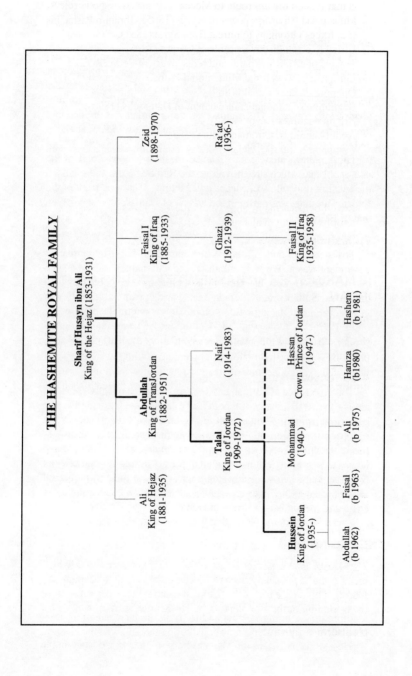

THE HASHEMITE ROYAL FAMILY

Sharif Husayn ibn Ali
King of the Hejaz (1853-1931)

Zeid
(1898-1970)

Ra'ad
(1936-)

Faisal I
King of Iraq
(1885-1933)

Ghazi
(1912-1939)

Faisal II
King of Iraq
(1935-1958)

Ali
King of Hejaz
(1881-1935)

Abdullah
King of TransJordan
(1882-1951)

Naif
(1914-1983)

Talal
King of Jordan
(1909-1972)

Hassan
Crown Prince of Jordan
(1947-)

Mohammad
(1940-)

Hussein
King of Jordan
(1935-)

Abdullah
(b 1962)

Faisal
(b 1963)

Ali
(b 1975)

Hamza
(b1980)

Hashem
(b 1981)

of the first Ottoman parliament. However this did not last long and two years later it was suspended, allowing the usual despotic rule to return.

Britain occupies Egypt

In 1882 Britain occupied Egypt, and it became a protectorate, although still nominally part of the Ottoman state. The Ottoman Empire was divided into provinces, or *vilayets*; both sides of the Jordan were part of the *vilayet* of Damascus. A *vilayet* was sub-divided into *sanjaks*. The region east of the Jordan was divided into three of these provinces: the *sanjak* of Ajlun, the *sanjak* of al-Balqa and the *sanjak* of al-Karak.

The southern area, from Maan to the Red Sea was part of the *vilayet* of Hejaz which stretched along the Red Sea coast and included the Muslim holy cities of Mecca and Medina. The west bank of the Jordan, Palestine, was partly in the *vilayet* of Damascus, and partly in that of Beirut.

Turkish nationalists

Towards the end of the 19th century, a Turkish nationalist movement was active in Istanbul. These nationalists wanted a state that was more Turkish than pan-Muslim, more modern politically than the current Sultan-ruled Ottoman one. Turkish national identity was to be achieved at the expense of other nations within the empire.

In 1908 this movement, the Committee of Union and Progress (CUP), also called the Young Turks, aided by the Turkish military, overthrew Sultan Abdul Hamid.

Arab renaissance

This emergence of Turkish nationalism created a negative reaction among the Arabs, many of whom had tolerated the Ottoman Empire because it aspired to be the empire of Islam. For over 50 years there had been something of a renaissance among intellectual Arabs. In particular there had been a revival and revitalization of the Arabic language, something that had declined sharply during the centuries of Ottoman domination. Increasingly conscious of their own cultural identity, history and national rights, secret groups had sprung up in Syria and Mesopotamia (Iraq) and the Hejaz.

And it is here in the Hejaz that the story of modern Jordan begins.

THE BEGINNING

The Hejaz is the western part of the Arabian peninsular which includes the Muslim holy cities of Mecca and Medina. Its capital was Jeddah. This area, a part of the Ottoman Empire, had been ruled since the beginning of the 19th century by Hashemite Sharifians.

Hashemite dynasty

Husayn (or Hussein) ibn 'Ali was born in 1853 in Constantinople

(Istanbul), a scion of the Hashemite dynasty and a nephew of the then Sharif of Mecca. The sharif was the religious ruler of the most holy place in Islam, and although there was a sultan appointed governor *(vali),* in practice it was the sharif who held the power.

In 1891, Husayn was ordered by Sultan Abdul Hamid II to come to Istanbul where he was made a member of the council that advised on various matters. During his stay in the Ottoman capital his four sons, Ali, Abdullah, Feisal and Zeid were given a modern education, something that would have been impossible in the deserts of Arabia.

the capable son

Of his four sons, Abdullah showed himself to be the most capable, entering the Turkish parliament as the representative for the Hejaz. His education and political acumen had become indispensable to his father, and he acted as his political advisor.

Sharif Husayn

When in 1908 the CUP overthrew Abdul Hamid, Husayn was allowed to return to Jeddah, having been confirmed as the Sharif and Emir. Husayn found that during his absence from Mecca the Turkish *vali* had taken over almost complete control, leaving the office of Sharif no more than ceremonial. Husayn quickly regained the power traditionally held by a sharif.

THE FIRST WORLD WAR

When the Great War erupted in 1914, the Ottomans sided with Germany. Since seizing power in 1908, the CUP government had slipped into a rather ruthless military dictatorship, with all power concentrated in the hands of three men; Enver, Taalat and Jemal. Husayn by that time was not only ruler of the Hejaz, but as the senior member of the Hashemite dynasty, was looked upon by many as a focus for Arab aspirations.

British want uprising

The British, from their bases in Egypt, realised that an Arab uprising would greatly facilitate the removal of Turkey from the war. A British officer (and Arabist), T.E. Lawrence (Lawrence of Arabia), recommended that contacts be made with Husayn to ascertain whether the Arabs would participate in the fight against the Ottomans. After initial communications, the British minister in Egypt, Sir Henry McMahon, participated in an exchange of letters (the McMahon Correspondence). The most important letter was dated 24th October 1915 and confirmed that, subject to certain reservations, the Arabs would get independence in their lands liberated from the Turks.

Lawrence's vain hopes for the Arab cause

Further negotiations were held by Abdullah in Cairo, and T.E. Lawrence was designated the British officer to co-ordinate their fight.

But, as he wrote at the end of the war, *"It was an Arab war waged and led by Arabs for an Arab aim in Arabia."* *(Seven Pillars of Wisdom, 1926.)* The romantic Arabist firmly believed that the ousting of the Ottomans would lead to true Arab independence: *"I meant to make a new nation, to restore a lost influence, to give twenty millions of (Arab) Semites the foundations on which to build..."* *(Seven Pillars of Wisdom, 1926.)*

King of the Arabs
On 29th October 1916, in the Great Mosque of Mecca, Husayn was proclaimed *Al-Malak al-Bilad al-Arabiyah*, King of the Arab Countries, and the Arab revolt against the Ottoman Empire began.

treachery of Sykes-Picot Treaty
In the same year, 1916, unknown to the Arabs and in complete variance with the McMahon letter, other events were taking place. A treaty was being drawn up between the British and French on how the area would be carved up on the conclusion of the war. Georges Picot for France, and Sir Mark Sykes for Britain outlined a memorandum which became known as the Sykes-Picot Agreement. Under this, the area that comprised Syria, Palestine and Mesopotamia was to be divided up: the British and French would control the coastal districts; in the inland region they would set up either a confederation or a single Arab state, with French and British spheres of influence, i.e. control.

Balfour Declaration
An additional blow to Arab aspirations came in late 1917 when the British foreign secretary, Arthur James Balfour, issued his famous declaration indicating that the "British Government viewed with favour the establishment of a Jewish national home in Palestine..." (Palestine meaning both sides of the river Jordan).

Ottoman rule ends
Meanwhile the Arab army had taken Aqaba in July 1917, and fighting their way north for the next 15 months entered Damascus, their greatest prize, on 1st October 1918 with Feisal, Husayn's third son, at the head of the Arab army; Ottoman rule that had endured for four centuries was finally over.

POST-WAR SETTLEMENT

Feisal, King of Syria
Feisal, now in control of Syria, began to set up an Arab administration. Syria was divided into eight areas called *liwas*. One covered all of central Jordan while the north became part of the *liwa* of Hauran, and the south the *liwa* of al-Karak. In March 1920 a Syrian National Congress meeting in Damascus proclaimed an independent Kingdom of Syria with Feisal as king. Simultaneously, a group of Iraqi delegates elected Abdullah King of Iraq.

Mandate imposed

The British and French would have nothing of these unilateral actions, wanting these territories for themselves. As Winston Churchill said, the British Government could not be indifferent to territorial gains; the nation looked for some compensation for its terrible losses.

A month later at an Allied conference in San Remo it was decided to put the entire region under a mandate. The northern part of Syria (i.e. Syria, Lebanon and parts of southern Turkey) was to go to the French; the southern part (Jordan and Palestine) was to be administered by the British, who also received the mandate for Iraq. In July 1920 French forces forcibly entered Damascus and Feisal was exiled.

British divide TransJordan

Meanwhile in the south, the British were busy establishing their rule over Palestine and TransJordan. They wanted to separate Palestine proper from the areas east of the Jordan. To achieve this, three distinct areas came into being, each having its own adminis-tration. In the north was the Government of Ajlun, centred on Irbid; the central area was under the Government of Salt, and centred on al-Salt, whilst the southern sector up to the border with Hejaz, north of Maan, acquired the rather strange title of the Arab Government of Moab, with al-Karak as its headquarters.

Major Kirkbride and the mukhtars of Moab

The administrations in Ajlun and Salt were essentially the same as that installed by Syria under Feisal, whereas Moab's was a mixture of village *mukhtars*, headmen led by a young British officer, Major Alec Kirkbride, who was yet to play a more important role in Jordanian affairs. (For a fascinating account of his experiences during this time see his book, *A Crackle of Thorns*, listed in the bibliography at the end of this book.)

Abdullah returns to Hejaz...

After the war, and with the collapse of the British undertaking to Husayn who was recognised only as King of the Hejaz, Abdullah returned to Jeddah where he became one of his father's advisors.

...and raises another army

Unable to stay in the Hejaz he resolved to raise another Arab army and liberate Syria once again. On November 21st 1920 he arrived, together with a force of 2000 Bedouin at Maan, then part of the Kingdom of the Hejaz. He announced that it was his intention to expel the French from Syria, and have himself installed as ruler. Abdullah was at this time 38 years old and already had a great deal of political and military experience. As the son of the prestigious Sharif, he commanded much loyalty from the Bedouin tribes all around.

sights on Damascus

In February Abdullah left Maan and travelled, with his army, to Amman — then no more than a large village. In the meantime Abdullah made it clear what his purpose was, to occupy all of Trans-Jordan as a prelude for the re-taking of Damascus.

The French were agitated. They were already experiencing difficulties in establishing their authority over Syria, and the last thing they wanted was more trouble from a Hashemite Emir.

Abdullah meets Churchill

The British, in order to restore credibility in Arab eyes, wanted to undo

King Abdullah

some of the wrongs they had caused the Hashemites and saw in Abdullah a way to effect this. He was invited to meet Winston Churchill, at that time British Colonial Secretary, in Jerusalem.

British proposition

There he was told that he could become the Emir of TransJordan on condition that he gave up his quest to invade Syria. He was also told that he must renounce his claim to the Iraqi throne in favour of Feisal, who likewise had to be placated. Abdullah's counter-demand for the unification of Palestine and TransJordan was rebuffed on the grounds that the mandatory obligations Britain had towards Palestine would not make that possible (i.e. the obligation to establish a Jewish national home).

offer he couldn't refuse

However, Abdullah was informed that TransJordan would be made into a separate mandate and the provisions of the mandate as regards the Jews would not apply there. The Emirate of TransJordan would become a distinct state, although until the British considered it ready for full independence it would be supervised by the British Government in the person of the high commissioner in Jerusalem. Abdullah, who already considered himself ruler of TransJordan, had no choice but to agree.

consolation prize

And so the Hashemites, who had raised the banner and joined the Allied war against the Ottomans in order to gain a unified Arab kingdom of Greater Syria (Syria, Jordan and Palestine), had lost the main components, Syria and Palestine. As a consolation prize they were given the supervised rule of a territory that the British termed as "unallocated" and comprised of over 80 per cent desert!

16

THE HASHEMITES

The Hashemite rulers of Jordan trace their ancestry back to the Prophet Muhammad. Muhammad belonged to the Hashem clan of the al-Quraysh tribe, but the term Hashemite is reserved for those who are descended from the Prophet through his daughter, Fatima, and his cousin 'Ali who was also Fatima's husband. They had two sons, Hassan and Hussein. The house of the Hashemites trace their lineage through Hassan.

'Ali was the last Caliph to be directly descended from the Prophet. The Abbasids, whose dynastic caliphate lasted from 750 to 968, claimed descent from the Prophet's uncle, Abbas.

Because they are from the Prophet's line, the Hashemites are termed *Sharifian,* that is of noble descent, and they carry the title *Sharif* or nobleman. Although it was not always a *Sharifian* who ruled the Hejaz, the position developed the title Sharif.

The present Sharifian Hashemites can be traced back to the mid 17th century and the house of Dawi Aoun. Sharif Aoun was the first in this line and was the great grandfather of Sharif Husayn. Although directly descended from the 4th Calpih 'Ali (who is especially revered by Shi'ite Muslims), the Hashemites are Sunni Muslims.

European creations

Many states in the Middle East are European creations, but none more so than Jordan. The fledgling state had no natural capital; indeed no cities! The final frontiers were yet to be agreed. There was no 'Jordanian' people as such, and the ruler had been born in the Hejaz and brought up in Constantinople. Even the name was not clear-cut, TransJordan being translated *Sharqi al-Urdan* or East of the Jordan in Arabic. The area was not strategic, the population very small and there were no viable resources.

demanding task for Abdullah

The Hashemite Kingdom of Jordan, although not yet called thus, created by the British, would take Abdullah another two years to weld into something that could be called a state. The regional governments had disintegrated and the different Bedouin tribal chiefs had reverted to their historical feuding. The British expected – indeed required – Abdullah to bring the territory under the control of a central authority, a task they knew would be very difficult to accomplish themselves.

first Government

In April 1921 *al-Hay'a al-Markaziyah*, or the Central Authority, was organised in Amman, which was selected as the capital over al-Salt which had been the Ottoman administrative centre. None of the appointed officials were natives of TransJordan, but hailed from Syria, Lebanon, Iraq and Palestine. Most of these officials were pan-Arab nationalists, members of the Istiqlal party.

formation of the Arab Legion

Abdullah then set about the formation of a security force which could be used to restore law and order should other means of persuasion fail. Unwilling to give it a definite TransJordanian title he called it *al-Jaysh al-'Arabi*, the Arab Army or Arab Legion.

British resident

The high commissioner in Jerusalem, aware of Abdullah's ambitions, which remained pan-Arab, appointed a 'Resident' whose task was to make sure the Emir did not stray from policies that were approved by the mandatory power.

Besides the problems of bringing local leaders under the control of the central authority, Abdullah had to look to both the security of his Emirate and his relationship with the British — who were after all the real masters of the territory.

Abdullah's charm

In spite of local rebellions like that of the Kura region in 1921, when the local chieftain refused to acknowledge the right of the government to exact taxes, Abdullah, by his charm, diplomacy and understanding of Arab tribal traditions, was able to bestow a semblance of order on TransJordan.

warring Wahabis

Border security in the south was a different problem. The Wahabis from Najd were repeatedly crossing into the south of the country, causing a grave menace to Abdullah's control there. His Arab Legion was unable to repel these murderous incursions which continued until the British were able to intervene.

Emirate of TransJordan

In 1923 Britain officially pronounced TransJordan to be an emirate, with Abdullah as its Emir. However the provisions of the mandate were still to apply, with the high commissioner in Jerusalem being the representative of the mandatory power.

British foot the bill

Talks were held to finalise the frontiers between Syria in the north and Ibn Saud's kingdom in the south. The British agreed to provide £150,000 sterling a year as a subsidy to the Emir's government. The Arab Legion was to be placed under the command of a British officer,

Captain Frederick Peake.

In 1925, just before the fall of the Hejaz to the Saudis, the districts of Aqaba and Maan were ceded to Abdullah by his brother Ali, the last Hashemite king of that area.

a treaty of sorts

In February 1928 a treaty was negotiated in Jerusalem which many thought might result in the Emirate's independence. The treaty fell far short of this; Britain was to retain full control over all the important facets of government, foreign affairs, finances and the army among them. Independence was not on the agenda.

The treaty also provided for a constitution, which was promulgated in April the same year. Under it there would be a representative assembly with largely advisory powers. Of the 21 members only 14 were to be elected; the others, including the prime minister, would be appointments. By 1934 an amendment had been made to the treaty giving the Emirate the right to appoint consular officials in other Arab countries.

Glubb takes over and World War begins

Frederick Peake remained in command of the Arab Legion until 1939, when John Bagot Glubb, a British officer serving in Iraq was called to take over. The outbreak of war in 1939 prevented any further steps towards independence. In 1943 the Emirate participated in talks that eventually led to the formation of the Arab League.

Abdullah, King

In 1946 talks were held in London which resulted in a new treaty. In May 1946 Abdullah was proclaimed King of the Hashemite Kingdom of TransJordan, an independent nation. The country, however, still depended on Britain for its financial support.

Abdullah had never given up his dream of a 'Greater Syria' under Hashemite rule. For him the union of Syria, TransJordan and Palestine was the ultimate aim. But now there was opposition from within the Arabs. Syrians were mainly republican, and the Jews were obviously totally opposed.

PARTITION AND AFTER

Palestine partitioned

In November 1947, the United Nations voted to partition Palestine between Arab Palestinians and Jews. This made conflict between the Jews and the surrounding Arab states inevitable, although Abdullah, unlike other Arab leaders, was aware of the Jewish military capability and was not eager to put it to the test.

Israel statehood proclaimed and war ensues

On May 15th 1948, the final withdrawal of the British from Palestine took place and the State of Israel came into being. Abdullah sent Glubb and the Arab Legion across the Jordan. At the same time Egyptian, Iraqi and Syrian forces advanced into different parts of Palestine.

lone success of Arab Legion

Only the Arab Legion acquitted itself well in this conflict, and by the time the UN ordered a cease fire on October 23rd they had secured the Old City of Jerusalem and the area we now call the West Bank. Egypt, whose invasion had been soundly thwarted, pulled back to Gaza where there was a large Palestinian population made even greater by the influx of refugees. Unwilling to incorporate this area into Egypt proper, a quasi govenment was set up there.

"King of Palestine"

In December, in response to this action, Abdullah had himself declared King of all Palestine. By February 1949, after extensive talks on the island of Rhodes, a Jordanian-Israeli armistice was signed. The cease fire lines became armistice lines, and these held until 1967.

West Bank annexed

In April 1949, the areas of Palestine held by the Arab Legion were annexed and the Kingdom's name changed to The Hashemite Kingdom of Jordan. Abdullah was the only Arab leader who tried to come to an arrangement with the Zionists – a fact that was to cost him his life.

success of assassin's bullet

On Friday, 21st July 1951, while entering Jerusalem's Al-Aksa Mosque in the *Haram al-Sharif* (noble enclosure or Temple Mount as Jews and Christians refer to it), Abdullah was shot and killed by a dis-gruntled Palestinian assassin. His grandson, Hussein, was by his side.

Talal, the unstable king

In September, his son Talal, who suffered from a mental illness, was proclaimed King. In 1952 a new constitution, which gave more powers to the Legislative Council, was promulgated. Jordan also joined the Arab Collective Security Pact, which Abdullah had declined to do.

Hussein, the young king

However, Talal's condition deteriorated, and it became clear that he would be unable to cope with the stress thrust upon him. After being examined by a panel of doctors he was prevailed upon to abdicate. On 12th August 1952, while on holiday in Switzerland, Talal's eldest son, Hussein, learned that he had been proclaimed king; he was just short of his 17th birthday, and then a student at Harrow public school near London.

turbulence and change

Hussein came to the throne at a time of great change, not only in

THE END OF SHARIF HUSAYN

By way of a postscript, the final part of the story of Husayn must be told. By 1919 Abdul al-Aziz al-Saud and the Wahabis had cemented their hold on the Najd and other parts of central Arabia. In 1920 he occupied part of Asir, the area south of the Hejaz, and Husayn's kingdom was under constant pressure.

Husayn, who in 1916 had proclaimed himself King of the Arabs, still aspired to that position even though events had irrevocably changed the situation. He was now only recognised as the King of Hejaz, and although the holy cities of Islam were in his realm, it was a much diminished title from the one he once planned for himself.

In March 1924 the new republican Turkish government abolished the office of Caliph, a post held for centuries by the Ottoman sultan. Seeing himself as the only person who could hold that office, Husayn had himself proclaimed Caliph in Jedda that month. This action angered most of the Muslim world and infuriated the Wahabis who saw themselves as the strict guardians of the faith. Abdul Aziz, intent on taking the holy cities, intensified pressure on Hejaz, forcing Husayn to abdicate in favour of his eldest son, Ali. He retired to Aqaba, then part of the Hejaz, but the British would not allow him to remain in the area, and the next 6 years were spent in exile on Cyprus. In 1930 he went to Amman where he died a year later. He is buried on the *Haram al-Sharif*, in Jerusalem

After his departure Ali could do nothing to stem the Saudis. In 1925 he was induced by Abdullah to cede Aqaba and Maan to Trans-Jordan. In early 1926 the Hejaz passed into Saudi hands. Ali retired to Baghdad where his brother was king. He died there in 1935.

Jordan, but throughout the Arab world. The loss of Palestine was a severe setback, as was the huge influx of refugees who had fled their homes in Israel. Radical regimes had taken over the governments of both Syria and Egypt, where anti-western sentiment was growing. In contrast, Jordan remained firmly pro-western, and declined any major contact with the Communist countries.

The next few years were ones of instability in the government. In the face of many problems, prime ministers came and went. In December 1955 there were no fewer than three changes of leadership as the question of Jordan's membership of the Baghdad Pact was fought over.

Glubb Pasha sacked

In March 1956 in an attempt to show the Arab world that Jordan was no longer dominated by Britain, Hussein announced that Glubb — or Glubb Pasha as he had come to be known — was dismissed, as were all other British officers serving in the Jordanian Armed Forces. This started a process of Arabising the Forces.

leftist government

In October 1956 elections were held against a background of increased tension in the Middle East following the nationalisation of the Suez Canal by Nasser and the Anglo-French-Israeli collusion that ensued. A pro-Nasserist government under Suleiman Nabulsi came to power which, besides removing the last British troops from Jordanian soil, attempted to open diplomatic relations with the USSR and China, something that Hussein opposed. Fearful that this marked the beginning of a Nasserite plot against him, Hussein dismissed Nabulsi, appointing in his place Ibrahim Hashim, a traditionalist. Unrest throughout the country erupted, which was dealt with very firmly by the Army. Martial law was proclaimed, curfews established and all political parties were banned.

Arabs "unite"

In 1958 Egypt and Syria formed the UAR, the United Arab Republic. Shortly after, King Feisal of Iraq, Hussein's cousin, announced the merger of the Kingdoms of Iraq and Jordan. Both unions were shortlived.

bloody coup in Iraq

In July that year, a military coup in Iraq resulted in the death of Feisal and most of his family. Hussein was shocked, but by the end of the month the new regime had obtained legitimacy. Concerned for his own throne, which he believed was in imminent danger, Hussein appealed to the British and Americans for help. Within hours British paratroops from Cyprus were in Amman.

Palestinian contribution

The Palestinians were now a substantial part of Jordan's population. By and large they were more skilled than their counterparts from the east bank, and included engineers, doctors, chemists, technicians and particularly teachers. They were an essential part of Jordan's economy. While some had settled into their new homeland, the majority lived either in refugee camps or on the west bank, often within sight of their dispossessed villages and towns. More radical than the population of the east bank, they had been kept in a state of limbo by the Arab States, who constantly promised that one day they would return to their homeland.

In January 1960, Hussein criticised Egypt and Syria, the UAR, who had never recognised Jordan's annexation of the west bank, for their strategy towards Palestinians. The following month Jordanian citizenship was offered to all Palestinians who wished to apply. This action was condemned by the UAR, with whom diplomatic relations had recently been restored.

Prime Minister assassinated

In August 1960 the Prime Minister, Hazza Majali, and other government officials were blown up by a bomb. The Jordanians suspected that this incident had been orchestrated in the UAR.

formation of the PLO

In September 1963 the Arab League approved the establishment of a 'Palestinian entity'. Jordan was strongly opposed to this as it threatened her annexation of the West Bank, which no Arab country had recognised. (In fact only Britain and Pakistan had done this.)

In May 1964 a congress of all the Palestinian groups took place in East Jerusalem. The result was the formation of the Palestine Liberation Organisation, or PLO. The leading group was the Harakat al-Tahrir al-Watani al-Falastin, more usually known as Fatah (an acronym of the first letters of each word, reversed). It had been founded in 1957 by a young engineering graduate of Cairo University by the name of Yasir Afafat. Ahmad Shukairy became the first head of the PLO, but by 1969 Arafat had assumed the position.

prelude to the June 1967 war

Guerrilla raids into Israel increased during 1966, and Jordan was fearful of a stinging Israeli reprisal. The Fatah had been using the west bank as its base for these attacks, though others were launched from Syria. In a bid to stem the raids, Hussein closed the PLO office and Ahmad Shukairy was deported. Further Syrian action in shelling Israeli settlements below the Golan Heights exacerbated the situation. Hostilities seemed inevitable.

On 13th November 1966 the Israelis launched an attack on the small village of Samu, 16 kilometres south of Hebron and just inside the armistice line. Relieving Jordanian soldiers were caught in an ambush, and more than twenty were killed with many more being wounded. After evacuating all the villagers, the Israelis demolished the entire village.

fear of Israel's ambitions

This Israeli attack, among other things, convinced the Jordanians that the Israelis' aim in any future conflict would be to wrest all the territory on the river's west bank, including Jerusalem, from Jordanian control. Other events, including the shooting down by Israel of six Syrian planes, inflamed tensions and in a bid to mend Arab discord King Hussein flew to Cairo to conclude a mutual defence agreement.

When Nasser closed the shipping lanes to Israel's Red Sea port of Eilat, hostilities were certain.

the June war — six day disaster for Jordan

The Israeli pre-emptive air strike against the Egyptian Air Force on 5th June 1967 settled the outcome of what became known as the Six Day War, even before it began. For Jordan it was an utter disaster; without the Egyptian air support the Jordanians had been promised, the Army could not prevail against the far stronger Israeli Army and Air Force. All her territory west of the Jordan River including Jerusalem, where the defending Jordanian Army put up stiff resistance, was lost. By the end of the brief war the Jordanian armed forces had lost most of its tanks, planes and heavy guns; the economy was in tatters, and to top it all over 200,000 more Palestinians had been turned into refugees. If there was ever any doubt, Israel had once again proved that she was militarily superior to the combined Arab armies, a fact that would and could not easily be forgotten by the Jordanians in the future.

the three Noes

In August 1967 the Arab States met in Khartoum. The resolution of the three Noes was its most significant outcome; *no peace; no recognition; and no negotiations* (with Israel). Jordan was a party to this resolution.

decision time for Arafat

A very volatile situation developed along the Jordan river cease fire line with Israel. Badly shaken by the outcome of the war, which left many Palestinians without much hope for the future, it was for Yasir Arafat a decisive moment. He was determined to continue the struggle, whatever the means and cost. (For this writer who has witnessed the events since then unfold with great interest, whatever one may think of him as an individual, it is only through his tenacity and single-minded devotion to the cause of Palestinian nationhood that the events of today's times have come about.)

In the period after 1967 this determination to continue an armed struggle against Israel became one of the main factors in Jordanian politics. As this developed into a confrontation with the government, Hussein was forced to balance his cabinet carefully between his supporters and the Palestinians.

financed by oil states

The guerrilla groups received both financial aid and armaments from the Gulf states and Saudi Arabia. The refugee camps became virtual commando bases, and so strong was their position that they posed a direct threat to the government. In November 1968, on the anniversary of the Balfour Declaration, a major confrontation broke out, which was only settled by the government giving in to certain Palestinian demands. Continuing incursions by Palestinian *fedayeen* (martyrs) into Israel and the West Bank were fraught with danger for Jordan as the Israelis threatened massive reprisals.

Israelis cross the Jordan

A base for many of these raids was the refugee camp in the village of Karameh, in the Jordan Valley. After a period when the *fedayeen* had been able to kill and injure a number of Israelis, a large retaliatory raid was launched against Karameh on 21st March 1968. Although they managed to kill many of the guerrillas, they were intercepted by the Jordanian Army, who on this occasion acquitted itself very well, forcing the Israelis to withdraw with difficulty. In spite of the losses it was a psychological victory for the PLO and even more so for Arafat.

Government undermined

In July 1970 a peace plan proposed by the US in which Israel would withdraw from the territory captured in 1967 in return for Arab recognition of her frontiers was praised by Jordan and Egypt. Most of the Palestinian groups rejected it outright, and a major showdown between them and the government seemed unavoidable.

airliners hijacked

In September 1970 events started hotting up. On 1st September King Hussein was ambushed while driving to Amman Airport. He escaped unhurt.

Almost a week later, on Sunday the 6th, the PFLP, the Popular Front for the Liberation of Palestine, a small but fanatical group led by George Habash, carried out their four-airliner hijacking drama which resulted in all four aircraft being destroyed, three of them in Jordan. Arafat was opposed to this action, but in the face of a sudden upswell in PFLP popularity there was little he could do.

Black September

In mid September severe fighting between the army and the Palestinians erupted. Since the end of the 1967 war Jordan had been under martial law, and on 16th September Hussein formed a military government to handle a situation that could not continue. The Palestinians were no match for the trained Jordanian Army, and the casualties among the *fedayeen* were very high. In spite of various truces brokered by Nasser, by the summer of 1971 Hussein had managed to expel most of the *fedayeen* from Jordan. This episode became known as "Black September".

embittered reaction

This conflict had cost the fighting Palestinians very dearly, and it left a legacy of bitterness that would last a long time. In September that year three unsuccessful attempts were made to hijack Jordanian airliners, and on 28th September the Prime Minister, Wasfi al-Tal, was assassinated by the Palestinian splinter group which called itself "Black September" after the events of the previous year.

salaries paid

Meanwhile Jordan continued to regard the Israeli occupied areas of the West Bank as an integral part of Jordan. The Government continued to pay local officials and teachers their salaries and provide Jordanian passports to citizens there. Despite the fact that Israeli currency was now in circulation in these territories, the Jordanian dinar was still the main money used. Both countries allowed, subject to some restrictions, travel between the west and east banks.

"Yom Kippur" war

Jordan was not directly involved in the war that began on 6th October 1973, but she did send a detachment of troops to the Golan Heights to assist Syria.

Rabat conference

During 1974 a pronounced change occurred in the attitude of the other Arab states as regards the Palestinians. In October that year twenty Arab heads of state, meeting in Rabat, Morocco, recognised the PLO as the sole legitimate representative of the Palestinian people, with the right to claim national authority over any areas of Palestine that may be liberated. Jordan went along with this agreement, but Hussein had still not given up, entirely, his claim to the West Bank.

all power to the King!

In the aftermath of the Rabat summit Hussein took sweeping powers to reorganise his country and reduce the influence of the Palestinians. He acquired powers to rule without recourse to the National Assembly, which was later dissolved. Elections, due in March 1975, were postponed and in February 1976 the constitution was changed allowing them to be suspended for an unspecified period.

Sadat takes the plunge

In 1977 President Sadat of Egypt made his surprise visit to Israel, which was followed by a peace treaty in March 1979. Like most other Arab countries, Jordan severed diplomatic relations with Egypt in protest against the making of a separate peace.

first Gulf war

When Iraq and Iran went to war in 1980, Jordan sided with the former whilst her northern neighbour, Syria, supported Iran. This state of affairs led to an extremely tense situation on the frontier. At one stage danger of hostilities between the two edged very close. When Iraq's initial superiority seemed to be fading under a fanatical Iranian onslaught, Hussein attempted, unsuccessfully, to broker a negotiated settlement.

Reagan goes for peace

In 1982 President Reagan proposed a Palestinian-Israeli peace plan which would see the creation of a West Bank autonomous Palestinian authority confederated with Jordan. This was rejected by Arafat and Hussein, who probably liked it but treated it with scepticism as it would have antagonised other Arab countries.

recall of National Assembly

Worried that Jordan's position vis à vis the West Bank was being irretrievably lost, Hussein reconvened the National Assembly in 1984 in a bid to restore to the West Bank Palestinians a say in Jordanian affairs. In March the first elections for 17 years were held, and women were allowed to vote. The result was such that the majority of Deputies rejected any solution for the West Bank based on the Reagan plan.

relations with Egypt restored

In September 1984, to the consternation of the militant Arab countries, Jordan restored diplomatic ties with Egypt. At the same time Hussein refused Israel's offer of negotiations without the PLO, demanding that the organisation should be treated on an equal basis with other states in the region. Hussein reiterated the requirement that Israel must accept the concept of "land for peace". Between 1985 and 1987 a peace plan worked out by Hussein and Arafat came to nothing when Israel refused once again to have any dealings with the PLO, and also opposed the idea of the US doing likewise.

the start of the Intifada

An incident on the border between Israeli-occupied Gaza and Israel proper in December 1987 prompted the spontaneous outbreak of a violent *intifada*, or uprising, throughout Gaza, the West Bank and east Jerusalem. This was to last for some five years, and proved to be the catalyst that eventually enabled Israel and the PLO to reach an agreement.

Hussein renounces claim...

Towards the end of July 1988, Jordan withdrew a billion dollar-plus development plan for the West Bank, a plan that in any event had not attracted sufficient funds. On 30th July the King announced the severance of Jordan's legal and administrative ties with the West Bank, and dissolved the House of Representatives where West Bank deputies held 50 per cent of the seats.

...and Arafat renounces violence

On November 15th 1988 the Palestine National Congress (PNC) proclaimed an independent state of Palestine, and indirectly recognised Israel. Over sixty countries gave recognition to the Palestinian state. In December that year Yasir Arafat, while addressing the UN General Assembly, renounced violence as a means of solving interstate problems. In spite of the fact that the then Israeli leader Yitzhak Shamir called this declaration "deceitful" it was clear that in the end Israel and the PLO would have to negotiate.

road to democracy

In the Jordanian general election that took place on 8th November 1989, nearly 650 candidates contested the 80 seats. All were classed as "independent" since the 1963 ban on political parties was still in force. Over half the deputies elected were from groups recognised as "opposition", including 20 from the Muslim Brotherhood. Although the government which took office afterwards had a radical slant to it, no members of the religious extremists participated.

In June 1991 the ban on political parties and activities was revoked on condition that the parties pledged allegiance to the Hashemite monarchy. At the request of the Prime Minister, Taker al-Maori, on 7th July 1991 King Hussein issued a decree lifting martial law which had been in force since 1967.

Iraq annexes Kuwait

After Iraq's annexation of Kuwait on 2nd August 1990, the Palestinians gave their support to Saddam Hussein. Jordan, too, did not condemn Iraq's action and Jordanian public opinion was squarely behind the Iraqi leader. The Jordanian stance was surprising to the western countries, as they had always considered King Hussein to be a staunch supporter of the West. However, they acknowledged he was placed in a difficult dilemma.

Iraq's invasion of Kuwait led to a massive influx of refugees, migrant workers, into Jordan. By October the country was overwhelmed, as nearly one million people passed through Jordanian territory.

second Gulf war

The King invested a great deal of effort in the search for a peaceful solution to the crisis, but to no avail. When the war broke out on 16th January 1991, Jordan was quick to denounce the bombardment and brutal onslaught of an Arab and Muslim nation. Huge anti-western demonstrations were held throughout the land, as the people continued in their near total support for Iraq.

When the war ended Hussein's image in the west, and in the rest of the Arab world, had been somewhat tarnished, but gradually this was repaired.

ROAD TO PEACE

opening moves

On 12th October 1991 in the face of opposition from the House of Representatives, King Hussein announced that Jordan would participate in a Middle East peace conference to be held in Madrid. A few days later the Central Council of the PLO approved the formation of a joint Jordanian-Palestinian delegation, thus circumventing Israel's long-standing refusal to talk directly with the PLO. The delegation was headed by Kamel Abu Jaber, who had recently been made Jordan's Foreign Minister. In his address Abu Jaber stated that although Jordan had wanted a separate Palestinian delegation, "we have no objection to acting as an umbrella for our Palestinian brethren". He continued, "Jordan has never been Palestine and never will be so".

The negotiations in Madrid, and later in 1992 in Washington and Moscow, produced no substantive progress.

that historic handshake

The breakthrough came in early 1993. Secret talks between Israel and the PLO directly had been taking place in Norway under the auspices of the Norwegian Foreign Minister. On 19th August that year a Declaration of Principles was agreed by both sides. This accord was duly signed on the White House lawn on 13th September. At the ceremony, the till then unimaginable occurred: Israeli Prime Minister, Yitzhak Rabin and PLO Chairman, Yasir Arafat shook hands—an event that eventually cost Rabin his life in November 1995.

Jordan's turn

In late 1993 King Hussein met with the Israeli Foreign Minister, Shimon Peres, in an attempt to work out a peace deal. Towards the end of April 1994 the Jordanian Prime Minister announced that his country would be willing to sign agreements settling individual items between the two countries and enter into multilateral negotiations that could lead to a peace treaty.

With the stage once again set in Washington, on 25th July 1994 King Hussein and Israeli Premier Rabin signed the so-called "Washington Declaration" which ended the state of war between Jordan and Israel.

American sweetener

The United States, keen to get a peace treaty signed as soon as possible, leaned heavily on Jordan by promising to cancel the $700 million debt Jordan had accrued. As only the King had the stature and authority to present a peace treaty to the Jordanian people, its speedy conclusion became all the more imperative because of his declining health.

On 26th October 1994 in a tent that straddled the Jordanian-Israeli border in the Arava, the two neighbours finally made peace.

2. Geography

THE LAND

Shaped like a pistol, the handle pointing towards Iraq and the hammer being the protusion in the north between Syria and Israel, Jordan is a small country of only 92,140 square kilometres; and of this 90 per cent is desert. The distance from Syria in the north to Aqaba on the Red Sea measures less than 400 kilometres, and from the Jordan river to the Iraqi frontier – the country's widest extent – less than 500.

almost landlocked

The Kingdom is bordered by Syria to the north, by Iraq in the north east, and by Saudi Arabia in the east and south. The River Jordan forms the western frontier, where it divides Jordan from Israel and the Palestinian entity and, further south, Wadi Arava which it shares with Israel. Apart from the western boundary, no topographical features mark the frontiers, which were often drawn in straight lines to suit the convenience of the former European occupiers. Jordan's only coastline is a diminutive strip some 26 kilometres long on the Red Sea, sandwiched between Israel and Saudi Arabia.

three main regions

The country can be divided into three main geographical areas all extending in a north-south direction: the Jordan Valley, the western mountains and plateau, and the arid eastern plateau. The last two are essentially part of the same plateau that slopes easterly towards the deserts of Arabia. These two regions are roughly delineated by the main highway running from the Syrian border to Amman and the desert highway to Aqaba.

Only the western uplands and plateau is suitable for settlement on a significant scale, as the climate is good, the soil fertile, and there are sufficient rains in the season.

✦ The western mountains and plateau

Stretching from the Syrian border southwards towards the Red Sea, this area is Jordan's most valuable, as it contains the majority of the urban centres and arable land.

The western side forms an escarpment above the Jordan Valley, Dead Sea and the Valley of the Arava, whilst the eastern side continues as a desert plateau out towards Saudi Arabia. The mountains of the north vary in altitude from 700 to 1000 metres, with some in the south being much higher.

spectactular gorges

From the northern frontier to Wadi Hasa, south of Kerak, the mountains are limestone, whilst further south they gradually change to sandstone. The region is crossed laterally by a number of seasonal watercourses which empty either into the Jordan Valley, the Dead Sea, or peter out in the wastes of the Arava Valley. These watercourses have in many places cut deep, steep-sided gorges into the landscape, the most spectacular being at Wadi Mujib, the Arnon of the Bible.

The dark soil here is generally rich and fertile. In winter there is usually enough moisture for farming, mainly the growing of wheat and other cereals, especially in the south, where wide, flat expanses of land are under intensive cultivation.

deep drops

The plateau ends, rather abruptly, at Ras Naqab, with a plunging descent towards the Red Sea. South of Amman the western edge of the plateau faces the Dead Sea, part of which is under Jordanian sovereignty. Both here and further south where the heights overlook the Arava Valley, they again terminate in a precipitous drop.

✦ The eastern plateau

This vast expanse, constituting most of Jordan's land, is nearly all wilderness. In the north east, below the (Syrian) Hauran plateau, it is mainly basalt rock. To the south near Azraq, Wadi Sirhan, a broad, level valley which was once well watered, heads off in a south-easterly direction into Saudi Arabia.

Further south the plateau becomes total desert, covered by flint and limestone chips. This wasteland continues until relieved by the high mountains – Jabal Ramm at 1,754 metres is Jordan's highest – and the beautiful valleys of south Jordan.

✦ The Jordan Valley (Ghor)

This flat valley, no more than a few kilometres wide and through which the River Jordan flows, is part of the Great Rift Valley, the geological fault that runs from northern Syria into Africa. The Jordan valley begins by Lake Tiberius and terminates at the Dead Sea, into which the river empties, 108 kilometres to the south. The meandering

of the river is such that its length through the valley is over double
that distance.

below sea level

Nearly all of the valley lies below sea level. As the surface of
Lake Tiberius is minus 210 metres and the surface of the Dead Sea
minus 400 metres, the valley slopes down in a southerly direction.
There are no main towns on the Jordanian side of the valley, the main
urban centre being Jericho, in the Palestinian entity.

The fertile alluvial soils, together with the year round warm clime,
enable the growing of three or four crops each year, thus making it
Jordan's most dominant agricultural region.

DRAINAGE

There are no fresh water lakes in Jordan, and the Kingdom has very
limited access to the waters of the River Jordan. The largest quantity
of above ground water available to the country flows from the River
Yarmouk whose waters are shared with Syria. The bulk of the rest of
the fresh water is drawn from wells. The Dead Sea, part of which is
in Jordan, is situated at the lowest point on earth and its water is so
saline that it can support no life or vegetation.

CLIMATE

In general Jordan's climate has hot dry summer days, with cool
evenings. There are, however, regional variations.

✦ Amman and the northern heights

At an altitude of c900 metres Amman is cold in winter, but the low
humidity in summer makes the heat at that time of year generally very
comfortable. Average daytime temperatures range from 17°C in April
to 23°C in June and 26°C in August. The summer nights are pleas-
antly cool. There can be the odd shower in late October or the
beginning of November, but the rainy season only really gets underway towards the end of November. Usually by late April the rains
have finished.

✦ Petra and the south

chance of snow

Because of its lofty altitude Petra is cold in winter, and occasionally
snow falls. However, from March to the end of May and October-
November the climate is near perfect. Summers are extremely hot
with temperatures normally above 32 degrees. Precipitation is rare
between March and the beginning of December.

hot and dry

Aqaba is mainly a winter resort and daytime temperatures in
December and January are often above 18°C. In April they reach 26°

or more and by August rise to blistering highs of 38° to 40°! Humidity is very low, and rainfall negligible.

✦ The Jordan Valley

Because this area is below sea level an almost tropical climate prevails. From May to November it is torrid, unbearably so in high summer. Winters are very mild.

The hot wind

Throughout the country a few times a year, particularly in the spring and autumn, a strong, easterly wind blows, laden with fine dust and sand picked up as it crosses the desert. Temperatures soar, often by 10°C or more, the sky turns dark and humidity drops to around 10 per cent, causing considerable discomfort. This wind is called locally *khamsin* (Arabs claim there are fifty such days in a year, consequently the name *khamsin* which means fifty — I doubt there are quite so many!), and can last from 1-4 days or more.

FLORA AND FAUNA

Perhaps suprisingly, parts of Jordan are covered in an amazing carpet of colour for a few weeks in the spring. This is especially so after a winter of bountiful rains. The entire western part of the Kingdom is transformed to such a degree that it has to be seen to be believed: anemones, cyclamen, poppies, hollyhocks and more enchant the eye.

the black iris

The most acclaimed of all the flowers is a deep purple iris (locally called a black iris), adopted as Jordan's national bloom. These lovely flowers can be found in the hilly regions, albeit not in the profusion of some years ago.

blossoming desert

Stretches of particular beauty are found near seasonable watercourses after the flows of winter. The contrast between the arid summer landscape of these wadis and the spring transformation is

almost miraculous. Sadly this riot of colour is all too brief; with the first *khamsin* wind (see above) they wilt and are quickly gone, awaiting the rains of the next year. Wild oleander is to be found most of the year near all the watercourses, and in the rocks of Petra.

not many trees

The northern hills were once covered in forests, but felling over many centuries denuded them. In recent years reforestation means there are once again wooded hills in many regions. Citrus and olive are the most important fruit bearing trees.

Most animals are domestic, but in the desert there may still be a few jackals and hyenas. In the northern hills some wild boar still roam. A poisonous viper lurks in rocky places but other reptiles are harmless. Gazelle and ibex once inhabited the Arava region.

THE JORDANIAN PEOPLE

The indigenous Jordanians are Arabs, similar in ethnic origin to the desert peoples of Syria and the Arabian peninsular. There is also a small minority of Circassians, Muslims from the Caucasus who settled in the area as refugees in the late 19th century.

lots of youngsters

In 1993, the population of Jordan was just under 4 million, and is increasing. As in most Arab countries where large families are the norm, young persons under 15 make up the largest age group. The natural rate of increase of about 3 per cent annually is high, especially for a country with very limited usable land and resources.

mainly Muslims

Over 92 per cent are Sunni Muslims, and a very small number are Shi'ite Muslims and Druse. About 6 per cent of the population are Christians, mainly Eastern Orthodox (similar to Greek Orthodox, but with Arabic as their liturgical language).

western influence

Although Arab traditional dress is still very evident in Jordan, especially among women, it seems to be waning somewhat, principally in the cities. Overall fewer men still wear the typical Arab garb as a matter of course and, apart from amongst the Bedouin, a veiled woman is a rarity. Aspects of westernisation can be seen everywhere.

Unlike some other of their Arab neighbours, Jordanians are exposed to the western way of life through tourism and, more pronouncedly, through television. Not only does Jordan TV screen western progammes, but Israel's broadcasts, many of which are culled from the west, can be received in most parts of the Kingdom.

less tradition

Additionally, Jordan does not have "old" or "traditional" quarters in its cities. Less than 70 years ago cities did not exist, Amman being no more than a village. When J.L. Burckhardt, the explorer who discovered Petra (see biographical details in chapter on Petra), visited in 1812, the place was almost deserted. In other Arab countries such as Syria, it is in the old or historic parts of the great cities like Damascus and Aleppo that the traditional way of life is perpetuated through the souks, mosques, tea houses and hammams etc. Jordan lacks this continuity of history, and as such is more open to change.

THE MAIN GROUPS

Among Jordan's Arab population two groups, the Palestinians and the Bedouin, stand out and are worthy of separate discussion.

✦ The Palestinians

During the British Mandate all those who lived in Palestine, Arab and Jew alike, were considered Palestinian. After the division of the area between Israel and Jordan, all the Jews and those Arabs who remained in Israel became Israeli citizens, while those Arabs who remained in their homes on the Jordanian west side of the river became Jordanian.

simply complicated

Then who are the Palestinians? Generally speaking they are those Arabs who lived formerly in what is now Israel and either fled or were expelled from their homes. They are also those Arabs who still live on the West Bank and Gaza Strip, together with the ones who were driven out in the wake of the Israeli occupation in 1967. Perhaps a simpler way of putting it would be that today's Palestinians are those who live in the area of Palestine that is not now Israel, plus those who either live in Jordan or other countries and still think of Palestine as their homeland.

the assimilated and the refugees

Although Jordan no longer claims any part of her former territory on the west bank of the river, there are still many Palestinians living in the country, although these people must now be called Jordanians. Most have integrated fully into the life of the state, but others are still classed as refugees, and receive payments and other services from UNWRA (United Nations Works and Relief Agency). Of the integrated Palestinians, some have reached the highest political office and many run substantial businesses.

hands across the river

Even those who are assimilated into mainstream Jordanian life still preserve strong ties with their relatives across the river, and some I have spoken to would want to return there if the political conditions were right. Jordan may have severed its political and legal ties with the Palestinian homeland, but strong emotional links bind many of her citizens to that area. When an indepedent Palestinian state arises from the present temporary entity, there is no doubt that it will have very strong ties with Jordan, perhaps in a confederation of sorts.

✦ The Bedouin

The eastern desert areas of Jordan are almost exclusively inhabited by the Bedouin, or Bedu in Arabic. (The singular is Bedoui.) Bedu live in most of the Arab countries of the Middle East including Israel, and can be considered less ethnically adulterated than other Arabs. Since ancient times the Bedu have lived as nomads, wandering the deserts of Arabia with their flocks of sheep and goats or herds of camels.

nomadic highwaymen

A warlike people, they have always had a history as raiders, particularly of caravans and villages. In the past travellers were often forced to make their way with a military escort to avoid being harassed by these desert dwellers.

There has been much romanticising of the Bedouin, often presenting a distorted picture. In fact they have two temperaments: one is indeed the hospitable knight of the desert whose tent is always open to the wayfarer; the second is the desert raider who until the 1920s was apt to maraud and plunder not only passing caravans and travellers, but also villages which were unable to protect themselves. One reason why the Ottomans wanted the Hejaz railway was so that they could transport troops quickly to restore order to the lawless regions of the desert.

polygamous patriarchs

Bedu are a fiercely independent people and have always nurtured a distaste for central governments. Their loyalty and obedience has been to their tribal sheikhs, and this combined with their patriachal, and polygamous, way of life has prevented them from achieving any unity to their overall benefit.

The Bedouin family is a very close-knit unit. Most of the men have more than one wife, as permitted in Islam, and consequently there are many children. All, women and offspring alike, are very obedient to the family head. The women are usually hidden from visitors and are rarely allowed to sit with the menfolk.

tribal conflicts

Internal feuding is also a problem amongst the Bedu. Any misdeed by one family or one tribe against another has to be repaid in kind. This sort of tit-for-tat quarrel can get very bloody and go on for years until the sides agree to make a *sulkha* or peace. Good fighters and trackers, the Bedu were the main force in the 1917 Arab Revolt, and are still an important component in Jordan's army today. They are among the King's most loyal subjects.

rite of hospitality

By custom and nature the Arabs are one of the most hospitable of peoples, but the Bedu take this hospitality much further, even to the point of ritual.

ceased to roam

Very few of Jordan's Bedu are still true nomads, though some may be classed as semi nomads. The majority, however, have settled in villages especially built for them. Many have been quick to seize on tourism as a livelihood, especially in Petra and Wadi Rumm, as you are sure to experience!

The two largest Bedu tribes in Jordan are the *Howeitat* and the *Banu Sakr*. There are perhaps seven or eight smaller or lesser tribes. The town of Maan in the south is the main gathering place for the Howeitat, and in the surrounding area there are many permanent Bedu settlements.

RELIGION

✦ Islam

Islam is the religion that burst out of Arabia in AD 630, preached by Muhammad, who according to Muslims was the last of God's prophets, a list which includes Abraham, Moses and Jesus. Islam means submission (to the will of God) and is, like biblical Judaism, a total way of life, encompassing a social system and code of values. Islam's holy book, the Koran, was not actually written down by Muhammad, but some time after his death. It is a collection of his teachings and revelations as told to his followers and remembered by them. The Muslim era, and the year from which its calendar is counted, started with the flight of Muhammad from Mecca to Medina, the *hijra*.

There are basically two streams in Islam. The orthodox, who are called Sunni and the breakaway Shi'ites. This can be likened to Catholics and Protestants within Christianity. In Jordan practically all Muslims are Sunni.

call to prayer

The orthodox Muslim is called to prayer five times a day:

fajr	-	dawn;
dhuhr	-	hour before sunrise;
'asr	-	noon;
maghreb	-	sunset;
isha	-	hour and a half after sunset.

There is no god but God

The call is made from the minaret of the mosque. In days gone by the call was by voice with the caller, the muezzin, walking around the minaret parapet so that he could be heard in different parts of the city. In today's technological world it is done via tape, amplifier and many speakers. The call starts with the words *"Allah Akbar!"*, "God is great!" and finishes, *"La allah illa Allah"*, "There is no god but God".

Jesus the Prophet

Allah is Arabic for God, and He is the God of Judaism and Christianity. Jesus figures prominently in Islam, but as an important prophet, not the Son of God. All the prophets of the Old Testament are revered by Muslims, and Muhammad is revered as the last of the prophets in that he received the revelation of the Koran from the Archangel Gabriel.

The Five Pillars of Islam

Islam rests on five fundamental pillars:

shahada -	this is the profession of faith: "There is no god but God (Allah) and Muhammad is his prophet";
salat -	prayer five times a day;
zakat -	the giving of alms;
sawn -	sunrise to sunset fasting during the month of Ramadan;
haj -	the pilgrimage to Mecca, at least once in a lifetime.

The day of rest for Muslims is Friday, and the main service in the mosque is at noon. Non Muslims are not allowed into the mosque at that time. Business is permitted after the noontime prayer; indeed the downtown area of Amman, which contains the city's main mosque, is at its busiest then.

Ramadan

> *"...and eat and drink,*
> *until the white thread*
> *of Dawn appear to you*
> *distinct from the black thread.*
> *Then complete your fast*
> *till the night appears."*
> The Koran, Sura 2:137

The fourth pillar of Islam, *sawn,* is celebrated in the 9th month of the Muslim year, Ramadan. During this month the devout — and the not so devout — abstain from food and drink (and smoking) during the hours from sunrise to sunset. It is not a holiday though activities do slow down somewhat. Government offices keep shorter hours, and often people arc in a lethargic mood. If the fast falls in the hot summer months it can prove quite a trial as drinking is prohibited.

As the Muslim calendar is lunar, with no leap year compensation, all dates based upon this calendar move back against the Gregorian calendar by 11 days (and consequently against the seasons).

The fast-breaking meal, eaten immediately after sunset and called *iftar*, literally break-fast, is a very celebratory affair. The family table is set with plates of food, while everyone waits for the moment that sunset is proclaimed, usually by a radio announcement, a call from the mosque or the firing of a cannon. Immediately everyone tucks in! Go to a typical Jordanian restaurant like the ones in downtown Amman and see how the tables are laid and the hungry customers wait, looking patiently at the food spread before them!

(For information on how Ramadan affects the tourist, and its dates see the chapter **General Information**.)

3. Jordan Today

GOVERNMENT

The official name of Jordan is **al-Mamlaka al-Urdunniya al-Hashimiyya** or The Hashemite Kingdom of Jordan. The King (Head of State) is His Majesty King Hussein ibn Talal, the great-grandson of King Husayn of the Hejaz. The monarchy is hereditary, and the King has the right to choose his successor from within the Royal Hashemite House. He designated his brother Hassan in 1965, who since then carries the title of Crown Prince. Hassan also acts as regent in Hussein's absence from the country.

King at the top

Jordan is a constitutional - monarchy, but not in the European sense. The simplest way to describe the King's position is that of a lifetime executive president.

Parliament is the dual chamber *majlis al-umma*, the National Assembly, comprised of an elected House of Representatives, elected (since 1984) by universal suffrage, with 80 members and a Palace-appointed Senate of 40 members.

King Hussein

Considerable political power is vested in the King which he can either exercise himself or through the Prime Minister whom he appoints. After appointment the Prime Minister selects a Council of Ministers (cabinet) in consultation with the King. All the ministers have to be approved by the monarch, and then by the *majlis al-umma*. The present Prime Minister (end 1995) is H.E. Sharif Zeid Ben Shaker.

Although legislative powers are mostly conferred on the House, all laws have to be approved by the King, and it would take an impossible-to-muster two thirds majority in both houses to override his veto. The Senate members must be at least 40 years old, and are usually former senior political figures.

Jordan is divided into eight *muhaafazat*, or Governorates. These are Amman, Irbid, Zarqa, Balqa, Karak, Mafraq, Ma'an, and Tafila.

ECONOMY

Jordan is not a rich country. There is no oil, little arable land, and an expanding population. Dependence on foreign aid and loans makes Jordan open to political leverage.

loss of West bank and resources

Traditionally, Jordan's economy has been agriculture based, but the loss of the areas west of the river in 1967, where about 50 per cent of the farming activity was concentrated, greatly affected the Kingdom's agricultural output. The Israeli occupation of Jerusalem caused the loss of most of the Kingdom's tourism revenue as Petra, Jordan's tourism jewel, was difficult to reach and lacked facilities. The West Bank, especially around Nablus, also contained most of the manufacturing capability.

money from abroad

Massive loans and aid from other Arab states, combined with expatriate earnings, helped Jordan overcome these difficulties, and by the late 1970s the country was experiencing a short period of economic growth. Mining and manufacturing off-shoots became the sectors of priority and investment, together with the generation of intensive agriculture, based in the natural hothouse of the Jordan Valley.

need for loans

This period of comparative economic stability did not persist, and in the second half of the 1980s Jordan's economy took a turn for the worse and she was forced to seek loans from the IMF (International Monetary Fund). One of the conditions for these being granted was the cancellation or curtailment of subsidies on staples. The implementation of this caused a great deal of resentment throughout the country and in Ma'an there were serious riots. Coupled with this, the Jordanian dinar (JD) was devalued, and for a time there was a ban on the import of certain luxuries. For a small country with limited economic potential, Jordan's external debt is huge, and some relief from this was essential.

better off than in Egypt

The majority of the people are in the lower income level, while at least 30 per cent fall below the poverty line. However, in spite of this the overall standard of living is higher than in, say, Egypt, and in Jordan you will not see the very poor and homeless that you will find

41

there. This picture is not reflected in the smarter surburbs of Amman, where there is a monied class which does not represent the general Jordanian economy. As is usual in many Arab countries the entrepreneurial spirit is strong, and many people strive to open a small business.

✦ Industry

The three main industries are phosphates, potash and agriculture —

Phosphates: Jordan is the fifth largest producer of phosphates in the world and the third largest exporter. The augmentation of this industry has been at the forefront of most of the Kingdom's development plans. The main mines are situated in Wadi Hasa in the desert between Amman and Ma'an, and at Shidiya, south east of Ma'an where reserves are in excess of a billion tons. Industries based upon phosphates form a significant part of Jordan's industrial base. A large fertiliser plant near Aqaba produces diammonium phosphate and phosphoric acid. Other plants capable of producing phosphoric acid are being set up in partnership with India and Pakistan.

Potash: Although formed in 1956, the Arab Potash Company really only started to produce in the 1980s. The works are located at Ghour al-Safi, at the southern end of the Dead Sea. Its output grows steadily, with the 1990 figures being 21 per cent higher than the previous year. The same company also produces potassium sulphate, and plans to expand to bromine derivatives, as the Dead Sea is the richest bromine lake in the world.

Agriculture: At least half the population are engaged in this important branch of the economy, although it only provides 13 per cent of the GNP. It is very export oriented, with large quantities of fruit and vegetables destined for the Gulf states. Three quarters of the activity is in the irrigated Jordan Valley, while the rest is concentrated in the precipitation-watered western plateau. The former area has mainly fruit and vegetable crops, while the latter is more suited to cereals (in which Jordan is not self sufficient).

Further expansion of the agricultural sector will depend on water resources, which at the present time are very stretched. The settlement with Israel may bring about some change in this.

Gulf casualty

As Iraq was Jordan's main trading partner, the sanctions imposed against Iraq by the UN after they occupied Kuwait in the summer of 1990 were difficult for Jordan to fulfil. The previous year almost 25 per cent of the Kingdom's exports had gone to Iraq, who in return supplied 80 per cent of Jordan's oil needs. There was also an important transit trade through Aqaba port which dried up by the summer's end.

oil from Syria

When the war began all deliveries of Iraqi oil ceased, and Jordan had to rely on Syria who supplied at a much higher price. After the war ended Iraqi supplies were resumed on a barter basis for food, and although this was condemned by the US, Jordan maintained that as no cash was involved sanctions were not being broken.

no remittances

A vital part of the Jordanian economy had always been money sent home by Jordanians working abroad, particularly in Kuwait and other Gulf states. By 1992 most of these workers had returned home, and although a large amount of money came with them further remittances soon ceased. Many of these returnees were educated people who could fit into the local economy, whilst some had the capital to open businesses. But numerous others served only to swell Jordan's unemployment figures, currently running around 30 per cent.

you're helping!

Tourism is now an important part of the economy. Over the past decade or so the infrastructure has been enlarged and improved. New roads and the paving of dirt tracks have made the sites of antiquity more accessible and the government has sanctioned a great deal of restoration work, which is ongoing.

Israel crosses the Jordan

Tourist numbers have greatly increased now that groups of Israelis are allowed to visit Jordan, and for the next few years they may actually be the majority of non Arabs who visit the country. It's hard to give actual tourist figures as those put out by the government include all arrivals, but it is safe to say that this is a growth industry.

EDUCATION

School attendance is compulsory until the age of 14, with about 75 per cent of the children studying in state schools and most of the rest at schools run by UNWRA. A small number attend missionary and private schools. For an Arab country Jordanian children are well educated and the literacy rate is over 80 per cent, compared with 65 per cent in Syria (which is considered high in the region).

Jordan has three state universities: the University of Jordan in Amman, Yarmuk University in Irbid and Mu'tah University in Karak, which tends to concentrate on military disciplines.

many graduates

Surprisingly, Jordan has one of the highest proportions of graduates in the world. Many of these are Palestinians who are, perhaps, the most educated of Arabs. A lack of job opportunities forces many to seek positions abroad, and Jordanian and Palestinian teachers and engineers are found all over the Arab world, and beyond.

EVERYDAY LIFE

Over the past couple of decades there has been a strong movement from the land to urban centres, particularly to Amman, which seems to be constantly spreading. Life is not easy for many, and the downtown streets are full of people hawking all manner of goods. Sometimes you'll see someone just selling a few socks or individual cigarettes. While not as pronounced as in some Arab lands, the difference between the rich and poor is noticeable, especially as the two often meet in the busy commercial areas of the centre.

the very simple life

In the rural areas poverty stands out even more, and while you will not find hungry people in Jordan, often a family with children will live in a single room, without running water or electricity. On a recent journey through the Jordan Valley, I was invited to drink tea by a resident of a small village. He, his wife and two small daughters lived in a single-roomed dwelling just outside the village. Apart from a large wardrobe there was no furniture, the mattresses for sleeping were stacked during the day, and cushions put on the floor for sitting. Water was drawn from a well about a hundred metres' distant and stored in a large earthen container. The "kitchen" was in a hut outside and consisted of a single kerosene stove and a wood burning oven. Washing facilities were very basic, and also outside. In spite of this the place was spotlessly clean and the daughters well cared for and well fed.

little extremism

Although Jordan does have a Muslim fundamentalist movement which has many representatives in parliament, religious extremism is not very prevalent, being mainly directed against the accommodation with Israel. However, religious influence cannot be ignored, and part of Jordan's legal code is based on Shari'a (Koranic) law.

Whether or not most Jordanians really love their King is impossible to determine. Suffice it to say that His Majesty's picture is in almost every establishment, and daily television coverage is full of his comings and goings.

LANGUAGE

Modern Standard Arabic (MSA), derived from classical Arabic, is the official language of Jordan. This is the language understood from the Persian Gulf to the Atlantic. MSA is used for all literary purposes including journalism.

local variations

Additionally, every region has its own colloquial Arabic which is used for verbal communication only. The version spoken in Jordan is the same as is spoken on the West Bank, and almost the same as that used in Syria. It is noticeably different to the colloquial of Cairo. (Refer to the **Language** chapter for more information).

English is spoken extensively, and you will be hard pressed to find someone who cannot speak it to some degree. French is also widely used. This notwithstanding, Jordanians will be delighted if you know a few words in Arabic, so if you don't already speak it, study the vocabulary section of this book!

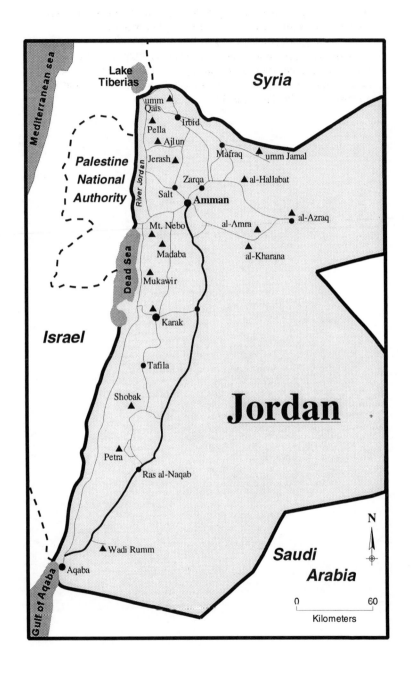

Mediterranean sea

Lake Tiberias

Syria

umm Qais ▲

Pella ▲

Ajlun ▲

Irbid ●

Mafraq ●

umm Jamal ▲

Jerash ▲

al-Hallabat ▲

Palestine National Authority

River Jordan

Zarqa ●

Salt ●

Amman ●

al-Azraq ▲

Mt. Nebo ▲

al-Amra ▲

Madaba ▲

al-Kharana ▲

Dead Sea

Mukawir ▲

Karak ● ▲

Israel

Tafila ●

Shobak ▲

Jordan

Petra ▲

Ras al-Naqab

N

Wadi Rumm ▲

Saudi Arabia

Aqaba ●

Gulf of Aqaba

0   60

Kilometers

PART II
TOURING JORDAN

4. Planning Your Itinerary

HOW LONG DO YOU NEED?

For sightseeing purposes, you can cover most of Jordan in about 10 days, but this will not leave any time for relaxation. A few extra days will enable you to explore more thoroughly or simply enjoy the leisure activities and beaches of Aqaba or the Dead Sea. Both places are ideal for this in spring and autumn. Snorkellers or divers may want to spend longer in Aqaba.

SUGGESTED ITINERARIES

Place names in italics are overnight stays.

✦ 14 days

Day 0: PM arrival. Pick up car if there is time. *Amman.*
Day 1: (Pick up car?) Mabada, Mt. Nebo, Hammamat Ma'in *Amman.*
Day 2: Jordan Valley tour, visiting al-Salt, Deir Allah, Tabqat al-Fahl (Pella), al-Hammah, Umm Qais (Gadara), *Irbid.*
Day 3: (From Irbid), Umm al-Jimal, Jerash, Ajlun, *Ajlun or Amman.*
Day 4: Desert Palaces and Azraq, *Amman.*
Day 5: Sites along the King's Highway, especially: Mukawir, Dhiban, Wadi Mujib (Arnon), Kerak, Hammamat Afra, Shobak, *Petra.*
Day 6: Tour Petra, *Petra.*
Day 7: Tour Petra, *Petra.*
Day 8: Wadi Rumm, *Aqaba.*
Day 9: Relax in Aqaba, *Aqaba.*
Day 10: Relax in Aqaba, *Aqaba.*
Day 11: Return to Amman via Desert Road to al-Karak, and then descend to Dead Sea and travel north towards Amman. *Dead Sea Rest House .*

Day 12: Dead Sea. *Rest House or Amman.*
Day 13: Wadi Seir, Amman, *Amman.*
Day 14: As you please.

✦ 10 days

Day 0: PM arrival, Pick up car if time.
Day 1: (Pick up car?) Mabada, Mt. Nebo, Hammamat Ma'in *Amman.*
Day 2: Tour Jordan Valley visiting al-Salt, Deir Allah, Tabqat al-Fahl (Pella), al-Hammah, Umm Qais (Gadara), *Irbid.*
Day 3: (From Irbid) Umm al-Jimal, Jerash, Ajlun, *Ajlun or Amman.*
Day 4: Desert Palaces and Azraq, *Amman.*
Day 5: Site's along the King's Highway, especially: Mukawir, Dhiban, Wadi Mujib (Arnon), Kerak, Hammamat Afra, Shobak, *Petra.*
Day 6: Tour Petra, *Petra.*
Day 7: Wadi Rumm, Aqaba. *Aqaba.*
Day 8: Relax in Aqaba. *Aqaba.*
Day 9: Return to Amman, tour Amman. *Amman.*
Day 10: Dead Sea, *Amman.*

A visit to Wadi Seir, just ouside Amman can be made late one afternoon as time allows. Day 4 would be suitable.

✦ 7 days

Day 0: PM arrival. pick up car if time. *Amman.*
Day 1: (Pick up car?) Umm al Jimal, Jerash, *Amman.*
Day 2: Mabada, Mt. Nebo, King's Highway etc to **Petra** (this will be a long day so leave early, selecting the places you visit carefully; Hammamat Ma'in and Afra could be missed, as could Dhat Ra). *Petra.*
Day 4: Tour Petra. *Petra.*
Day 5: Wadi Rumm, then return to *Amman.*
Day 6: Desert Palaces, and Azraq, (possibly Wadi Seir late in the day). *Amman.*
Day 7: Dead Sea, Amman. *Amman.*

If you want two full days at Petra (recommended) skip Day 6 tour.

5. Amman

INTRODUCTION

In the majority of Middle Eastern countries, the capital city is usually one of the high points of interest. Not so in Jordan. Though steeped in a rich history that goes back to early biblical times, today's Amman is a new city with very few signs remaining of its past.

main touring base

Having said that, Amman is also where most visitors arrive, and its position makes it an ideal base to see all the country except the south. It is also the home of a good proportion of the Kingdom's population, and the only city in Jordan that can boast every amenity the modern world can offer.

hilly city

Situated at a height of about 900 metres, 40 kilometres east of the river Jordan and on the fringe of the eastern desert, Amman is built on seven main hills *(jabaal)*. In fact when travelling around, in nearly every direction, you are either going up or down! And because of the valleys between the hills, lateral travel often requires a most circuitous route.

grew from village

When the Emir Abdullah established his administration here in the early 1920s, Amman was really just a large village with a population of no more than a thousand. By 1963 this had grown to a quarter of a million, and in 1994 was officially 1.2 million, although the unofficial figure may be much higher.

In spite of this rapid growth, Amman remains an essentially low rise city with few multi-storey buildings. The growth has been mainly around the girth, with new areas springing up all the time. Except for downtown and the areas close to it, the city is new – and looks and feels that way.

round in circles

When the city began to expand from the valley up towards Jabal Amman, traffic roundabouts (locally called circles) were built along the main road. Thus the first circle is that closest to downtown, and the eighth, the furthest from it. However, I warn you that most of the "circles" have now been replaced by traffic lights and flyovers, with only the first, second and third remaining as roundabouts; they are all, though, still called circles! If this confuses you, you are not alone!

clean and tidy

Although other writers have found the residential areas dull and uniform, I am not one of them. Having lived in a number of cities in this part of the world I find that, for a modern metropolis, Amman is extremely pleasing with many fine homes and bright apartment buildings. To Western eyes some of the architecture may look over-done and the Eiffel Tower TV antennas may summon a smile, but they bear a stamp which identifies them as a part of their own culture. What really stands out is the cleanliness, very unusual for the Middle East - or for that matter many a European capital!

public transport problems

A difficulty, especially for those visitors who do not have a vehicle, is transport around the city. This is mainly provided by *servees* taxis and often long queues form for these. The main routes are listed in the Amenities chapter.

Ordinary taxis are quite easy to stop and the fare is cheap. This may prove to be your best way of getting around this sprawling maze of a city even if you have rented a vehicle. Make sure the meter is activated; some drivers will quote you a price for the journey when you get in, but don't accept — the meter price is always lower!

snow sometimes

Because of the altitude the weather varies from being very cold in the winter, mild in spring and autumn and not too hot even in summer. It can, and often does, snow in winter, and the spring and autumn can be marred by the occasional hot dusty day caused by the strong east wind from the desert, the *khamsin*.

plenty of Palestinians

Over half the population is Palestinian in origin, the result of three wars with Israel plus nearly 30 years of quite restrictive Israeli control over the Palestinian areas of the West Bank. Their origin is often reflected in the names given to their shops and other businesses: Haifa Hotel, Nablus Restaurant, Jerusalem Sweets etc. Many people you will come into contact with will hail from these areas. The owner of a car rental agency I frequently use came to Amman from Nablus as a youth of 15 after fleeing with his family in the wake of the Israeli occupation which followed the 1967 war. Hard work and enterprise, for which many Palestinians are renowned, enabled him to save money, open his business and prosper. When I asked him about the future he told me that if *real* peace came he would like to open a branch of his firm in Nablus, *"inshallah* [God willing]"!

no Cairo

Don't expect to see a city of oriental *souks* or other eastern delights as found in profusion in Cairo, Istanbul, Damascus or Aleppo. The closest you'll come to this is perhaps in the side streets of the old downtown area, especially on Friday after mid-day prayers.

down in the valley

When I say downtown, I mean exactly that! For this district lies in a valley, surrounded by the heights of Amman's *jabaal* (mountains); to the south are Jabal al-Nadhif, Jabal al-Ashrafieh, Jabal al-Jaufeh and Jabal al-Taj; while to the north are Jabal Amman and Jabal Hussein. Jabal al-Qala'a rises directly to the northwest, topped by the ancient citadel. To get downtown by almost any approach you have to descend markedly, often via narrow roads that switch back again and again.

river covered

Through this valley once flowed Wadi Amman, or Wadi Abdun as it is also called today. The water emanated from a spring to the west, and although a short section was covered in Roman times, modern construction has meant that it is now more or less completely covered over, and what is left is pumped dry. The wadi emerged in the north west of the city, eventually joining the upper course of Wadi al-Zarka (the Jabbok).

water from the desert

Once upon a time, the springs that fed this flow supplied Amman's daily water needs; now with a population of 1.2 million, large quantities have to be pumped from elsewhere, with much of this coming from the springs of Azraq, the oasis in the eastern desert. When flowing the wadi must have been very abundant as Amman is referred to as "the city of waters" in the Bible (II Samuel 12:27), an appellation that would hardly be appropriate today.

HISTORY

The centre of Amman's ancient past has always been Jabal al-Qala'a, or citadel hill. This is a rather small triangular plateau north of the wadi that is today's old town centre. Excavations there have shown that this site was used as early as the Middle Bronze Age, the 17th to 16th century BC, and perhaps in the Old Bronze Age, 2000 years BC.

King Og's bed

Amman is referred to in the Bible variously as "Rabbah of the sons of Ammon" (Deuteronomy 3:11 and II Samuel 12:26), "the city of waters" (II Samuel 12:27) and Rabbath Ammon. It was the city that possessed the "iron bedstead" of King Og, the last of the Anakim or giants (Deuteronomy 3:11).

David and Batsheba

Around 1000 BC, King David besieged the city and captured it (II Samuel 12:29). It was during this seige that Uriah, the husband of Batsheba who David seduced, was killed after David deliberately had him sent to the front line.

Conforming to the usual Old Testament biblical practice in victory, David acted with great cruelty: *"He brought out the people who were in it* (the city) *and set them under saws, sharp iron instruments, and iron axes, and made them pass through the brick kiln..." (II Samuel 12:31)*

prophets of doom

Henceforth Rabbath Ammon, together with the Ammonites in general, were periodically vassals to the kings of Israel and Judea. Between the 8th and 6th centuries BC the biblical prophets of doom took turns in forecasting Ammon's destruction (as well as that of Israel and Judea). *"So I will kindle a fire on the wall of Rabbah, and it will consume her citadels..."(Amos 1:14)*. And, *"...the days are coming...that a trumpet blast of war will be heard against Rabbah of the sons of Ammon; and it will become a desolate heap, and her towns will be set on fire..."(Jeremiah 49:2)*. Later Ezekiel, after prophesying all manner of nasties for Israel and Judea also turned his attention to Ammon: the first seven verses of chapter 25 are devoted to its destruction.

None of these prophesies were fulfilled until the demise of the kingdom of Israel in 722 BC at the hands of the Assyrians, and the taking of Jerusalem by the neo-Chaldean or Babylonian ruler Nebuchadnezzar in 586 BC.

Ammon briefly allied to Nebuchadnezzar

The Ammonites were allied to Nebuchadnezzar when his army invaded Judea. *"In his days Nebuchadnezzar king of Babylon came up...And the Lord sent against him* [Jehoiakim, king of Judea] *bands of...Ammonites. So he sent them against Judah to destroy it..." (II Kings 24:1-2)*. The defeated Judeans were taken into captivity. But the Ammonite flirtation with the Babylonians did not last and before long they too were put down by them, and many of them exiled.

Persians and then Greeks

In the next centuries the history of Amman parallels the history of Jordan and the region with the Achaemenid Persians the masters.

This Achaemenid rule continued until 333 BC when they were defeated by Alexander at the Battle of Issus.

Thus began the Hellenisation of the Middle East, and when Alexander died ten years later his empire was divided between the Ptolemies and the Seleucids, the former gaining control of most of Jordan, including Amman, and Egypt.

original Philadelphia

The second Ptolemaic ruler, Ptolemy II Philadelphus (reigned 285-247 BC) took a special interest in Amman, rebuilding it in Greek fashion and giving it the name **Philadelphia** (brotherly love). Rivalry between the Ptolemies and the Seleucids was constant, and in 218 the city fell to the Seleucid king, Antiochus III, after a long seige.

Although Philadelphia was one of the Decapolis cities (see box, page 107), in the last century BC it was occupied by the Nabateans, and seems to have been excluded, at least initially, from the Roman conquest of the area by Pompey in 64 BC. During this period the old Semitic name, Ammon, may have been revived, or at least used alongside Philadelphia. Herod the Great took the city from the Nabateans in 31 BC, and as he was a Roman protegé the Romanisation of the city probably began from then.

Romans redecorate

After the Romans took over the city was again rebuilt, this time along Roman lines, and practically all traces of the past were erased. On the important *via nova Traiana*, the route which connected Bosra with the Red Sea, Amman was a city of some importance.

Byzantium precedes Islam

During Byzantine rule Philadelphia was a bishopric and a centre of Christian activity. In the 6th century the Ghassanids, a Christian Arab tribe, ruled the city for a period. AD 614 saw Philadelphia overrun by the Sasanian Persians, but it was soon back in the hands of the Byzantines.

This respite was short-lived as Amman fell to the invading Muslims in 635. For a while the city continued to exist, but by the 10th century one Arab traveller described it as a "desert harbour and a place of refuge for the Bedouins." In the 15th century it was described as a field of ruins and was totally deserted.

Caucasian refugees

In the late 19th century Circassian Muslims fled to the Muslim Ottoman Empire after the Russian conquest of their Caucasus homeland. Some were settled in the vestiges of the former Roman city of Philadelphia, which now became the poor village of Amman. Many remains of Greco-Roman edifices seen by early travellers, and described in particular by J.L. Burckhardt, were destroyed totally as the settlers used the materials to build their houses etc.

Abdullah's capital

After the First World War, when the British made the Emir Abdullah ruler of TransJordan he choose Amman to be his capital after considering also Salt, which had been the centre for the Turkish administration.

THE VISIT

As already mentioned, Amman, in spite of a long history, has few sites. Almost all the remains are Roman or post Roman, everything earlier having been obliterated — and much of what did survive the many centuries has been lost in the last 100 years of frenzied development. This can be deduced from Burckhardt's journal of 1812 in which he records the existence of many monuments that are no more.

site improvements

What has endured has now been carefully preserved and researched. In recent years, the tourist drive has made the authorities even more aware of the interest that historical edifices provide and, few though they may be, the restoration has rendered them very worthy of visiting. They are all in the downtown area so once you are there they can mostly be visited on foot. How long it takes depends on your degree of interest and fascination; including the museum, at least 3 hours, but perhaps a good half day should be allocated.

► ## Al-Husseini Mosque

We'll start our tour from the **Al Husseini Mosque** on Al-Malak al-Talal Street, on the corner of Al-Malak al-Faisal Street. This mosque, with twin minarets, is the largest and one of the most important in Amman. Constructed in 1924, it was erected on the site of a 9th century Abbasid mosque which in turn was built over the Byzantine cathedral of Philadelphia.

King prays here

Every once in a while King Hussein prays here. On Friday it is very busy, as is the entire surrounding area, which then becomes a huge street *souk*. The large area in front of the mosque is especially lively and you will see and hear many animated conversations going on there.

► ## The Nymphaeum

Walking east from the mosque for about 500 metres you will come to the Roman theatre and the monuments around it. On the way you pass by Amman's most recently restored monument — Philadelphia's **Nymphaeum**.

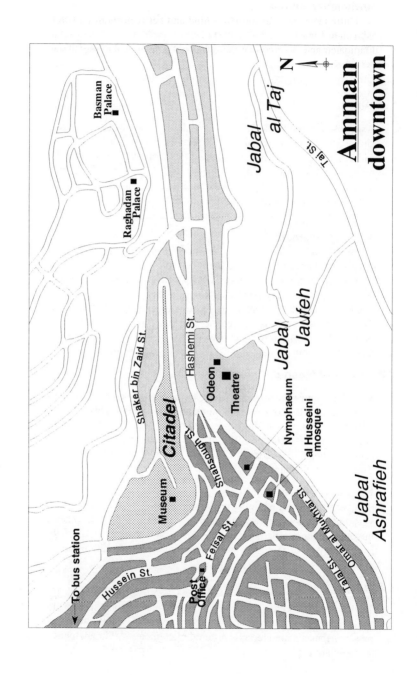

Amman downtown

N

Jabal al Taj

Taj St.

Basman Palace

Raghadan Palace

Jabal Jaufeh

Shaker bin Zaid St.

Hashemi St.

Citadel

Odeon

Theatre

Nymphaeum

al Husseini mosque

Jabal Ashrafieh

Museum

Shabsough St.

Feisal St.

Omar al Mukhtar St.

Jabal St.

To bus station

Hussein St.

Post Office

newly revealed beauty

Until 1995 this was hidden behind and between shops and was difficult to locate. Even for those who did find it, the edifice was so dilapidated and covered that there was not a great deal to see. Now the Department of Antiquities has decided to restore it. Some surrounding buildings have been demolished and, since the excavations, the edifice has been exposed and the sheer size is astounding. At the time of writing restoration work is continuing but even prior to its completion the nymphaeum is worth a visit.

You'll find it by crossing over the main road just past the al-Hussein Mosque, and taking the first passage on the right. A clothing store, al-Shamaan, is on the corner; the monument is at the end of the passage.

running waters (once)

The nymphaeum stood on or near the bank of the flowing wadi, and in its day was a handsome structure. Alas, though it may be made beautiful again it will never stand by flowing water!

Abdullah's office

Until a few years ago, facing the theatre was the old Philadelphia Hotel, one of Amman's first "real" hotels. The Emir Abdullah, then ruler of TransJordan, had his office next door to the hotel. The river rolled right by. This small enclave *was* Amman in those days, an Amman with no paved streets, a commercial activity that was no more than a *souk* and a very decidedly oriental ambience.

▸ The Roman Theatre

This very impressive theatre was built in the mid second century during the reign of Emperor Anoninus Piustime, AD 138-161.

built into hillside

As with many Roman theatres, the hillside has been partly cut away, and the structure built into the cavity. The *cavea* which seats about 6000 spectators is divided into three *maeniana* with the first and second, and second and third separated by a level space. Above these *maeniana* is a small structure that could have been a box for special visitors or even a shrine for a deity. The *cavea* was entered through vaulted passages that opened onto the level areas, and thus to the seats. Restoration of this monument began in the late 1950s, and was finished in 1970. The

Jordanian Department of Antiquities has made a pretty good job of it, and it is frequently used for performances.

sound engineering

Of special interest are the acoustics. Try standing at one end of the curved stage area and put your ear to the low wall. Get a companion to speak softly at the other end, also close to the wall. You will be able to hear each other perfectly! This "whispering gallery" effect is particularly intriguing as the wall is not entire, having an entranceway cut out of it half way round!

Another feature is the echo. If you stand centre stage towards the back your voice will echo strongly, but you must be in the exact centre. A small cross is engraved on the ground to show you where to stand. A few centimetres either way and there will be no echo!

public plaza

Outside the theatre, to the north, is a colonnaded forum, now partly restored. North of this, where the road now runs, was the flowing wadi which is still marked on maps of the late 1950s. The theatre was approached by a bridge across this stream. The area has again been turned into the modern equivalent of a Roman forum with trees, benches, cafes, kiosks and fountains dotted around. It is a very enjoyable spot to relax in.

risen from ruins

On the east side of the forum is a small **odeon** which was heavily ruined. Until the demise of the Philadelphia Hotel it adjoined its gardens. Restoration is not quite complete but you can get a view inside.

► Museums at the Theatre

In the wings of the theatre are two small museums with similar themes. The **Folklore Museum**, in the right wing, shows the traditional way of life of the Jordanian people, particularly the Bedouin. There is even an authentic goat hair tent (many used today are just made of fabric!) complete with all the living paraphernalia.

In the left wing is the **Museum of Costumes and Jewels.** Here, the traditional garbs of the Jordanian people are displayed together with their jewellery, a very important item for Bedouin women. On marriage an Arab woman is given much jewellery, mainly gold, by her husband. Many a young man has to work and save hard to acquire the funds for the *mohar* or bride price and for the requisite jewellery. (As a result he is often not so young by the time he takes his bride!)

► Jabal Qala'a, Citadel Hill

On top of the town

Just northwest of the theatre area and about 100 metres high above it, is **Jabal Qala'a** or Citadel Hill. Looking up from the theatre area you can see part of the remains, including an arch on top. From the summit you get a superb view over downtown Amman, and this is one of the reasons for the ascent! Although the very energetic could scramble their way up the hillside, I recommend that you take a taxi. Just ask for *al-Qala'a*, the citadel. For those who want to walk, save it for the descent! This acropolis was in use as early as the Bronze Age, but all the visible remains are from the Roman, Byzantine and early Muslim periods.

precipitous drop

The citadel area is a triangular plateau on the south of the mountain. Its sides are quite sheer on all boundaries except the north where it is joined to the rest of the mountain. The plateau was surrounded by a wall, and stretches of this have survived. During 1995 some of these were being restored.

Christian or Muslim?

Of the ruins, the largest is the rectangular one known as the **Palace,** sited towards the centre. Noted in the 1950s as "rather dilapidated", renovations have much improved on that description. It either belongs to the period of the 6th century Christian Ghassanid tribe or to the 7th and 8th century Omayyad era. The structure is in the form of a Greek cross inside a square surround.

fallen roof

Originally it had a cupola roof, but this has now gone and it is open to the sky. All around the inner walls are small decorative arches and niches ornamented with arabesques, palms and vines. The arms of the cross interior are vaulted. The purpose of this structure is not clear, but it may have been a reception or audience palace. To the south of this building you can see what is left of a **Byzantine basilica**. It dates from the 6th century and when it was excavated a mosaic floor was discovered. This has now been covered over for protection.

Herculean height!

In the south west corner stood a **Roman temple** dedicated to Hercules. Partly restored in recent years, it dates from the last half of the 2nd century during the reign of Marcus Aurelius. At one time a huge statue of Hercules stood by the temple, and from fragments found, it is estimated that it was almost 10 metres high.

King's homes

To the east of the hill you can see the Raghadan and Basman palaces, two of the modern royal palaces.

▶ **National Archaeological Museum**

Dead Sea Scrolls

The National Archaeological Museum on Citadel Hill, although small, offers some interesting exhibits. Among these is a replica of the

Mesha Stone (see box, page 149) and some of the Dead Sea Scrolls, the significant documents from the first century BC/AD which were found in caves near the north west shore of the sea. Near the entrance is a head of the patron deity of the city, the goddess Tyche. For the interested there is much else besides.

► **The modern city**

There are only two places of general interest in the modern part of Amman, and they are very near one another.

blue and white marble

The **King Abdullah Mosque** is just off King Hussein Street not far from the Abdali Bus Station. This mosque, completed only a few years ago, is worth a visit. Faced with blue and white marble it can be seen from most of Amman's high points, and is destined to become a city landmark.

no camera!

Opposite is the new **National Assembly Building,** still not quite finished (as of late 1995). Security is very tight here and not only are you not permitted to enter, but unfortunately photographing the building is also prohibited.

NEAR AMMAN

Many places described elsewhere in this book are close to Amman and can easily be reached in day trips from the city. However, returning to Amman may not always fit in with your itinerary and you will have to decide if it would be applicable. But there is one very interesting site just west of Amman which is definitely preferable to visit while staying in the capital. If you have a vehicle a couple of hours should suffice.

► **ARAQ AL-AMIR (Cave of the Prince) or Qasr al-Abed (Palace of the Servant)**

Alluring alcazar

About 18 kilometres west of the city in the area called Wadi al-Seir is **Araq al-Amir,** also known as **Qasr al-Abed**, the Palace of the Servant. This is a fascinating place with an equally fascinating history.

fruitful valley

Impressively built of unbelievably massive blocks of quarried stone, I do not know why so few tourists venture the short distance to visit it. I urge you not to miss it, especially as the wadi in which it is situated is so fertile. If you have just returned from the desert, this trip will be in stark contrast.

How to get there

Take the road that leaves Amman to the west, signposted to Wadi Seir. In the city the signposts are few, but most people, especially taxi drivers, will point you to the right road. Once out of the city the route is clearly signposted (although some say Iraq al-Amir), so keep an eye out for them.

By bus: To get there by public transport take the bus from near Ali bin Abi Taleb Street, west of the Hussein Mosque, to the large village of Wadi Seir. From here another one, unfortunately irregular, will take you to Araq al-Seir, very close to Araq al-Amir. Qasr al-Abed is a short walk from there.

verdant vale

The road descends the whole way into the valley, and eventually reaches the village of Wadi Seir, populated mainly by Circassians. From here the road continues down into a valley that is particularly beautiful in the spring when it bursts with colour, but is even verdant in summer due to the many springs in the vicinity. You will quickly see why it is a choice picnic and excursion area, especially on Fridays, for those who dwell in the crowded metropolis.

rock facade

A few kilometres past the village, on the right, you can pick out the remains of an archaic **aqueduct**. Soon on the left you pass a rock facade known as **al-Deir**, the monastery, but there is nothing there to indicate why it acquired this title. Inside are so many small niches that it was in all probability an ancient dovecote.

cavernous caves

Nearby, on the right, is **Araq al-Amir**, the caves of the prince (this name is generally used to describe both the caves and the palace, even though they are some distance from each other), hewn from the cliff face and in two rows, one above the other.

The upper row consists of a gallery some 300 metres long, and runs along the rock face. The rest of the caves can be accessed by way of passages and steps, and all told there are 14 of them.

They are not very well cut, and with the exception of a couple, are undecorated. These are on the lower level and have doors. By the doors, carved in old Hebrew or Aramaic characters, is the name Tobias. According to the Jewish historian Josephus, these caves were hewn at the same time as the palace was built (see below).

affable custodian

The edifice called **Qasr al-Abed** is at the end of the road, and fenced off. There is a guardian, a very pleasant character who will show you around. Unfortunately he does not speak English so if you want to avail yourself of his services it will have to be in Arabic or by sign language!

Hebrew name

The building as well as the caves appears to be the work of the influential Tobiad dynasty who were powerful in the Amman area from the time of Xerxes, the Achaemenid Persian ruler between 486 and 463 BC. The family came from the area north and west of Ammon where they built the Araq al-Amir fortress. The first Tobias (Hebrew *Tuviah* meaning "goodness of God") we know about is mentioned in the Bible during the Judean exile in Babylon in the reign of Xerxes, where Nehemiah twice in Chapter 2 (vs 10 & 19) refers to *"Tobiah the Ammonite official [or servant]"*. This reference could possibly be the reason why the fortress is called Palace of the Servant.

Jerusalem's walls

If so, this Tobiah would have been the governor of Ammon who opposed, fruitlessly, the rebuilding of the walls of Jerusalem. A later Tobiah is recorded in the reign of Ptolemy II Philadelphus, (283-246). This one was linked with the priesthood in Jerusalem as he was married to a sister of Onias II the high priest (Josephus, Antiquities, 12:160).

During the time of his son, Joseph, who according to Josephus *"...was still a young man but because of his dignity and foresight had a reputation for uprightness..." (Antiquities, 12:120)*, the Tobiads reached the zenith of their power and influence.

suicide of Hyrcanus

In 218 BC the Seleucid Antiochus III, took Philadelphia from the Ptolemies. Joseph's son, Hyrcanus sided with the Ptolemies, actually establishing a small anti-Seleucid state west of Philadelphia and around the Tobiad castle. He was only reduced when the succeeding ruler Antiochus IV (the Seleucid ruler associated with Judas Maccabeus and the Feast of Lights) sent a force against him. After being defeated, Hyrcanus killed himself in 175 BC. The dynasty then fades from history.

slipshod writing

Josephus further relates that Hyrcanus *"built a strong fortress, which was constructed entirely of white marble up to the roof, and had beasts of gigantic size carved on it... He also cut through the projecting rock opposite the mountain, and made caves many stades in length; then he made chambers in it, some for banqueting and others for sleeping and living...and when he had completed the place in this manner, he named it Tyre." (Antiquities, 12:230-233).*

Josephus, often a careless writer, undoubtedly got some of this wrong. Ancient papyri clearly show that this building was completed long before Hyrcanus' time, possibly in the lifetime of Nehemiah in the 5th century. The white marble was probably an exaggeration. "Tyre" is the Greek form of the Aramaic *tura,* mountain, which becomes *seir* in old Hebrew and Arabic, thus corresponding with the name of the valley, Wadi al-Seir.

ruins restored

When first discovered, the qasr was in ruins, due mainly to the method of construction. Initially excavated in 1903-4 by the Princeton Archaeological Expedition, further research was conducted in 1976 by French and Jordanian archaeologists prior to partial restoration, a process completed in 1987.

how did they do that?

Qasr al-Abed is built from huge blocks of stone, some weighing more than fifty tons! During restoration, the largest cranes available were used to replace some of those that had fallen, and often two cranes were needed to lift one block! The gigantic pieces still on the ground outside the entrance could not be raised by any available equipment! These massive blocks, some 7 metres long and 3 metres high were only very narrow, often no more than half a metre thick. They were set up, peculiarly, on an equally narrow ledge in such a manner that even minor earth tremors were able to dislodge them!

Inside are remains of columns and capitals, and one large block has been cut for steps indicating that the palace had a second storey. The blocks were originally quarried about 5 kilometres away, so we can but wonder how they reached this spot!

pink lion

In keeping with Josephus' description, the palace was once covered with carvings of animals. The best of what survives are found in the north west corner. The carving on the east side was a lion fountain with the water issuing from the paws. There were three entrance doors. On the right of the southern one there is the figure of a lion, carved in pink and white breccia. The excavations have shown that the building was used in Byzantine times, when the interior was so changed that the original layout cannot be determined for certain.

I'm sure you'll agree that the short journey to reach this unusual site was well worthwhile.

6. Madaba and vicinity

INTRODUCTION

Madaba is the first stop on the route south known as the King's Highway (chapter 11), but as there is so much to see there and at nearby Mt Nebo, I recommend that if you want a thorough visit to both these places plus time to explore all the sites along the King's Highway, you should visit the Madaba region separately. You can also travel to the hot springs of **Zerka Ma'in** at the same time, as these are east of Madaba.

How to get there

Madaba is an easy drive of some c30 kilometres south west of Amman.
By car: Take the road to the airport and Aqaba and after about 20 kilometres a right hand signposted fork points to Madaba.
By bus: For non-drivers, there is a fairly good and regular bus service from the Wahadat bus station in the south of the city. In Madaba the bus station is at the entrance to the town, on the King's Highway.

HISTORY

biblical town

Originally an Ammonite and later a Moabite town, the centre of Madaba sits on the *tell* of the town of antiquity. The earliest signs of habitation date from the 13th century BC. Built on a slight elevation on the plateau that comprises most of Jordan, the centre has been raised even higher by the *tell* of the ancient settlement. Often mentioned in the Bible when it was known as Medeba, the town was captured by the Israelites during their wanderings:

> *"But we have cast them down, Heshbon is ruined as far as Dibbon, then we have laid waste even to Nophah, which reaches to Medeba." (Numbers 21:30)*

And again when Canaan was divided between the tribes of Israel:

> "...the Reubenites and the Gadites received their
> inheritance...beyond the Jordan...from Aroer which is on the
> edge of the valley of the Arnon...and all the plain of
> Medeba..." (Joshua 13:9)

fluctuating fortunes

King David defeated an army of Ammonites there (I Chronicles 19:7ff), but it must have been recovered either by the Ammonites or Moabites later as the Mesha (or Moabite) Stone (see box, page 149) records in line 7 that the Israelite king, Omri (who the Bible tells us did *"evil in the sight of the Lord, and acted more wickedly than all those before him."* (1 Kings 16:25), had taken possession of it. The stone then records that Mesha recaptured the town (line 9). Perhaps during this action Madaba was badly damaged as Mesha had to rebuild it (lines 29 & 30 of the Stone).

By the time of the Maccabees, Madaba had long been restored to Ammonite rule but in 110 BC, according to Josephus, John Hyrcanus restored it to Hasmonean (Jewish) control after a lengthy siege. The town remained under the control of the Hasmoneans throughout the reign of Alexander Yannai. Hyrcanus II presented it to the Nabatean king, Aretas III for his help against his brother Aristobulus.

finally the Romans

Like everywhere else in the region, Madaba became part of the Roman Empire in AD 105 and was incorporated into *Provincia Arabia*. The Romans replanned the city along their typical lines, and it became a classic small Roman provincial town with colonnaded streets, baths and temples. Under Byzantine rule, Madaba was a flourishing Christian town, and is reputed to have had 13 churches. It became a bishopric and was represented at the Council of Chalcedon in 451. Justinian built a huge cistern in the north of the town, and his name can still be seen on the walls near the Greek Orthodox Church.

Madaba disappears

Madaba continued as a Christian town well into the Islamic era, and it remained a settlement into the Mameluke era. After that it appears to have been abandoned.

the re-discovery

In 1807 the explorer Ulrich Seetzen visited the ruins but noticed only two columns with a lintel. The local people called this *al-Mishnaqa*, the gallows, so we are left in little doubt what they were originally used for!

In 1812 J.L. Burckhardt passed through and what he found was very scant:

"I observed many remains of the walls of private houses...but not a single edifice is standing. There is a large birket (cistern) which, as there is no spring at Madeba, might still be of use to the Bedouins...On the west side of the town are foundations of a temple, built with large stones, and apparently of great antiquity...At the entrance of one of the courts stand two columns of the Doric order..."
(J.L.Burckhardt, Travels in Syria and the Holy Land).

Christians re-settle

In 1880 a Christian community from al-Karak resettled the town, and the modern Madaba dates from then. As the town grew it covered most of the relics of the past, and only in the last 30 years or so have many of these come to light. Like most towns in Jordan the population has expanded considerably during the past 20 years, and although the centre which mostly stands on the *tell* is very pleasant, urban sprawl at the edges is beginning to show.

THE VISIT

Town of mosaics

Despite the lack of structural remnants, Madaba is known for the many Byzantine mosaics which have been uncovered in churches and private homes and if you have a great interest in this form of art, spend some time here.

▶ THE MADABA ARCHAEOLOGICAL PARK

In 1991 the Jordanian Ministry of Tourism and Department of Antiquities, in conjunction with the American Centre of Oriental Research, started to plan an Archaeological Park that would encompass most of Madaba's Roman and Byzantine remains. At the time of writing this project has not been completed but many of the sites can still be visited. As they are mostly in the centre of town, on the *tell* of the original town, they are easily accessible on foot. All the sites described below are encompassed within the Park.

▶ CHURCH OF ST GEORGE

famous map of the Holy Land

Of all the mosaics in Madaba, the most renowned is the mosaic map which is incorporated into the floor of the Greek Orthodox Church of St George in the town centre. It was discovered in 1884 when the modern church was being built over the ruins of a Byzantine church that stood on the site. Unfortunately, it was not brought to the notice of scholars until several years later by which time it had been partly ruined, so today only sections survive. The 6th century mosaic depicts the Holy Land and much of the Middle East in the form of a decorative map, and is certainly the most impressive item to survive from the Byzantine era.

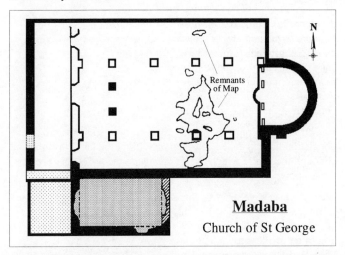

N

Remnants of Map

Madaba
Church of St George

from Lebanon to the Nile

It is orientated to the east, with the Mediterranean Sea at the bottom. The complete map depicted the area from Tyre (Lebanon) in the north to the Nile Delta (Egypt) in the south, and from the sea in the west to the desert (Jordan) in the east. The texts give the (then) contemporary Greek names of places as well as the biblical ones. In some sections there is a historical note together with the appropriate verse taken from the Septuagint (the Greek translation of the Old Testament). Because of the realistic relief nearly all the named locations have been identified.

Jerusalem characterised

It is the section depicting Jerusalem which is particularly interesting. Clearly seen are two colonnaded streets, one being the recently restored charta. The Church of the Holy Sepulchre is given most prominence, although other churches like those on Mount Zion are clearly depicted. When laid the map measured 22 metres by 7 metres and covered most of the church's transept.

pictorial embellishments

The artists have incorporated such features as springs in the Jordan Valley, palm trees at Jericho and fish in the river Jordan. Even the castle at al-Karak is there. It is interesting that Jerusalem has been placed in the centre as if the city was truly the centre of the Christian world.

This mosaic was restored by a German team in the mid 1960s. Try not to miss it as it is one of the treasures of Jordan.

▸ THE ROMAN STREET

South of St George are most of Madaba's ancient relics, and these are grouped around two uncovered sections of the Roman road that ran from the east to west gates. In late Byzantine and Omayyad times this road was covered by a layer of beaten earth, and the columns which flanked it were recycled into later buildings. When constructed it consisted of large flagstones, many of which have survived due to the earth covering. Most of this thoroughfare has been built over by the modern town, but the two excavated sections are interesting.

The first section is reached by turning south outside the Church of St George and following the road around to the west. This is al-Hussein bin Ali Street. About halfway down on the right is the Madaba Society Shop, where souvenirs etc are on sale. By the side a passage leads to the tourist office, but don't count on this being open. Behind it you'll see part of the Roman road which appears more like a courtyard. The second section is to be found further east (see below).

▸ THE BURNT PALACE

This ruined building is at the east end of this first stretch of Roman road behind the tourist office.

In 1905 an archaeologist discovered a mosaic here and deduced that the building was

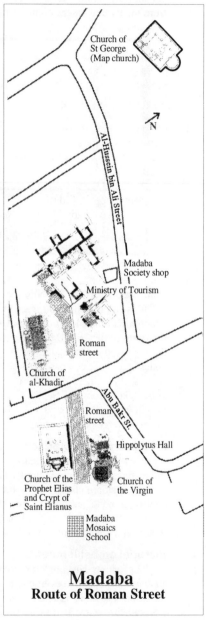

Madaba
Route of Roman Street

that of a church. Further excavations were conducted in 1985 by Fr. Michele Piccirillo of the Custodia Terra Sancta which revealed that the building was in fact a grand residence or palace. Other mosaics were uncovered in different sections and some of these are quite outstanding. The palace was erected in the late 6th or early 7th century, and evidence of devastation by fire points to it being destroyed by the earthquake of AD 748. The mosaics have been removed for restoration so you will not see them in situ though they should go on display when the park is completed.

▶ CHURCH OF AL-KHADIR

To the south of this stretch of road, up against the wall, are the very scant relics of the Church of al-Khadir. It was uncovered in the first years of the 20th century, and the non Byzantine name was locally acquired. Excavations in 1966 have dated it to the 6th century. It was a basilica and the builders re-cycled Roman columns into its design. A fairly well-preserved mosaic was found, although like many others elsewhere in Madaba, this has been removed for treatment.

▶ THE CHURCH OF THE VIRGIN AND HIPPOLYTUS HALL

These are on the second piece of the Roman thoroughfare. As modern buildings and streets cut the two sections off from each other, to get there return to the street of the Madaba Society shop and turn right. Continue down to the end of the street, turn right and then immediately left into Abu Bakr Street. The walled-in buildings can be seen over on the right. Extensive work is being carried out here in preparation for the Park, due for completion during 1996.

new packaging

Both the Church of the Virgin, and Hippolytus Hall are housed in a new glass and stone structure with internal raised walkways to enable easy viewing of the mosaics. The church is at the west end and the hall at the east. In reality the church was built on top of part of the hall.

Hippolytus Hall was the hall of an early 6th century house. Part of it discovered in the early 20th century, while the rest was only unearthed in 1982 by Fr. Michele Piccirillo. The roof of the hall was supported by arches, the remains of which are still visible along the northern and southern walls. A border of acanthus scrolls containing various pastoral scenes are in the mosaic's centre. Other panels depict flowers, plants and birds.

Greek tragedy

The hall gets its name from the portion of the mosaic that shows some of the characters from the tragedy of Phaedra and Hippolytus, a story by Euripides. Captions identify the names of those depicted in a scene showing maidservants assisting Phaedra. Another portion shows Hippolytus accompanied by his ministers, and a groom holding his horse. This latter section is partly destroyed. In another section Aphrodite is seated on a throne next to Adonis. The other figures are the Three Graces and cupids. Pastoral emphasis comes from the scene of a girl carrying a basket of fruit on her shoulder and a bird in her hand.

three cities

Along the east wall there are representations of three cities and two sea-monsters. The cities are Rome, Gregoria and Madaba. Each is shown as a Tyche seated on a throne with a cross and staff in the right hand.

The Church of the Virgin, dating from the end of the 6th century, was partly constructed over a Roman monument. The church had a circular nave and an apsed presbytery. The mosaic in the nave has been dated to two periods. The earlier consists of flower blossoms and buds running along the edge and is concurrent with the original mosaic from the late 6th century

strong exhortations

The better preserved and later section dates from the Omayyad period of the 7th century. It comprises of a rectangular frame decorated on the outer edge by a series of serrated points. In the centre is a round medallion with an inscription that reads, *"If you want to look at Mary, virginal Mother of God, and to Christ whom she generated, Universal King, only Son of the only God, purify with your mind, flesh and works! May you purify with your prayer the people of God."* Another inscription in front of the chancel records that the mosaic was laid in the time of a Bishop Theophane, and continues, *"thanks to the zeal and ardour of the people who love Christ in this city of Madaba...".*

As noted, the two above edifices are jointly housed and they should be open to the public in the near future, along with a wide array of other restored mosaics of Madaba.

▶ CHURCH OF THE PROPHET ELIAS

To the south of the above and on the other side of the Roman road behind a wall is the Church of the Prophet Elias with the **Crypt of St Elianus** below it. The church, discovered in 1897 in a state of ruination was further destroyed in later years as Madaba was rebuilt. Excavations were undertaken in 1992 and some mosaics were found. The crypt, discovered at the same time, is reached by two flights of stairs from the church. Both flights end on a mosaic decorated landing. The apse and nave have mosaic floors and the one in the nave bears the dedicatory inscription, *"The Christ God has erected this house at the time of the most pious Bishop Sergius, for the care of Sergius, the priest of St. Elianus, the year 490 (this corresponds to AD 596)...".* At present both places are closed, but who knows...?

► CHURCH OF THE APOSTLES

To the south east of the town, covered by a new building with a red tiled roof, is the **Church of the Apostles.** You will find it on your right across traffic lights, just before you leave town south on the King's Highway. At the time of writing all the mosaics in this church are covered with protective sand while renovations, which include walkways for viewing, are carried out. Maybe by the time of your visit this will have been completed as there are some fine mosaics here. Originally a Byzantine church, it was discovered early this century by a Roman Catholic priest. It has been dated to 578 when a certain Sergius was Bishop and was built as a basilica with a central nave and two flanking aisles.

mermaid mosaic

The central feature of the mosaic in the nave is a depiction of the sea in the shape of a woman appearing from the water surrounded by fish and other sea creatures. Very unusual for a church, the woman is shown with half her body and one breast uncovered. The word *thalassa*, Greek for sea, is above her head. The aisles have patterned mosaics, both different.

► MADABA MUSEUM

There is also a museum where the main items on show are – you guessed it – mosaics. This is located not far from the above church in the direction of the town and is clearly signposted.

► Mosaics in homes

Many of the towns mosaics are located in private residences. With the help of a guide, available from the museum, some of these can be visited. Of particular interest is **Beit Mitri al-Masarawa** in the east of Madaba. Here there is a perfect floor mosaic depicting animals and a female head in the centre.

► MOUNT NEBO AND VICINITY

"Now Moses went up from the plains of Moab to Mount Nebo, to the top of Pisgah, which is opposite Jericho. And the Lord showed him Jericho and all the land..."

Deuteronomy 34:1

How to get there

Mount Nebo, *Jabal Niba,* lies about 10 kilometres north west of

71

Madaba. It is easily approached by road from Madaba, and the route is well signposted. Unfortunately, those without their own transport may have a problem. The nearest village is **Faysaliyah** and a minibus that starts near the Madaba tourist office goes there. Mount Nebo is some 4 kilometres further on and barring hitching a lift there is no alternative but to walk.

Introduction and history

Mount Nebo ascends from the plateau, and consists of a number of peaks. The highest is **al-Mukhayyat** on the southeast which reaches 790 metres. The other significant crest, **Siyagha**, reaches 710 metres. It is surrounded by Wadi Afrit on the east, Wadi Ayoun Musa on the north and the Jordan valley to the west. The important peak for visitors is Siyagha, and it is here that the **Memorial to the Prophet Moses** is situated.

dramatic setting

The site, comprising of an ancient basilica and monastery, is on the plateau precipice, and provides a dramatic backdrop to match its history.

Jerusalem visible (sometimes!)

On a clear day you can see across the Jordan to Jericho, and those with very keen eyesight may be able to make out the spires on the Mount of Olives, just east of Jerusalem. It is also possible to pick out Bethlehem, just south of Jerusalem, and Herod's stronghold of Herodion immediately to the south of that city.

Down below is the Dead Sea and Jericho lies slightly to the north of it. Looking down into the valley and northwards, you can see Ayoun Musa (see below), and the route of the Roman road that connected the ancient cities of Esbous (Hesbon) to the NE and Livas (Tel-Rameh) in the Jordan Valley below.

Stele at entrance to Basilica on Siyagha (Memorial of Moses)

Moses' last view

Nebo constitutes part of the heights of Abarim (Deut. 32:49). Although we are told that Moses went to the highest point – "pisgah", it is generally accepted that this was Siyagha because of the view which that crest affords: *"Go up to this mountain...Mount Nebo...and look at the land of Canaan..." (Deut. 32:49),* The extent he is supposed to have viewed cannot be seen from the higher peak of al-Mukhayyat.

prehistoric finds

Perennial springs in these wadis have enabled habitation in the area from the earliest times and tools, tombs and more that have been found here attest to this.

Siyagha has always been associated with Moses, and the Franciscan Custody of the Holy Land managed to purchase the site in 1933. Since then they have extensively excavated it, restoring the mosaics and turning the area into what it is today.

tomb of Moses?

Christians have venerated this location from at least the 4th century when the first church was built. It was rectangular with three apses and a vestibule entranceway and was constructed from blocks of limestone. The floor was mosaic, and fragments of this lie near the altar. To the north and south were funerary chapels and to the west an open courtyard bordered by monastery offices. A pilgrim Egeria nun who passed by in 394 described a church that "contained the tomb of

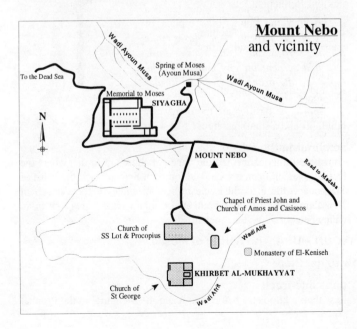

Moses". This is at variance with the biblical version, *"So Moses the servant of the Lord died there in the land of Moab...but no man knows his burial place...".* *Deuteronomy 34:5-6.*

travellers' rest

The site is recorded again in the early 6th century when the church, now much larger, was accompanied by other buildings. Six centuries later, a traveller on his way from Ein Gedi (at the southern end of the Dead Sea, on the west side) to Shobak, stayed the night at the monastery. Jumping forward another 400 years to the mid 16th century, according to a monk who visited the mountain the buildings were in ruins and abandoned.

THE VISIT

▸ THE BASILICA (Memorial to the Prophet Moses)

Covered by a modern structure the basilica as seen today is basically that of the enlarged 6th century church. The building is oriented east/west, the apse being at the eastern end. Parts of the aisle columns are still in place. Some of the mosaics from the floor have been removed and are now on the walls; others are still in situ and can be viewed from wooden walkways.

Outside, in front of the basilica overlooking the valley is a replica of Moses' bronze serpent: *"And Moses made a bronze serpent and set it on a standard; and if a serpent bit any man, when he looked to the bronze serpent, he lived."* *(Numbers 21:9)*

The Bronze Serpent

Below the basilica are the monastery buildings and a small rest house.

celebrating the feast

Interestingly, this is the only ancient church in Jordan where the liturgy is still implemented. The fourth of September is the Feast of Moses according to the ecclesiastical calendar of the Church of Jerusalem. On that day Christians from all over the area join in an ancient celebration at an ancient site.

▸ AYOUN MUSA, The Spring of Moses

How to get there

passable track

Less than a kilometre before you reach the Memorial to the Prophet

Moses, just opposite the rest house, a signposted track leads from the right as you ascend (north) down to **Wadi Ayoun Musa**, the Valley of the Spring of Moses. The track is stony, steep and very winding, but an ordinary vehicle can use it. Drive carefully, and on the way up don't rev the engine too much or you'll spin the wheels in the sand. Keep away from the track sides as the ground there tends to be more stony and the sand looser. It's 2.5 kilometres to the main spring, and well worth the detour.

still cultivated
On the way down you can see at various places to the right green fields cultivated by the local Bedouin. These have been farmed since ancient times, and the travelling nun, Egaria, who visited in 394 commented on them. There is plenty of evidence that this valley has been occupied since the 3rd millennium BC, and in an area where water was scarce the valley's springs were very important.

After c2.5 kilometres the drivable track terminates at the gate of a walled enclosure. Park your car here.

Bedouin watering place
The gate is closed, and inside are a few buildings and some remains of a Byzantine church. Walk around and over to the left below the wall you will see one of the main springs. Water from here is pumped up to Siyagha. Most likely there will be Bedouin girls with goats and sheep, filling their containers with the cool fresh water that gushes from a spring under a curved recess at the base of the wall.

Further down in the valley to the west are large patches of greenery, and the local Bedouin bring their flocks to the stream that flows from the spring.

The whole locality is very picturesque and may provide you with some authentic Bedouin photographs!

Roman milestones
On a ridge above the spring, to the north, is a track which was the Roman road from Esbous, the Heshbon of the Bible (Numbers 21:26-27, Judges 11:19), to Livias, Tel-Rameh, in the southern Jordan Valley. Some Roman milestones are still visible along this track as is what is left of an Iron Age fortress, al-Mushaqqar, on a crest to the north.

► KHIRBET AL-MUKHAYYAT
How to get there

About 3 km before the Nebo site a narrow road branches off to the left (S). (There is a signpost pointing to Mukhayyat, but this can only be seen travelling west, so if you intend to visit these ruins after the Memorial on Mt Nebo, make a mental note of it's position on your way up.) The road descends for a few hundred metres before arriving at a fork. The main one is left, and this is easily noticeable. It soon begins to climb, and a kilometre further ahead is a small building enclosed by a perimeter fence. Drive around the hill to the right and you'll arrive at a car park. Walkers can climb the path over the hill to reach the same place.

History

The ruins are part of the ancient town of Nebo, and today bear the collective name **Khirbet al-Mukhayyat**, the Ruins of Mukhayyat. The town of Nebo is mentioned several times in the Bible (I Chronicles 5:8, Isaiah 15:2, Jeremiah 48:1&22). At some time before the 7th century BC it must have been in Israelite hands as lines 14-16 of the Mesha stone record how the Moabite king conquered the place.

7,000 slain
Nebo was quite a large town for its time, as the Stone records that 7000 people were slain there.

During Byzantine times it was, together with Madaba, an important Christian centre with numerous churches. Over the centuries they were all buried and lost. Re-discovered in 1863, the area was not examined in detail until 1901 with the first major discovery, the mosaic in the Church of SS Lot and Procopius in 1913. The *tell* was bought by the Custodia Terra Sancta in 1935, and detailed archaeological excavations began.

five churches
Five churches have been discovered on or around the *tell* but only three are worth a visit. Inside the new building are the remains of the **Church of SS Lot and Procopius.**

Behind it, high on a hill, you can see the **Church of St. George**, and just to the east in Wadi Afrit the **Church of Amos and Casiseos** and the adjacent **Chapel of Priest John**.

► Church of SS Lot and Procopius

Of the three, only this church has its mosaics in situ, and they are among the most beautiful yet discovered in Jordan. The mosaics date from c562 when a certain John was Bishop of Madaba.

Not too many people come here and the building's door is often kept locked. However a guardian is usually lurking around, and as he can speak a little English will be able to explain some things to you.

It was in 1913, during the building of a private house that the mosaics were first discovered. The present shelter was constructed in 1935, and this has enabled the mosaics to be kept where they were found. The enclosing building is entered from the west side.

two nave mosaics
The small church had an apse and two side aisles which were separated from the nave by three pillars on each side. The bases of

these can still be seen. The floor was covered with mosaics, most of which survive.

The altar, before the apse, was approached by two steps and has a fine mosaic of two lambs facing a tree. (The lambs' bodies resemble horses, but the heads are clearly of sheep!) The nave is decorated with two main panels with an edge pattern all the way round although incomplete at the NW corner.

an offering of bulls

The panel at the west end, the smaller one, is composed of four trees with pairs of animals between them. The east side of this panel depicts two bulls before an altar with a burning flame. An inscription in front of it translates *"Then young bulls will be offered on Thine altar."* (Psalm 51:19)

byzantine inscriptions

The larger panel is mainly pastoral, showing a shepherd with his dog and sheep, a youth spearing a bear, a wolf eating grapes(!), wine making scenes, a hunter and his dog and an archer who has just shot a lion. At the altar end of this panel is an inscription that reads *"At the time of the most holy and most saintly Bishop John, your holy place was built and finished by its priest and sacristan in the month of November in the 6th indiction, O God of Saint Lot and Saint Procopius receive the offering in the presence of the brothers Stephen and Elias, the children of Comotisa...etc".*

The spaces between the pillars depict various scenes, the one nearest the entrance depicts a church building with a boatman on one side and a fisherman on the other.

The mosaics in the aisles were patterned, and the southern aisle terminates at the eastern end with the inscription *"O St. Lot, receive the prayer of Roma, Porphyria and Mary, your servants".*

no mosaics to be seen here

On a nearby hill is the **Church of St George** which formed part of a small monastery, which has yet to be investigated. This very ruined structure dates from c536, and was only discovered in 1935. Like the Church of SS Lot and Procopius it was decorated richly with mosaics. These were removed for restoration and some are on display at Siyagha. The church was built in rather a strange form, but was roughly square. The aisles were separated from the nave, which terminated in an apse, by two rows of pillars. At the eastern end of each of these was a small chapel. When excavated, mosaics were found in the nave, part of both aisles, the presbytery, and the southern (aisle) chapel.

church in the valley

To the east of the Church of SS Lot and Procopius, on the slopes of Wadi Afrit is the **Church of Amos and Casiseos**, and joined to it

the **Chapel of Priest John**. To get there, return to the fork and take the east fork. The church, the oldest yet discovered in the town of Nebo, was paved with flagstones and had been used as a house until acquired by the Custodia. The column bases of the altar are still visible on the raised presbytery beneath the easily identifiable apse.

same artists

The area on the north side is the Chapel of Priest John, and was a 6th century addition. This chapel, terminating with an apse, had a mosaic floor which when discovered was almost complete. Unfortunately it then suffered considerable damage until being removed for restoration. Photographs taken in 1939 show it was indeed a fine piece of art, probably executed by the same mosaicists who decorated the Church of SS Lot and Procopius.

High on a hill to the east of the town of Nebo are the meagre remains of the **Monastery of El-Keniseh**. It is not worth a visit.

► Way to the Dead Sea

By way of a postscript: You may have noticed when visiting the Memorial to Moses at Siyagha, a road (omitted or shown as a track on maps) to the left of the shrine pointing to the Dead Sea. This narrow road winds its way, often hair-raisingly, down to the southern end of the Jordan Valley and the northern tip of Dead Sea. Although it starts off promisingly this soon evaporates, and not just because of the heat! The surface is badly deteriorated and full of pot-holes. Still, it is better than a track. About halfway down the route veers to the right with a minor road continuing ahead. Make sure you keep to the right. Once down in the valley the road is unfinished (as of my last visit in October 1995), but the route is there and passable, if not yet sealed.

► HAMMAMAT MA'IN, Baths of Baaras

Back at Madaba an excursion to the hot springs at **Hammamat Ma'in** might be worthwhile if time allows. Now the site of a luxury hotel complex, Hammamat Ma'in is a series of hot springs emanating from the deep and very sheer canyon of **Wadi Zarka Ma'in.** The springs were known to the Byzantines as the *Baths of Baaras* and have a temperature in excess of 40°C. The whole area has been "landscaped" into the grounds of the hotel which has taken over the site.

desert waterfall

A feature of the springs is the waterfall. Set in a gorge above the Dead Sea, it is a sight to see the water as it cascades down the mountainside. Facilities have been constructed to enable visitors to enjoy the waters in a modern environment. Besides the expensive hotel located here, cheaper overnight accommodation in static caravans and a chalet-type hotel is available. There is an entrance charge into the spa.

How to get there

drive carefully!

Hammamat Ma'in is about 35 kilometre south west of Madaba, and the route is well signposted. The latter part of the journey can be heartstopping for its dramatic views and sharp descent, with Wadi Zarka Ma'in on the right. Some of the gradients are as much as 15% so drive with care!

By bus: For those who are travelling by bus the only way I know of reaching the Hammah is by JETT bus from Amman. It leaves from the terminal near the Abdali Bus Station. You should check the schedule beforehand. Otherwise once you are in Madaba you may find a "servees" taxi but this would be irregular.

the way to ancient Callirhoe

Just before the entrance to the spa, which is marked by a gate across the road, a new road, not complete at the time of writing, makes its way a further c4 kilometres down to where the Wadi empties into the Dead Sea. (Before attempting to use it ask at the gatehouse what its condition is.) Here is Ain Zara, which could be the classical Callirhoe. (See chapter on the **Dead Sea**.)

Herod bathed here

It was to Callirhoe that Herod would go, from his palace at Machaerus, to bathe in the waters in an attempt to heal his diseases.

▸ Ma'in village, Baal-Meon

Gift to tribe of Reuben

Between Madaba and Hammamat Ma'in is the village of Ma'in. Today there is hardly anything to see but for interest's sake this was the biblical *Baal-Meon* (see Numbers 32:38 and Joshua 13:17) where it is related that it was given to the tribe of Reuben. The location is also recorded on the *Mesha Stone*. Ma'in gets a later mention in the 4th century from Eusebius and had some importance in Byzantine times.

7. The Jordan Valley and Umm Qais (Gadara)

INTRODUCTION

Part of the great rift valley that stretches from northern Syria south into Africa, the Jordan Valley, or Ghor (as it is called in Jordan), is situated below sea level. Beginning at Lake Tiberias (the Sea of Galilee) in the north, even its high point is 210 metres below sea level. It extends south to the Dead Sea, some 400 metres below sea level, where it ends as it joins the depression south of the Dead Sea called Wadi Arava.

Through this valley the River Jordan flows. Rising in the Anti-Lebanon (mountains) in Lebanon and Syria, the river enters the northern end of Lake Tiberias, leaving it at the south for its journey through the Jordan Valley. The winding river is over 350 kilometres long, though spanning no more than 200 as the crow flies.

no deep river

The River Jordan, so romanticised in song and literature – and perhaps the most famous river in the world – may conjure up in your imagination a mighty watercourse. It may well once have been, but not in living memory; the river of today is hardly more than a stream! Centuries of change have doubtless had an effect and the Israelis, for whom Lake Tiberias is their main water source, only allow a small flow to pass from the lake into the river southwards, except in a very rainy winter when they open the lake's sluice gates. (I can remember once crossing the bridge between the Israeli held West Bank and Jordan with a party of American pilgrims. They were sorely disappointed when the bridge turned out to be a few metres long and the water beneath no more than a creek!)

troubled waters

The Jordanians, denied access to a fair share of the waters of the Jordan, rely on the River Yarmouk, a tributary river on the Syria-Jordan border. A canal, the Ghor or King Abdullah Canal, brings the water from this river down into the valley. There have been many disputes between Jordan and Israel over these waters, and only now, after the reconciliation between the two countries will Jordan, hopefully, get its share of this precious commodity.

rich agricultural land

Agriculture is intense throughout most of the area. In 1973 a separate authority, the Jordan Valley Authority (JVA) was set up to oversee agricultural expansion of the valley. The hot climate with only 2 or 3 months of a very mild winter allows three or four crops every year. In recent years so much use has been made of plastic field coverings and plastic greenhouses that cultivation is almost continuous.

The crops are very much the staples of the Middle East diet, tomatoes, cucumbers, aubergines, peppers, melons and of course citrus. Large quantities of the produce is exported, mainly to other, more arid Arab lands providing Jordan with much needed foreign currency.

plastic bubbles

As you descend into the valley, the fields of polythene deceptively look like rippling lakes of water! It is interesting to note that in this fertile valley where the most advanced methods of agriculture are practised, some of the earliest attempts by mankind at a sedentary life based upon the land began! In an expanse so rich in ancient settlement there are many archaeological sites. Only a few, though, have interest for the visitor – even the more inquisitive sort! And it is only to these that I shall direct you.

From Amman it is possible to visit the whole of the Jordan Valley and some of the surrounding heights and still be back in time for a late dinner. I would, however, recommend a less strenuous journey, spending the night in Irbid where there are a couple of comfortable hotels, and one of my favourite bargain restaurants!

HOW TO GET THERE

Take the road out of Amman in the direction of Suweileh past Amman University and the University Hospital. At the major intersection with a sign pointing right to Jerash, carry straight over. There are signposts towards al-Salt and the Jordan Valley (Ghor). The road passes through a busy commercial district for a couple of kilometres before becoming more rural.

After about 18 km there is a slip road exit for **al-Salt**. As it is scarcely off the main route, you may want to make a short detour to see this town.

By bus: A minibus from the Abdali bus station in Amman will get you as far as Suweima near the Dead Sea. From here, other minibuses ply most of the Jordan Valley. Please note that none of these services are regular, but hitch-hiking is a possibility.

➤ Al-Salt

During late Ottoman times, al-Salt was the administrative centre of the Jordan area. At that time both Amman and al-Salt were small provincial village-towns with perhaps al-Salt being a little busier. Being the administrative centre a number of Ottoman officials resided there and there were quite a few elegant, typical Turkish residences, some of which have survived to this day (though with neglect plus the growth of the town, they no longer merit that description!).

When King Abdullah chose Amman over Salt to be his capital it was the former which entered an era of frantic development, eventually acquiring its modern, "westernised" character, while al-Salt remained a town of typical Arab ambience. Apart from sampling this ambience, al-Salt has little to offer the visitor. However if time is available you might enjoy a half hour stroll around the centre, assuming you can find a place to park!

picnic in the woods

Return to the main road to continue down to the Jordan Valley (Ghor). Some 12 km west you reach the Zai National Park on the right. This pine-wooded park, opened in the late 1980s, is a favourite outing spot for Ammanis, and has many recreation and picnic areas. On Fridays and holidays the air is thick with blue smoke and the tantalizing smell of charcoal-grilled meats, picnics in this part of the world being strictly barbecue affairs.

temperatures soar

The descent towards the valley continues and passing the sea level sign the changing climatic conditions are quickly felt. If you left Amman on a crisp late winter or spring day, you'll soon be peeling off your sweater or jacket. By the time you have reached the flat valley you have descended about 1200 metres, and the temperature has increased by at least 10 degrees, perhaps much more. If you are travelling between mid May and October you will now feel the full impact of the oppressive Jordan Valley climate. I hope your vehicle is airconditioned! However, even if it is, as you will soon be stepping outside, it might be a good idea to turn the cooling off so you can begin to acclimatise.

At the end of the road (a T junction) turn right (north). You are now at a point some 35 kilometres north of the Dead Sea.

the house of God?

About 10 km further north you enter the village of **Deir Allah**, meaning the House of God. Deir Allah is a very ancient settlement as the large *tell* on the north side of the village testifies. You will find the stone-faced mound just past the filling station on the west (left) as you exit the village. It is this tell we shall now visit.

► Tell Deir Allah

History

There are two explanations as to why this place is called the House of God. The first is because a sanctuary was discovered on the site leading some to conclude that it may have always had pagan holy associations. But this is not very likely as the word Allah is reserved for the God of the Koran and Bible.

Jacob's ladder

The other reason, and the one which seems more likely, is that in Muslim tradition this may have been the place of Jacob's dream:

> *"Then Jacob departed from Beersheba and went towards Haran. And he came to a certain place and spent the night there...and he took one of the stones of the place and put it under his head, and lay down in that place. And he had a dream,...and behold, the Lord stood above... and said 'I am the Lord, the God of your father Abraham and the God of Isaac...' So Jacob rose early in the morning... and took the stone that he had put under his head and set it up as a pillar...and he called the name of the place Bethel..."*
>
> *(Genesis 28:10-19).*

Bethel, or Beit-El, is Hebrew for House of God just as Deir Allah is in Arabic. The Jewish tradition believes that this place, Beit-El, is just north of the Palestinian city of Ramallah on the West Bank; in fact they have built a new settlement there. It could quite easily be there. Both places are on a logical ancient route Jacob could have taken from Beersheba to Harran, which is situated in southern Anatolia. Which one? Well, there is no archaeological evidence for either site, or the story; so I'll leave that to you. You can, however, be sure of a wonderful view of the area from the flat summit.

The visit

The best way to climb the tell is to drive (or walk) around to the west side. Take the left turning by the side of the mound and after c50 metres on your left you'll see a sandy area to park. Ignoring the chicken and livestock sheds on this side of the artificial hill, scramble to the top. Although not very high, remember that, depending on the time of year, the ambient temperature might be between 38 and 42 degrees!

All the archaeological finds at the summit are dug-outs below ground level so don't expect any marvels. The main find is the large sanctuary dating from around 1500 BC which was destroyed some

300 years later by an earthquake. The *tell* was excavated some 20 years ago and during the excavations artefacts associated with the ancient temple were unearthed.

Continuing north

irrigated fields

Continue your journey north. The river Jordan is 5-7 km to the west and never comes into view. On both sides of the road there is intensive farming, with irrigation channels bringing water from the main canal. Fertile as the soil is, without this irrigation nothing would grow after the winter rains.

There are many army checkpoints along the route (end of 1995) in spite of the peace agreement with Israel, but old habits die hard. Sometimes these can be irritating. Just have your passport ready for inspection. I doubt whether many of the soldiers can read the document, but they like to check the photograph.

contrasts of climate

When J.L. Burckhardt entered the valley in 1812 he observed:

"...it's temperature is hotter than I had experienced...the rocky mountains concentrating the heat, and preventing the air from being cooled by the westerly winds...The barley harvest that does not begin to ripen in the upper plains [the Houran] *till...later we here found it nearly finished. The Houran, on the other hand, was everywhere covered with the richest verdure...while every plant in the Ghor was already dried up...there are few countries where the changes from one climate to another are so sudden as in* [then] *Syria...To the north was Djebel El Sheikh* [Mount Hermon] *covered in snow; to the east the fertile plain of Djolan* [Golan] *clothed in the blossoms of spring; while ...the withered vegetation of the Ghor seemed the effect of a tropical sun." (Travels in Syria and the Holy Land)*

Cultivation today hides much of the withering effect of the sun in the valley, but the heat is nonetheless withering to the traveller!

Our next stop is the famed Decapolis city of **Pella**, which flourished quite nicely in the fiery clime.

▸ PELLA (Tabqat al-Fahl)

Pella has not fared the ravages of time as well as Jerash, and consequently there is much less to see. Notwithstanding, the ruins, coupled with the rather lovely location, particularly in spring, makes the site definitely worthy of a visit.

How to get there

About 35 km north of Deir Allah is the large village of **al-Mashare**, and the ruins of Pella are just over one kilometre to the east, near the village of **Tabqat al-Fahl**. To get there drive through al-Mashare and just before the end of the dual road, take the right fork, signposted to Pella, for 1.5 kilometres. You know when you have arrived when you see the three columns on the left, all that's left standing of a **6th century church**.

By bus: From Deir Allah you can pick up one of the irregular buses north to Al Mashare which is also reachable from Irbid, and then its either a walk or (cheap) taxi ride to Pella. The whole Jordan Valley is accessible on the minibus route from al-Mashare, but as there are no fixed schedules be careful not to get stuck!

HISTORY

There are ample signs of human occupation in this area from the Neolithic and Chalcolithic periods, 5000 to 3000 BC. From around 2000 BC it appears that a walled town of some substance existed here. Egyptian papyri of the 17th century BC refer to the place as "Pihilum" or "Pahel". Later Egyptian texts dated around 1200 BC record that Pahel was the source of wood that was used for wheel spokes. There are also references to the town on early Akkadian tablets. Little else is known of this early city, as it is not mentioned in any of the period's conventional writings such as the Bible.

named after Alexander's birthplace

The city which history knows as Pella dates from post Alexandrian times. It was founded by one of the Seleucid rulers who inherited part of Alexander's empire. This was most likely Seleucus I Nicator who ruled from 304 to 301 BC. As the city was given the name Pella, the name of Alexander's birthplace in Macedonia, it could indicate that it was founded soon after the death of the great conqueror. Artefacts found during extensive excavations in the 1960s show that Pella was a city of wealth and importance.

pillaged by Hasmoneans

In the early years of the first century BC, according to Josephus' *Wars of the Jews*, Alexander Yannai, the Jewish Hasmonean ruler, demanded that Pella should adhere to Jewish religious laws; when they refused he crossed the Jordan and pillaged the city.

prosperity under Rome

The Roman annexation of the region in 64 BC freed the city, and it was rebuilt on a grandiose scale, becoming one of the Decapolis Cities. Fine Roman roads were constructed that linked Pella with the others in the league: Jerash in the east and Scythopolis (Beit She'an or Beisan) in the west. As elsewhere, the *pax Romana* enabled Pella to expand and prosper. Archaeological finds show that Pella became a refuge for Christians in the early years of the faith, fleeing to the city as early as AD 70, when the Romans destroyed Jerusalem.

more prosperity under Byzantium

During the early Byzantine era Pella reached its zenith. As a bishopric, her bishops attended all the great Christian councils. By the 5th century the population numbered around 25,000 and continued to expand into the 6th century.

the Battle of the Marsh

A major battle was fought near Pella between the Byzantines and the emerging Muslim army in 635. Known as the Battle of Fahl, the Battle of the Marsh, the Byzantine forces were defeated with colossal casualties. Pella came under Muslim control, and the city reverted to its Semitic name, Pihil, or Fahl, and by this name later Arab geographers refer to it. Subject to the usual conditions that the Muslims imposed upon those not of their faith, the Christians continued to live there peaceably.

devastated by earthquake

Fahl was devastated by a major earthquake in the middle of the 8th century, following which the city declined, though it remained populated into the 10th century. In the 13th century there must have been a small revival, as there are remains of a Mameluke mosque of that period. In early Ottoman records a village of "Fahl al-Tahta" in the area is mentioned. Today the nearby village is known as Tabaqat Fahl.

THE VISIT

The best place to get an overall picture of the ruins of Pella is from the rest house. Continue on the road as it veers left past the remains of the church with the three columns, following it as it continues to twist and climb. Along the way you will see a couple of signs pointing straight ahead to the rest house. Park in the small car park.

If you arrived here by public transport, your best bet is to skip the very long trek to the rest house and approach the ruins from the West Church as described below in the paragraph headed **"getting a closer view"**.

view from the veranda

Situated high on a ridge to the east of the ruins, the veranda of the pleasant building affords a sweeping panoramic view over the entire area. The rest house also provides food and drink, and the manager,

who speaks a good English, is a knowledgeable guide and will be pleased to point things out not, I hope, making my description dispensable! Pella – like most of Jordan – looks its best in springtime. The hilly terrain is clad in a covering of greenery and wild flowers. Later, these same hills revert to desert, with only goats and sheep finding pleasure in the dry thorns and scrub.

Looking south from the veranda, that is to your left, you can see a terrace with four pillars overlooking the entire Pella depression. This is the **Eastern Church** and was built towards the end of the 5th century. It was an impressive basilica, approached by a huge stairway from the wadi below. The floor was covered in marble, and some of it is still there should you decide to make the climb. Like most of the city, the church was destroyed by the mid 8th century earthquake.

Below in the heart of the depression is the area known as the **Civic Complex**. It acquired this name as it was the centre of the Roman city, and dates from the 1st and 2nd centuries. The only clearly visible remains from this era is the small **theatre** near the stream, but you may have difficulty locating this as all the stone seats have been removed, and it is little more than a shell. There are indications that a forum, a temple and other Roman functionary buildings once stood nearby

the main remnants

What you can see in the centre of the complex is the largest and most significant Byzantine church. It is called today the **Civic Complex Church** because of the location. It was built at the beginning of the 5th century using some material from former Roman structures. The church had a nave terminated by an apse, and two flanking aisles. On the west side was a colonnaded atrium. This atrium, partly restored by the Department of Antiquities, used twenty recycled Roman columns. It was approached by a wide monumental flight of steps fashioned from the theatre's stone seats.

If you look across the valley, ahead and to the right, you will see on the slopes the remains of a 7th and 8th century Omayyad residential area, and to the south of this an area of Byzantine houses.

getting a closer view

If you want to look at these more closely or view the ruins from a different direction, return with your vehicle to the **West Church** (the 3 pillars). Across the road to the south you can see a track climbing the mound. Drive or walk to the top. Over on the left is a white building. This is the Dig House, the quarters for the archaeologists and diggers who are excavating Pella. If you make your way over to the right — to the precipice — another fine view of the Civic Complex can be had. You are now standing over the ruined residential areas you saw from the Rest House.

Back on the road north

Return to al-Mashare, turn right and continue north. The road runs adjacent to the Israeli border. Some 20 km north the main road turns east towards Irbid, but our route continues north.

sensitive zone

This was till recently a particularly sensitive area, being so close to Israel — you can clearly see traffic moving along the road on that side. The uninformed visitor could be forgiven for thinking that a state of war still exists between the two countries, as passage on this road is controlled by a tight military checkpoint complete with boom! However don't fret; after checking your passport and ascertaining your destination – which is Umm Qais – the barrier will be raised and the drive along the narrow but soon-to-be-scenic road can continue.

no video cameras!

You are now just south of Lake Tiberias, and near the point where Jordan, Israel and Syria (occupied Golan, or al-Jawlan) come together. The road now ascends to the top of the river Yarmouk ravine which is the frontier between Jordan and Syria. On the way, to the right, is a parking place where you can stop to admire the vista. Regulations which may not have been changed prohibit the use of video cameras in this area.

About 10 km from the checkpoint the road reaches a T junction, with a small traffic island, usually occupied by the military. Left (E), leads down 3-4 kilometres to the hot springs of al-Hammah, while right (W), ascends still further to Umm Qais.

▶ AL-HAMMAH (Hammat Gader)

The hot springs and *thermae* of al-Hammah, **Hammat Gader** are split between Jordan and Syria, although those in Syria are since 1967 under Israeli occupation. I have visited both, and I must say that those presently under Israel's control have the actual Roman *thermae* buildings. Hoping to keep them for good (doubtful) they have turned the baths and the surrounding area into a veritable recreation park. But we are in Jordan, and until now investment in this place seems to have been practically nil!

How to get there

To reach them turn left at the road junction and continue on the descending road till its end. You are now almost on the frontier, and although a track continues you cannot. The springs are on the right, which except for the slightly sulphurous smell, could be mistaken for a swimming pool.

taking the waters

There is one large outdoor pool and three smaller ones indoors. The temperature of the sulphurous water in these pools is between 25 and 42 degrees. Sadly the whole area is not very inviting, but as most people who come here are Jordanians there is a local mood about the place. The baths alternate between use by men and women every hour or so. On Fridays they are especially crowded, even in the winter

months as a real winter is rarely felt here, and the water is always hot!
By the "spa" is a rest house where you can rent a room, complete with
cooking facilities. It also serves refreshments and meals.
Return to the T junction to continue to the next stop on our tour.

▸ UMM QAIS (GADARA)

How to get there

Back at the T junction continue straight over for Umm Qais, ancient
Gadara, a few kilometres away. This is a steeply ascending and
winding road, with what could be a grand view being obscured by
trees. Just before the village another barriered road block will
probably be encountered. The entrance to the Greco-Roman site is
about fifty metres past this on the right.

Although it is possible to drive in, I recommend that you park a
little further on by the souvenir shops and walk, as there are things to
see on the way, and the distance is short.

By bus: If you're following our route, you will by now know the
drill for catching an irregular minibus or a lift. From Irbid, Umm Qais
can easily be reached by minibus.

HISTORY

*"And when He had come to the other side into the country of
the Gadarenes, two men who were demon-possessed met Him
as they were coming out of the tombs...now there was at a
distance from them a herd of many swine feeding. And the
demons began to entreat Him saying, ... 'send us into the
herd of swine'...and they came out, and went into the swine,
and behold, the whole herd rushed down the steep bank into
the sea and perished in the waters."* (Matthew, 8:28-34)

Umm Qais is the site of Gadara, a Hellenistic/Roman city situated on
a high headland overlooking Lake Tiberias (Sea of Galilee), al-Jawlan
(Golan Heights) and the Yarmouk ravine. On a clear day you will be
able to see the snowy peaks of *Jabal al-Sheikh* (Mount Hermon).
Gadara is about 475 metres above sea level, but the fact that the lake
lies a further 210 metres below sea level gives the effect of a much
greater altitude.

university city

As one of the cities of the Decapolis, on the road to Tiberias and
Scythopolis (Beisan or Beit She'an), Gadara was a flourishing city, in
its time a centre of learning and culture boasting a university. Some
well known intellectuals of the era were natives of Gadara including
the poet Meleager (c100BC), the philosopher Philodermos, who died
around 45 BC and the orator Apsines who lived in the 3rd century.

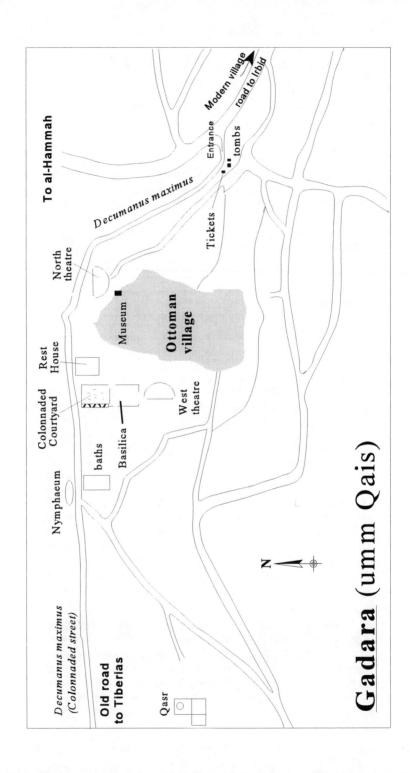

Gadara (umm Qais)

It is likely that due to its important location on the road to the Palestine coast, some settlement stood here prior to the Hellenistic one, although no firm evidence of this has been found.

While the name Gadara may be Semitic in origin, it appears that it was actually founded after the death of Alexander the Great in the year 333 BC. With his Middle Eastern empire split between two antagonists, the Seleucids and the Ptolemies, a fortified position was established by the Ptolemies.

much fought over location

In 218 BC it was captured by the Seleucid ruler Antiochus III, after a lengthy siege. Polybius, the second century BC historian, remarked that Gadara was the strongest place in that region.

The Jewish historian Josephus records in his *Wars of the Jews* that in the early part of the first century BC Alexander Yannai, the Hasmonean ruler, required ten months of seige to conquer the city, when most of the area came under Jewish control.

 Gadara remained under the Jews until 63 BC when the whole region was conquered for Rome by Pompey. The city must have been badly damaged in the Hasmonean seige because, again according to Josephus, Pompey had it reconstructed as a favour to Demetrius, a freedman and a significant figure in the Roman Republic. As a city of the Decapolis, Gadara had a self governing status and was entitled to mint its own coins.

unpopular gift

For his help in defeating Antony at the battle of Actium, Octavian (Augustus, the first Roman Emperor) gave the city to Herod the Great in 30 BC. This move was very unpopular with the citizens, who attempted to turn the Emperor away from Herod. Josephus records that the attempt was unsuccessful and that *"they killed themselves for fear of torture, some with their own hand, some flung themselves into the valley or drowned themselves in the river"*.

After Herod's death in 4 BC, Gadara was incorporated into the Roman Province of Syria. If at all, the events of Matthew chapter 8 took place during this time.

pleasure-seeking Romans

The *Pax Romana* that came with the Romans brought prosperity to Gadara and most of the remains that can be seen today are from this era. The great baths at *Hammat Gader,* renowned all over the Empire for the curative qualities of the waters, also date from this period. People came from far and wide to bathe in the therapeutic *thermae,* and there is plenty of testimony that the Romans, after soaking in the hot sulphurous waters, would retire to Gadara where the mountain air

was fresh and invigorating and, no doubt, the pleasures many. Gadara's theatres provided the entertainment.

As with other cities in the region, Christianity came to Gadara in the third century, and there are records of martyrs during the Diocletian massacres. In the fourth century a bishop from Gadara was present at the Council of Nicea. With the Byzantine defeat at the hands of the Muslims at Pella (Fahl) in 635, Gadara became part of the Islamic world. As it lay on one of the north-south routes to Mecca the city fared quite well, and Christians continued to reside there.

disaster strikes

After the demise of the Omayyad Caliphate and the shift of power to Baghdad, Gadara no longer stood on any major route and serious decline set in. Violent earthquakes in the 8th century, followed by disease in the 9th and 10th hastened this. By the 12th century it was no more than an isolated village called Umm Qais. In late Ottoman times a more substantial village was built among and atop the acropolis, and remains of this village still stand.

Ulrich Seetzen visited Umm Qais in 1806 and identified the site as that of Gadara, but no major exploratory work was carried out till almost the end of the century. Until the 1970s the site remained a heap of ruins. Since then a German team of archaeologists has carried out extensive excavations and the restoration work visible today.

The visit

After parking your vehicle, begin your walk among the ruins. Some 40 metres along the entrance track, on the left, is a booth where you will pay the 1 JD entrance fee. Just before it, also on the left are two Hellene/Roman tombs.

doors of solid stone

The first one, with an inscription on the lintel, is the **Tomb of Germani**. Preceded by a small courtyard, the sepulchre has two entrances, each secured by impressive, carved basalt stone doors. Inside, and with the aid of a flashlight you can go in, is a hall and stairs that lead to the two internment rooms. These have been partly restored. The inscription carved on the lintel gives the owners as a Quintus Publius Germanus and one Aulus Germanus Rufus.

Just west of this is the **Tomb of Lucius Sentius Modestus**. The lintel is carved with flowers at each end, and in the centre is a wreath with the inscription: *Lucius Sentius Modestus, Holy Hierokeryx of the city.*

take the decumanus maximus

The entrance path through the site was originally the **decumanus maximus**, and as you pass along it you will walk over sections where the Roman paving remains. The decumanus ran in an east-west direction eventually becoming the old Roman road that led down to

92

the valley and then to Tiberias and Scythopolis (Beisan or Beit She'an).

About 40 metres along the path (W), the outline of the **East Theatre** can be noticed on the left. Practically nothing remains of this, the larger of Gadara's two theatres. Over the centuries the seating stones were removed for other building purposes, particularly for the construction of the Ottoman houses above it. The semi-circular shape identifies it clearly, even if there are some Muslim graves there now. From this point you may get a glimpse of the southern tip of Lake Tiberias.

fine colonnaded terrace

Past the theatre you arrive at the heart of Gadara and also the modern (non-residential) Rest House. Walk around it and you come to the main part of the **decumanus maximus** with a **colonnaded terrace** on your left (S). This area, together with the west theatre to the south of it, form the best visual sector of the ruins, having undergone extensive restoration work (continuing). The terrace, measuring almost 100 metres by about 30 is braced on a construction that we will get to shortly.

The north end of this terrace is a plaza or forum with pale-coloured columns. Because of the elevated position a good view is obtained over Lake Tiberias, a view which is especially attractive in the glow of late afternoon.

cathedral church

At the southern end of the terrace stood a **Byzantine church**. The church was a rectangular black basalt basilica with a central octagonal arrangement fashioned from re-cycled Roman columns. When this church was built, in the late 5th or early 6th century, the western plaza would have become its *atrium* thereby making the whole terrace part of Gadara's main cathedral.

well-preserved theatre

Past the cathedral, at the extreme southern end of the terrace, through a door which was one of the *vomitoria,* is the **West Theatre,** where much of the original seating is well preserved. The rest, together with the stage area that was in ruins, is now in the process of comprehensive restoration. The entranceway through which you entered is original, and was also very well preserved, and as it led from the huge terrace could well have been an entrance for the VIPs of the day. Of special note are the nearly complete vaults that almost encircle the edifice below the seating area. The entire structure, seats and all, are constructed of the local basalt.

If you go back to the northern end of the terrace and walk around to its western side you'll find yourself in a side street with a number of vaulted shops with fallen facades, built underneath the terrace's structure. Like much else here renovation is in process.

bathhouses and water fountain

Continue west past the terrace along the main path. Just over 100 metres further along (W), on the left (S) of the decumanus, and also accessible from the side street with the vaulted shops, are the hard-to-discern fragments of the **public** *thermae*, baths. These date from the mid 4th century, and followed the usual pattern of bathhouses of the period. Although only excavated in the 1980s the site is so overgrown now that it is difficult to determine much.

Almost opposite, you can see the remains of a **nymphaeum** to the right of the road (N). This was in its time a very handsome basalt edifice. Its floor was covered in fine marble, and bits of a marble statue that adorned it have been unearthed. Behind it was a large vaulted cistern, which supplied the water for the fountain.

The road that branches off left just by the baths in a slightly S/W direction leads to what is left of a building known as *al-Qasr*, the castle. This site is unexcavated, and its use has not been identified.

▶ Ottoman village

Return to the terrace and behind it, to the east and towards the **Acropolis** is the **Ottoman village** still partly inhabited. These houses date from the end of the 19th century, and were built by a motley collection of people encouraged to move there by the Ottoman administration. The houses fell into bad disrepair and are largely abandoned, but some were renovated and used by the German archaeological team that excavated Gadara. A wander around this village is recommended.

The houses are built largely of stones from ancient Gadara, and it is strange to see such a house with Greek inscriptions and decorations on the door lintels! The abodes follow the typical Ottoman pattern, even if not as grand as many. Some have small shaded courtyards with the traditional *diwan* at one end.

▶ Museum

One Ottoman dwelling, white, and close to the top of the East Theatre, is known as *Beit Rusan*, and served as the quarters for the administrations official of the area. By any standards it is a fine building and now finds its use as Gadara's museum.

While not exhibiting the best of the finds at Gadara, this museum is worth a brief visit. Just inside the gate there is a larger-than-life-size headless statue of a white marble goddess. This statue was originally discovered on the seats of the West Theatre. It is thought to be a representation of Tyche, the goddess of Gadara.

Among the artefacts on display is an interesting Byzantine mosaic found in the crypt of a Byzantine era tomb. On one side of the courtyard, under a portico are fragments from various mosaics, but these are not identified.

a chance to cool off

The courtyard of this fine Ottoman residence is shady and cool. If you are tired and hot after walking around the ruins this could be an ideal spot for a short rest – even if the only seat you can find proves to be an ancient sarcophagus!

Where next?

If you have the energy you can return to Amman via Irbid, a distance of about 120 km and taking at least 2 hours. You could choose, however, to spend the night in Irbid, 25 minutes away, and avoid night time motoring. In either case head for Irbid by driving straight through modern Umm Qais and following the signs.

Some travellers might want to stay in Umm Qais, and there are two very basic, and cheap, hotels in the village.

▸ Beit Ras (Capitolias)

If you still have time, and are not too tired you can, on the way to Irbid make a brief stop at the village of **Beit Ras**, once the site of the city of **Capitolias**, a latter city of the Decapolis. Situated some 5 kilometres north of Irbid, don't be too upset if you don't have time, as there is little to see. What is left is spread out through the village, and consists mainly of rock tombs and items of fallen masonry, bits and pieces of which have been used in constructing some of the present dwellings. Of the fine temples, churches, and other buildings that graced this city nothing remains.

▸ Abila?

Irbid, itself, is sometimes identified with one of the later Decapolis cities, **Abila,** although archaeological finds perhaps indicate that this did in fact lie to the north of the present metropolis. These finds are located about 10 kilometres north of Irbid. There is little to see there, but for some a few Roman tombs may hold interest. To reach the area you'll have to return along the road to Umm Qais, past the village of Beit Ras, and turn right along the narrow road just beyond. The archaeological site can be seen about 6 kilometres along this road.

8. Umm al-Jimal

INTRODUCTION

The Hauran plain of southern Syria was legendary for its fertility in Roman times, so much so that it earned the appellation "bread-basket of the Eastern Empire". The result of volcanic upheavals in the late geological era, it was strewn with black basalt boulders and rock. Many towns in the region, the most notable being Bosra, now in Syria, close to the Jordanian border, were fashioned almost entirely out of this sombre black stone.

arbitrary frontiers

Near where the plain ends, and below the foothills of the Jabal al-Druze (now called Jabal al-Arab), is another ancient town built of the same basalt rock. Frontier delineation by the Great Powers after World War One has placed this one just inside Jordan, but it shares much of its history with the deservedly more well-known town across the border.

once neglected

Both sites, indeed the whole area, was excavated by the American archaeologist Howard Crosby Butler in the early years of this century, and it is through his work that the general layout of these places is known to us. Butler wrote that **Umm al-Jimal** was situated in the desert. Centuries of neglect had turned the once productive plain, in Butler's words, into a *"great white sea... not of sand but of dry exhausted soil... and the deserted ruin appears like a living town, all of black, rising from it."* Today, much of the damage has been turned around: modern deep water drilling has put large tracts of the arid land back into productive use, and the site is very accessible via new roads – in fact less than an hour by car from Amman.

not spectacular

Umm al-Jimal has no eye-catching splendours like Jerash, or massive Roman constructions like the theatre at Bosra. For all that, as a town which was inhabited for almost 1000 years, with an eerie atmosphere all of its own, it should be on the itinerary of every inquisitive visitor to Jordan. There is no record of a town of this name in ancient historical writings, but Butler thought it may be identified with the Thantia marked on a Roman map; others thought the name Surattha, quoted in Ptolemy's *Geography*, might be more appropriate.

best in the sun

Pick a fine day for your visit otherwise the blackness of the town's mainly basalt ruins just merges into a dull landscape and there is little to impress you.

HOW TO GET THERE

From Amman: Take the Zarka road, continuing on to Mafraq. At the main crossroads, turn east along the Baghdad road and after about 12 kms turn north along a recently paved track. (There may be a checkpoint here, it has been there for years, but who knows!) You will soon see the ruins on the left.

From Irbid: follow the straight road east to Mafraq, and then as above.

By bus: Take a bus (or servees) from Amman to Mafraq via Zarqa, and from there you can get a local minibus. To do it in one day start early. Bus travellers from Irbid should also make for Mafraq to pick up a local bus.

HISTORY

caravan stop off

Umm al-Jimal started life as a Nabatean settlement in the final century BC. It was most likely an intermediate stop on the trade route between Petra and Damascus. Practically nothing from that period has survived. In AD 105 Umm al-Jimal was annexed by the Romans and became part of *Provincia Arabia*.

date on gate

Under *Pax Romana* Umm al-Jimal was a fairly prosperous if rather insignificant town. Soldiers were stationed there, as the barracks testify, but the only dateable find has been the North West Gate where an inscription records that it was built during the reign of Emperor Commodus, 180 to 192.

first churches

Christianity found its way here very early. The Church of Julianus, dating from 345, is the oldest dated church known. During Byzantine times many more churches were built, and at least 15 have been uncovered to date.

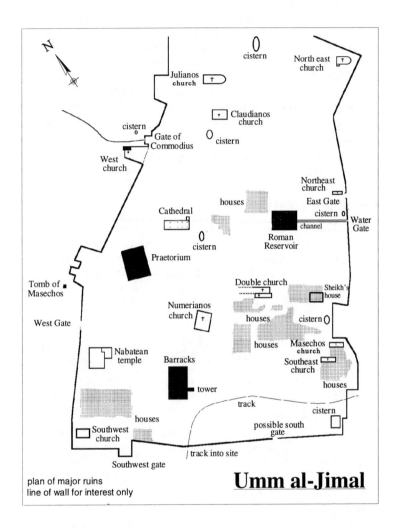

Mother of Camels

Umm al-Jimal remained inhabited until the 9th century. The area then suffered depopulation and general neglect, a situation that was not improved upon until almost modern times. Over the centuries the buildings were used by the Bedouin and Druse. At what time the town acquired the name Umm al-Jimal, which means the Mother of Camels, is not really known. Burckhardt, in the account of his travels, wrote, *"It had been my wish to visit the ruined town of Om El Djemal, which is 8 hours distance from Boszra, to the south..."*, so the name must have been in use for a long time prior to then. Why it was thus called can only be conjecture, but you will see many of these animals in the vicinity.

THE VISIT

From a distance the town does not look like very much. What can be seen on the approach road has the appearance of a blitzed, burnt ruin, and this impression remains until you actually start the exploration.

volcanic stone

Like so many other ancient sites in southern Syria the building material is almost exclusively the local black basalt and other lava rock. As there was no wood in the vicinity, none could be used, and corbelling was widely employed, especially in roofs. The ruined town was surrounded by walls, and where these cannot be readily seen they can be traced, albeit with some difficulty.

Umm al-Jimal covers a vast area, about 80 hectares. Large sections are strewn with ruined buildings, and other sections quite empty. For the most part the buildings remain in their ruined state although here and there some minor restoration has been done.

try to find the guide!

Of all the places you are likely to visit in Jordan, Umm al-Jimal will be the most difficult to find your way around as the paths are unclear, nothing is marked and many points of interest are located amidst uninteresting ruins. Yet accompanied by explanation it can be quite fascinating, so don't be put off visiting! Fortunately the Ministry of Tourism have provided a very knowledgable guide, **Sulemein Fais,** who is there every day until 14.30. He will guide you around without charge. This young man, a student of archaeology, knows Umm al-Jimal thoroughly and his explanations are very lucid. Other archaeological students (one of Jordan's universities is not far away), often hang around the place so it may not be too difficult to find someone to help. If you don't see anyone, they will probably find you as you wander about. The last time I was there I encountered a student majoring in Nabatean script!

pouring oil on trouble

You enter the fenced off site area near the structure known as **The Barracks**. Park your car near here. The guide, and/or a tourist policeman should be in the vicinity. The entrance to this edifice is on the southwest through a low doorway. The single slab stone door will, with a bit of effort, still pivot on its original stone hinges. Notice the machicolations above the door: defenders really did pour hot oil from here on to attackers! The building is late Roman, dating from AD 412, and it underwent rebuilding in the late 5th and 6th centuries.

tower of the archangels

The entranceway opens onto a sort of courtyard and the double-storeyed barracks were built around it. Most of what can be seen of these today is the rubble in the courtyard. In the southeast corner is a **tower**. Part of the top of this collapsed in the 1970s. According to the Hachette guide (Guide Bleu) of the late 1950s, this tower is then described as "remarkably well preserved". There were four rectangular bays at the top, one on each side, a feature that is not too evident today. Each bay was dedicated to one of the archangels, Michael, Uriel, Raphael, and Gabriel.

monks replace soldiers

The local Bedouin call this place *Al Deir*, the monastery, and in Byzantine times the place was used as such. On the tower are a number of crosses and Greek inscriptions. One is loosely based on Psalm 35:1, *"O Lord God, judge those who wrong us, and make war against them with thy might"*. Outside the main gate and on the east side is a chapel, which was added during the Byzantine era.

take correct path!

Two broad tracks or paths lead from the barracks in a roughly northerly direction; take the right hand fork. The first ruin you come to, about 50 metres on the left, is the very ravaged **Numerianos Church,** named for a bishop of the town. The church, once a very fine edifice, is from the 6th century. Originally there where three entrances but when it was converted into a mosque in the Omayyad period two of these were closed, as was the apse on the east side. This apse is still very noticeable, and was topped by three arches, no longer complete. You can see the *mirhab* which was built into the south wall.

mosaic vandalised

The church underwent thorough excavation in 1984 when a fine mosaic was discovered. Unfortunately, the place was not properly protected and children from the local village came to play and destroyed almost everything. The stones are lava stone and though appearing heavy, they are in fact quite light. They were bought to this site from a volcanic area some 25 kilometres to the east.

where the caravans have rested

Leaving the path, to the right, about 10 metres past Numerianos Church, it is possible to discern the remains of an area which included houses and a large stables. It is thought that this area could have been a caravanserai, as Umm al-Jimal was primarily a caravan town. Picking your way slightly further east you arrive at what is known as the **Double Church**, difficult to isolate because they both merge into the surrounding structures: look for the apses at the east ends.

It is not too clear why there were two churches adjacent to one another; popular theory is that the one to the north was a community building, while the other was a family prayer hall. The northerly one was built as a basilica, and, unusual for Umm al-Jimal, part of the roof may have utilised wood as well as the standard corbelling. The south church, somewhat smaller, was just a single hall without any elaboration. The former dates from the early 5th century and the other was added later. These churches also ended their useful lives as mosques.

grand dwelling

East of the Double Church, and approached through an archway on the south wall and then by walking around, is an edifice called the **Sheikh's House**. This house, with a large courtyard, acquired its name because of its size and excellence. Originally a Byzantine construction, it underwent some redesign in the Omayyad era. The eastern wall of this house is one of the best pieces of surviving building in Umm al-Jimal. High up, supposedly on the third floor, is a twin arched window, and below it a postern doorway with part of the door still in place. Outside is a vaulted covered cistern, and the doorway allowed access to it.

water storage

Our route now turns north past the east wall of the Sheikh's House following the open area between the ruins. After about 150 metres you come to an open space with an ovalish reservoir or cistern. There are many such reservoirs all over Umm al-Jimal and they were all fed from the main one by stone water canals. Just north of this is another smaller one, with vaulting, showing it was covered.

Al-Jimal Water Co.

Slightly to the northeast is Umm al-Jimal's main reservoir, originally Roman built. It has been resurfaced with concrete. This is still in use during the rainy season when the Bedouin water their camels here. The filter system is still there and it still works! From the Luss valley to the north east (the valley is at the foot of the Jabal Arab mountains, but still higher than Umm al-Jimal, so the flow is gravity fed), a seven kilometre canal channels the water into the first tank. The stones, grit etc fall to the bottom and, when full, the water overflows into the centre tank where the process is repeated. Finally the filtered water flows from the third tank into the reservoir, and when that is full overflows into the gaps at the sides into the conduits that in former times took it all over the town. The bottom of the reservoir slopes from all sides to the centre, and in the rainy season the water level reaches 12 metres deep.

built-in washroom

Almost due west of the Roman reservoir, amongst a number of ruined houses, is one that has been partially restored. I'm afraid it will not be too easy to locate so look carefully. The lower part of this house is mainly made up of a kitchen with a washroom and toilet in the far right corner (standing at the entrance). The corbelled ceiling is supported by an arch which is not original, but was built this century by Druze who used the place. The holes on the west wall provided ventilation, and the protrusion on that wall just by the entrance was designed to push food through to the animal shelter next door.

concealed floor

From this house continue west to the **Cathedral** which today is very ruinous. Constructed in 556, it had a mosaic floor that is now covered. The south side had three entrances, and the one on the right has an inscribed lintel which refers to Valentinian and Gratian who reigned as joint emperors in 371. As this is an early date for such a building it must be assumed that the stone was re-cycled.

mislaid stone

North west of the cathedral is the **Commodus Gate** in the city's western wall. The gate was thus named because of an inscription, now lost, which stated it was built at the time of the Emperor Commodus, (AD 161-192). Don't expect to see much that looks like a gate!

photogenic

Just outside this gate is the **West Church** which, as a funerary church was placed outside the walls. The remnants of this building are, perhaps, the most photogenic in all Umm al-Jimal. The four dramatic arches are what is left of the separation between  the nave and the southern aisle. They make a good sunset photo, or failing that picture them against the light. Inside the arches are carved some fine Byzantine crosses. North of this gate are the **Claudianos and Julianos Churches,** both very ruined. The Julianos church is the oldest dated church yet discovered.

being renewed

South west of the cathedral is the so-called **Praetorium**. One of the best buildings in the town, it is now undergoing restoration. You'll notice that some of the walls have stones with numbers on to assist the restoring workmen to fit each one back in its right place. Inside is a courtyard with cloisters around three of its sides. There were four Corinthian columns in the centre, the bases still in situ, and the shafts on the ground. There is also a large basilica type hall, and this makes some people believe the construction was really a church; the whole structure certainly has that air about it.

difficult directions

You may now continue to the southwest part of the town where there are so many ruined houses that it is difficult to give even reasonable directions. (This difficulty would be greatly eased if the Department of Antiquities would put up some signs!) As a consequence you may be hard pressed to find the following places but I would not be completing my task if I fail to mention them!

bi-lingual inscription

Proceed in a southwesterly direction from the praetorium, and your target is a house with entry into a courtyard where, on the ground, is an inscribed stone. The inscription is in Nabatean and Greek, and translates, *"This is the sacred stone which Masik, son of Awidha, made for Dushara"* (Dushara being the main god of the Nabateans, see box page 177).

On the west wall of the same courtyard is another inscribed stone which almost certainly was re-used in this position. The inscription is in Aramaic, and translates *"This is the tomb of Pher son of Sulaieh son of Judaima, King of Tannur"* (Tannur was a Nabatean temple just south of Wadi Hasa along the King's Highway).

fine frontage

If you found that house you may be lucky (or clever) enough to locate the **Nabatean Temple**. This is situated in a courtyard due south of the above. The temple is a kind of portico on the south side of the courtyard. In the Byzantine era the building was used as a house.

East of this, and on your way back to where you started, is a large Byzantine house. The north facade is still well preserved, and over the door above the circular window is a Byzantine type cross.

You are now west of where your tour began, and a short walk will bring you back to the barracks. Even if you were unable to find all the places I have described, you should have obtained a good overview of this very fascinating antique site.

9. Jerash

INTRODUCTION

Jerash, or to use its ancient name Gerasa, is *the* Roman city of the Middle East. Petra has some Roman influence, but remains unequivocally Nabatean. Palmyra, in the Syrian desert, has the feel of a Roman city, but its location by a desert oasis is as un-Roman as can be imagined. Jerash has it all: a Roman look, a Roman feel and, placed as it is in a valley below green, well-watered uplands, a decidedly Roman setting. The finest preserved example of a Roman provincial city anywhere, Jerash as such rates second only to Petra on the list of places to visit in Jordan.

easy to reach

Situated less than one hour's drive north of Amman, Jerash is easy to get to even for the traveller who is not touring the whole country. How long to spend there depends on how much one wants to see, and how thoroughly. I would say that three hours minimum is required but a whole day would not be excessive for such a fascinating place. An extra bonus for those who stay late is the *son et lumière* every night from May through October.

annual festival

In July and August there is a colourful 14 day festival, exotically staged among the ruins, which includes everything from folk dancing and music to Arabic drama and gymnastic displays. For the exact dates in any year check with the Jordanian Government tourist offices.

HISTORY

It is not known for sure who founded the city of Gerasa. Some attribute it to Alexander the Great, or his general, Perdicas, in the late 4th C BC after Alexander had defeated the Achaemenid Persians at Issus in 333 BC. However there is no record of this. Others say it was Ptolemy II Philadelphus (283-246 BC), the ruler of southern Syria and Egypt. It was he who Hellenised Amman and renamed it Philadelphia.

slow growth

Most likely the city emerged slowly over a period of about 100 years, each ruler adding a touch more. The transformation into a fully-fledged metropolis probably occurred around the end of the 3rd C BC when the area was under the control of the Seleucid king, Antiochus III Megas (r223-187 BC), who named the city *Antioch on the Chrysorhoas*, the Chrysorhoas (Golden River) being the rather grandiose name for Wadi Jerash. (The Hellenes seemed to have liked the name Chrysorhoas as they gave the same name to Damascus's river, the Barada.)

pre-historic finds

Long before this, though, there was settlement in the immediate vicinity. On the slopes of the nearby hills artefacts have been unearthed that show people lived here as early as 6000 BC. In other places there are traces of an early Bronze Age village from c2500 BC. On such a well-watered site it is more than likely that settlement was almost continuous.

The name Gerasa is of Semitic origin, and it is quite possible that whatever village stood there at the advent of the Hellenic period was the basis for the city that was to emerge.

the treasure of the tyrant Zeno

The first historical reference to Gerasa is from the Jewish historian, Josephus; he mentions Gerasa as the city captured by the tyrant rulers of Philadelphia (Amman), Zeno and his son, Theodorus, who took their treasure there and placed it for safekeeping in the Temple of Zeus in that city. It is not clear exactly what date this episode occurred but subsequent events would put it in the last third of the 2nd C.

emergence of the Hasmoneans

The Seleucid rulers controlled most of what is called *Greater Syria* which included all of modern Syria, Palestine, and most of Jordan. In 173 BC their rule in Judea was challenged by the Maccabees, whose leader Judah drove them out of the country, occupying areas in TransJordan and the Hauran. Judah was eventually defeated by the Seleucids at Elasa. In spite of this victory, the Seleucids did not regain control of Judea, which remained under the rule of the Hasmonean dynasty.

Zeno holds out...

In 102 BC Alexander Yannai, who was also High Priest of Jerusalem, became the Hasmonean ruler, and soon after attacked the Greek cities east of the Jordan, occupying some. But he was unable to take Gerasa which remained in Zeno's hands.

...but not his son

In 84 BC, Zeno's son Theodorus, now himself ruler of Gerasa, was defeated by Yannai and the city came under Jewish control. Gerasa remained mostly under Jewish rule until 64 BC. This period was punctuated by unrest following Yannai's death in 76 BC, and the subsequent in-fighting in Judea for the succession, a matter which was only really settled when Pompey recognised Hyrcanus as the Judean ruler.

Roman conquest

By 63 BC Pompey had completed the conquest of the region, which he divided into provinces, and Jerash became part of the Province of Syria, the capital of which was Antioch (on the Orontes). This was a major event for the city of Jerash, and henceforth it became a Roman city with Roman planning, and of the original Greek city practically nothing remains.

In the top ten

Gerasa was one of the Ten Cities or Decapolis, a loose federation of cities with a mainly Greek culture.

Rome brings peace

The whole region was transformed by the Roman presence. With the eastern and southern boundaries secured against Parthian and Arab threats, a *Pax Romana* descended on the Middle East. Such an all-embracing peace in the region had never been achieved before -- nor has it been achieved since!

With this new-found security the cities of the Decapolis were able to grow and flourish. Trade, the main source of Gerasa's wealth, expanded as did agriculture in the surrounds. Although, like the other Decapolis cities, Gerasa remained firmly Greco-Roman in its way of life, the Semitic influence of the countryside was never far away.

The building of the walls

In about AD 40 a plan was drawn up to rebuild Gerasa as a distinctive Roman city. A main street running approximately north/south, the cardo, was to be the focus, with two intersecting streets leading off it.

By AD 76 the city's walls had been constructed, determining the area that Gerasa was to occupy for the rest of its existence. An inscription found on the lintel of the north west gate confirms its completion in that year. Throughout the rest of the first century building activity continued and some of the great temples erected then constitute some of Gerasa's finest monuments.

In AD 106 Trajan annexed the Nabatean lands to the south, created a new province, *Provincia Arabia,* and reorganised *Provincia Syria*. Gerasa and Philadelphia became part of the new province whose capital was Bosra in (what is today) southern Syria. A great new highway was built, the *Via Nova Traiana* which linked Damascus, Bosra, Amman and Petra with Aqaba on the Red Sea.

The Decapolis

The Decapolis, or Ten Cities is the name given to a group of Hellenistic cities, all except one being east of the river Jordan. Historians are not sure when the group, or league, came into being but it was most likely at the beginning of Roman rule. Pliny, in his *Natural History 5:74* names the cities as Damascus, Philadelphia (Amman), Scythopolis (Beit She'an or Beisan), Gadara (Umm Qais), Pella (Khirbet Tabaqat Fahl), Gerasa (Jerash), Canatha (Qanawat) Hippos (Qala'at al-Husn) and Dium and Raphana (which have not been positively identified). Later on other cities joined the league, Arbila (near Irbid), Capitolias (Beit Ras), and Bosra.

One of the earliest mentions of the Decapolis is in the New Testament. After Jesus began His healing ministry and exorcised the demons from Legion at Gadara *".. he* [Legion] *went off and began to proclaim in the Decapolis what great things Jesus had done for him...". (Mark 5:20).* Mark also mentions the Decapolis in 7:31 as does Matthew in 4:25.

Most of these cities were captured by the Jewish Hasmonean ruler Alexander Yannai c80 BC. According to Josephus, Pompey removed these cities from Jewish rule and restored them to their own citizens under the Province of Syria (Josephus, Antiquities of the Jews, XIV.iv.4). The Romans generally allowed the Hellenised cities they controlled to retain a great deal of local autonomy.

Through the fame of the ten cities, the region between Philadelphia (Amman) and the Sea of Galilee became known as the "region of the Decapolis". They were mainly populated by people of Hellenistic background who chiefly welcomed Rome's coming. This made the Decapolis cities important to Rome as their Greek culture helped stabilize the entire province. They provided a location from which Roman forces could control the various Semitic peoples of the area who were constantly against Roman occupation. To emphasize their stature and semi-independence, they were allowed to issue their own coins. Provided they paid the required taxes and supplied the men needed for military duty, Rome interfered with them as little as possible, and they were able to prosper.

Of the ten cities, only a few remain as settlements of any size today, and of those only two, Damascus and Amman, can be called cities. Apart from Damascus and Canatha (Qanawat), both in Syria, and Scythopolis (Beit She'an) in Israel, the others are all situated in Jordan, with the finest remains at Jerash.

benefits of highway

Although Gerasa was not directly on this road it was connected to it by a branch road, and so shared most of its benefits. Additionally the city was linked to the Mediterranean via Pella and the Jordan Valley, by a good road from the west. Thus Gerasa was able to take advantage of its situation as a point for eastwards trans-shipment of goods to the west. Between Jerash and the sea there are no great mountains to cross.

imperial visitor

As more trade passed through the city so its wealth increased, enabling lavish buildings to be constructed. Prospering greatly during Trajan's reign (98 to 117), the city fared even better under Hadrian (117 to 138). He paid a visit to the city in 129-130, spending some time there. This imperial visit initiated fresh building activity including the **Triumphal Arch** which is also called Hadrian's Arch.

granite from Nubia

This was the beginning of Gerasa's "golden era" with the City Fathers planning ever-more building. The main thoroughfare was widened and lined with newer Corinthian columns. To achieve the magnificence they desired the Fathers had granite brought in from as far away as Aswan in Nubia. New temples to Artemis and Zeus rose up, and no expense was spared on their construction and decoration. The finest edifice of this period was probably the Temple of Artemis that was dedicated in 150.

Roman citizens

In 211 the new Emperor Caracalla made all the people of Rome's provincial cities full Roman citizens, raising the status of the cities to *colonia* and it was at this time that Gerasa's zenith was reached. But Rome's troubles were just beginning, and these soon had an effect on the lands in the east.

ominous stirrings from the east

The rise of the Sasanian Persians became a threat to the eastern frontiers, and the rule of less than capable Emperors did little to help matters. Internal difficulties and rivalries were tearing away at the empire's political stability, and its vitally important *Pax Romana*.

prosperity restored

In 284 Diocletian became Emperor and this ruthless but able, one-time general was able to arrest part of the Empire's decline. The Sasanian threat was removed and after reorganising the provinces of Syria and Arabia the prosperity of the Decapolis cities, which had fallen during the deterioration, began to return.

advent of Christianity

Most of the Decapolis had small communities of Christians as early as the late 2nd C and as the faith began to spread throughout the Roman Empire these communities grew. By the time of Constantine's edict of Milan in 313, Christianity was well established in Jerash. The Edict simply hastened the time when it became a Christian city. By the mid 4th C the cathedral had been built, and various Christian festivals were part of the city's life. The Christians of Jerash were represented at the Council of Seleucia in 359 and by Bishop Placcus at the Council of Chalcedon in 459.

churches replace pagan temples

By the time of, and during the reign of the Byzantine Emperor

Justinian (531 to 565), the former Hellene city had very many churches, built in the main from materials taken from the pagan temples which had either been destroyed or fallen into disrepair. Fifteen churches have been uncovered so far, and it is probable that more are still buried.

threat from the east materialises

Although Justinian had improved the fortifications of the *limes* (the frontier areas), the security from eastern aggression was not to last long. Whilst it did, the fortunes of Jerash were not too bad and, though not comparable with past splendours, the city continued to thrive.

In 573 the Sasanian ruler Chosroes I invaded northern Syria and before being repulsed took Antioch. The respite was short-lived. In 611 the Persians, this time under Chosroes II, attacked again and in 614 they occupied the city. There they remained until 630 when the Byzantines regained brief control.

Islamic conquest

The Arabs from the east, now fired with the fervour of Islam, had begun their conquests. In 629 the armed might of Byzantium and Islam met in southern Jordan. In this encounter the Byzantines prevailed. Seven years later, though, at the Battle of Yarmouk (636) the Byzantine army under Heraclius was defeated, and Roman-Byzantine rule in the entire region came to an end. Jerash, like every other city in the Middle East now had Islamic masters.

With the assumption of power by the Omayyads, and the centre of their new Empire at Damascus not too far away, there was still life left in Jerash. Various Muslim quarters have been discovered in the city and an Omayyad mosque of very modest construction has also been unearthed.

decline complete

A serious earthquake in 747 damaged most of the city, and when a few years later the Abbasids came to power and government shifted from Damascus to Baghdad, Jerash was left as little more than a backwater. A mixture of Christians and Muslims still lived there in the 9th C, but mainly amongst the ruins.

Crusader nastiness

In 1120 the Atabek of Damascus built a fort on the site of the temple of Artemis and stationed some soldiers there. This was captured and destroyed by Baldwin II, Crusader King of Jerusalem a few years later. A thirteenth century Arab geographer, Yaqur, described the place as a field of ruins, completely uninhabited.

Jerash re-discovered

In 1806, while exploring southern Syria, the German traveller Ulrich Seetzen became the first European to find and identify the ruins of the ancient city. J.L. Burckhardt spent some hours there in the late spring of 1812, and his account makes interesting reading. In 1818 while on a tour of the region, one that also took them to Petra, two Commanders in the Royal Navy, C.L.Irby, and J. Mangles visited many of the Decapolis cities spending a few days exploring and documenting Jerash. They were followed in 1826 by two Frenchmen, who like them would also visit Petra, the Marquis Leon de Laborde, and the engraver Linant who made drawings of the ruins. In the years that followed many other travellers were to visit and document the ruins.

Circassian settlers

In 1878 the Ottoman government decided to settle some Circassians there, and they built their village largely from materials gathered from the ancient buildings. This was the beginning of the settlement that exists alongside the ruins today.

serious excavations

By the end of the 19th C and the first years of the 20th many serious archaeologists had turned their attention to the region. The Germans Brünnow and von Domaszewski published their study, *Provincia Arabia* in the years 1904-9. In the late 1920s an extensive dig was undertaken by an Anglo-American group with the aid of Yale University, the British School of Archaeology in Jerusalem and others. The results of their research were published in 1938 by Carl Kraeling in a book entitled *Gerasa, City of the Decapolis*.

Other researchers who have worked there include the Briton Gerald Lankester Harding, who was director of the Jordanian Department of Antiquities for a time. Before he died in 1979, he requested that he be interred inside the Roman walls of the city.

VISITING THE SITE

► Hadrian's Arch

As you drive into Jerash from Amman the first monument you encounter, on the left, is the **Triumphal Arch** or **Hadrian's Arch,** as it is also known. It was constructed in 129/130 in honour of the visit of the Emperor Hadrian who was on a tour of his eastern empire. In fact he stayed most of the winter at Gerasa. Although this arch was not a gateway through the city walls, it was built in line with the southern gate so that the Emperor would have to pass through it prior to entering the city gate.

top has gone

This triumphal arch, a triple gateway, now stands at only half its original height. The central arch is 12 metres high, 6.5 metres wide and nearly 7 metres deep. A recently excavated street runs through the centre towards the southern gate of the city.

Both faces are similar, having semi-columns decorated with acanthus leaves above the bases. Atop the side arches you can see ornately decorated niches bordered by pilasters. At each side are pavilions built at a later time. These have niches that can be entered only from the north sides.

huge proportions

Just north of the arch a large hollow announces the site of the **hippodrome**. A very long oval in shape, the hippodrome had tiers of seats all around except on the south. The only ones remaining are on the west side. Now no more than a depression overgrown with weeds, it is easy to see that it was once a stadium of impressive dimensions, nearly 250 metres long and over 50 metres wide. It is estimated that there were about 15 rows of seats, and as many as 15,000 spectators were able to watch the events. There were at least six entrances, with the main one on the north side. This entrance, which you can still see, may have been the entrance through which the horses, etc entered the arena.

anyone for polo?

A semi-circular wall was built some way down from the northern end. Scholars believe this was erected by the Sasanian Persians during their occupation (614 to 630) as polo goal posts were found there. (Polo was a favourite Persian sport).

or water polo?

Water sports of some kind may also have been played nearby. To the east is another largish depression that seems to have been filled with water from nearby springs. This is not too easy to make out as time has levelled much of this area.

place to park

Continuing on the road past the triumphal arch you come to the site proper. This is preceded by a car park, a number of shops selling souvenirs and the like, and the Government Visitors Centre and Rest House. Here you can hire a guide and ask all manner of questions, although answers are not guaranteed! Hopefully, if I have done my job properly, everything you'll need to know will be found in this book!

get your ticket

Entrance to the site is via the **South Gate**. Before entering you must buy a ticket at the office facing. In late 1995 these cost JD2.50 per person.

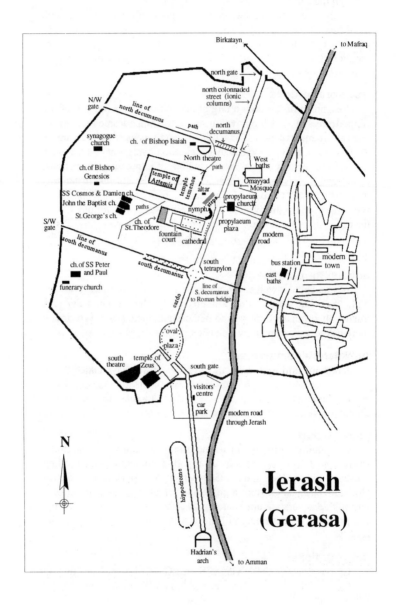

Jerash
(Gerasa)

▸ The South Gate

The gate is almost identical to Hadrian's Arch, but on a smaller scale. The two edifices are almost perfectly aligned, the road from Philadelphia passing through them both in a straight line. The gate was most likely built at the same time as the triumphal arch and replaced a previous, and less elaborate one built in the mid first century AD.

The central entranceway, just over 4 metres wide, stood between two smaller ones 2.25 metres wide. The two side pavilions are an integral part of the structure, and not added later as is the case with the triumphal arch. On the north side of the pavilions are doors that lead into interior rooms. The southern side has undecorated niches. All the entrances are bordered by engaged columns which, like those of the triumphal arch, have bases decorated with acanthus leaves. The remains of two towers, one each side, are additions from the Byzantine era.

expanding city

The gate is in line with the city walls whose length was roughly 3,500 metres, enclosing an area of c97 hectares (c240 acres). The area is rather irregular in shape reflecting many additions that were made as new quarters were built.

▸ The Oval Plaza

A short, slightly ascending walk from the South Gate brings you to the **Oval Plaza** or **Forum**. This area is one of the finest sights of Jerash.

Burckhardt's comments

When he laid eyes on it in 1812 J.L. Burckhardt called it *"a magnificent semicircle of columns"* (what we see today includes some restoration). This almost flat space with a rather strange semi-elliptical shape is c90 metres long and 80 metres wide.

Ionic columns

The plaza is surrounded by columns with capitals of the Ionic order. Except for two columns on the northeast side all are spaced uniformly around the plaza. Jerash's leading archaeologist, Gerald Lankester Harding, surmised that these two columns, closer together than the others, had been moved to make way for an arch across the entrance to the cardo. All the columns stand on blocks and support an architrave. The outer area is paved with large limestone blocks, while the inner area has blocks of smaller dimensions. These paving stones, in the majority of places, follow the curvature of the flanking colonnades. In the centre are the foundations of a rectangular plinth which once supported a statue.

unique outline

Harding thought that the unusual shape of the plaza was required to accommodate a pre-existing construction or natural peculiarity of the terrain, not now visible. Harding further suggested that the approach to the temple of Zeus must have also had an influence: entering the sunlit plaza, perhaps from the shaded porticos, the eye would sweep around towards the *temenos* of the Temple of Zeus above it to the south west.

hidden water pipes

By Byzantine times the plaza was no longer used as a public area, and houses were built over it. At one time a water cistern was built in the middle, with water reaching it via pipes concealed below the paving stones. The line of these pipes can still be seen on the north and west. On the sides of the cistern are what appear to be seats; the purpose of these remains a mystery.

debris conceals

After the city was abandoned the houses built in the Oval Plaza collapsed and when Jerash was re-discovered and excavated the whole area was full of rubble. Only in later years when this was cleared was the majesty of the arena appreciated.

▸ Temple of Zeus

"...I found the remains of a beautiful temple commanding a view over the greater part of the town." J.L. Burckhardt, writing in 1812.

To the west of the South Gate (or southwest of the Oval Plaza) is the **Temple of Zeus**.

treasure house

It may be hard to appreciate that the mass of ruins, fallen columns and capitals, and other bits of masonry at present on show, once formed a piece of refined and imposing architecture. Completed in the second half of the 2nd C AD (161-166) it was to this temple that the rulers of Philadelphia, Zeno and Theodosus, brought the treasure for safekeeping (see page 105).

The approach to the temple from the Oval Plaza was by a flight of steps which led up to the *temenos*, one of the terraces that make up the temple complex. This *temenos*, 100 by 50 metres, was enclosed by an arched portico with openings on the north, east and south. The terrace was supported by cavernous underground vaults. These were used to increase the height of the terrace, and can be seen on the west as you approach the Plaza from the South Gate.

view from the temple temenos

The upper terrace was reached by an impressive stairway that was nearly 30 metres wide! Sadly this has long gone, buried beneath tons of earth and fallen rubble, and you must climb up as best you can.

From this terrace more steps led up the *cella*. This was once flanked on all sides by Corinthian columns over 14 metres high: 8 at the front and back and 12 at each side. Earthquakes have taken their toll of nearly all but you can climb up to the three remaining ones, from where you will get a great view of the Oval Plaza and the site. The outside of the *cella* had 8 arched niches, and corner pilasters at the ends. The front entrance led into the main room, where the shrine is thought to have been located.

▸ The South Theatre

Some 50 metres west of the Temple of Zeus is the **South Theatre** which is among the most outstanding monuments in this wonderful ancient city.

commemorative statue

Dating from the beginning of the 2nd C, this is the larger of Jerash's two theatres, and could seat up to 5000 persons. There were 32 tiers, and those towards the bottom were numbered. An inscription in Greek on the wall beneath the last row of seats records a victory statue presented by officers who had fought in the Jewish revolt of AD 70, which Titus put down. (This rebellion resulted in the Roman rasing of Jerusalem). The statue cost 3,000 drachmae and was put up in the reign of Domitian (81 to 96).

split auditorium

The *cavea* is in two halves, with a dividing terrace. The lower part, comprising about half the rows, is further divided into 4 sections, each separated by stairs. Likewise the upper *cavea* has 8 sections.

The theatre was orientated towards the city so that the sun only faced the spectators for a short time in late afternoon. Entry into the theatre was (and is) from the front, via two vaulted passages that open into the orchestra. This also allowed access to the lower rows. The

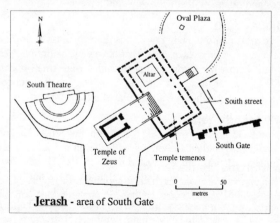

Jerash - area of South Gate

upper area was reached from four vaulted *vomitoria* situated at the rear of the building.

still used

The South Theatre including the decorated stage has been extensively restored, and some of the outer north wall is of entirely modern construction. In the manner of Roman theatres, the acoustics are very good. The theatre is regularly used for performances, especially during the Jerash Festival in July and August.

▶ The Colonnaded Cardo

Return to the Oval Plaza and you can now start the walk along **the Colonnaded Cardo** which extends from the plaza to the North Gate, a distance of some 600 metres.

resplendent route

This monumental street was originally set down around the middle of the first century AD, with the columns being Ionic. The cardo was the "High Street" of Gerasa, and is still today a splendid route to traverse. In the second half of the 2nd C this thoroughfare was widened, and the Ionic columns were replaced by the finer Corinthian ones, at least as far as the north tetrapylon.

Many of the bases and shafts used were from the original Ionic pillars, and have differing heights. As the columns carried an architrave this had to be corrected at various points.

covered walkway

In the places where a public building led directly off the street the columns were increased in height to that of the facade of the building, as for example in the front of the nymphaeum. (It should be noted that many of the columns you see have been re-erected.) For most of the way there were covered porticos on each side and from these shops, offices and other small structures would have led.

drains as well!

For most part the paving, which is limestone, is the original, and you can even see grooves made by chariot wheels. A drainage channel was laid below the cardo, and at the sides were small openings to enable the water to run off into the channel. The channel could be cleaned etc via manholes with circular stone covers.

newly found agora

Some 75 metres from the forum, on the left, four columns, somewhat larger than the others, indicate an entrance to a public building which was only excavated in the 1970s. These excavations unearthed a very large edifice that was flanked on the north and south by side streets that joined the Cardo. The excavators found engraved on one of the columns the word **agora**, market, and it is believed that this could have been the city's main commercial structure.

► South Tetrapylon

The intersection of the southern decumanus is another c75 metres along the colonnaded street. As was the usual practice this junction was marked by a huge **tetrapylon**. This comprised of four podiums, each about four metres square and each supporting four granite

The South Theatre

columns (no longer in situ) on which was a pyramid-shaped entablature. Each podium had a niche on each side and in the centre a manhole that allowed entry to Gerasa's sewer.

In the early Byzantine period the crossroads was rebuilt into a circular plaza, and shops and other buildings were erected around it.

To the west the decumanus reached the city wall and the south west gate, and to the east right down to the Chrysorhoas river which was spanned by a Roman bridge, three arches of which have been re-erected in the restored structure.

(Like so much in partly restored ancient sites like Jerash, much imagination is required if descriptions of areas like the one following or the Artemis complex later on are not to be seen as absurd!)

► The Cathedral and Fountain Court

Some 100 metres north of the tetrapylon, on the left, is the gate and stairs leading to the **Cathedral,** and next to that (north) the **nymphaeum.**

stone artisans

This gate and stairway was originally the entrance to the 2nd century Temple of Dionysus. It was rebuilt as the Cathedral Gate some time in the 4th century. A short flight of six steps leads up to the actual cathedral gate which is flanked by columns mounted on pedestals. The gateway is a very good example of Gerasa's stone craftsmanship in the 2nd century. Inside are four Corinthian columns to the side of which are remnants of two stairways which most likely led to the upper part of the shops lining the cardo.

first church

The cathedral, which is Gerasa's oldest church, is a basilica with a single apse and is in a very ruined state. The basilica design is still visible as are the bases of many of the Corinthian columns that separated the aisles from the central nave. These columns were reused from the earlier 2nd century structure.

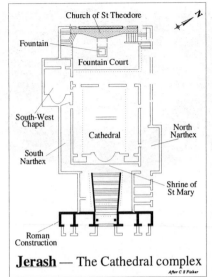

Jerash — The Cathedral complex

After C S Fisher

At the west end of the cathedral stood the **Shrine of Saint Mary**, a small niche-like structure with pilasters on each side. This little sanctuary is said to date from the 5th century, a time when the cult of the Virgin Mary was gaining ground.

water into wine

Just west of the cathedral is an *atrium* called the **Fountain Court**. The fountain in the centre is still there, built of pink limestone. Here the annual Feast of the Miracle of Cana took place which recalled the events of John 2:1-9 when Jesus turned the water into wine at a wedding celebration.

Immediately behind the fountain court (west of it) lie the ruins of the **Church of St. Theodore**, dedicated in 496 by Bishop Aeneas. Built on a terrace above the court it was approached from the north west by steps. The nave is separated from side aisles by rows of 7 Corinthian columns, one on each side, taken from Roman buildings of an earlier date, 2nd or 3rd century. On their bases are some Greek letters that may have been a guide for their erection. The apse of the church protruded into the fountain court. Originally there were arches which sprang across the colonnades supporting the roof that may have been part timbered. At the west end of the building was the *atrium* which stretched across the western wall of the church, and some of the adjoining rooms.

mosaics long gone

From the outside a triple doorway, of which only the middle one remains opened, led into a small vestibule with a mosaic floor. To the sides of this vestibule were other rooms also with mosaic floors. To the south west is the baptistry with a font in the eastern apse. Just by this baptistry were another series of rooms, each with mosaic floors.

▸ The Nymphaeum

Directly north of the Cathedral Gate is the **nymphaeum**, or public water fountain. Built at the end of the second century, it presented the local citizenry with a beautiful monument which, with its cool spring water, must have been a delight on a hot summer's day.

sumptuous decoration

The nymphaeum comprises of two storeys: the lower one is covered with marble, while the upper had painted plaster, of which orange and green fragments are still visible in the upper left niche. The whole structure was covered by a half-domed roof, probably decorated with mosaics, and was one of the most superbly decorated public buildings in the city, with especially fine carvings on the lower entablature.

The nymphaeum was fronted on the western colonnade of the cardo by two pairs of Corinthian columns which were considerably taller than those lining the street. Of the four you see today, three are original while one has been restored by the Jordanians.

The semi-circular fountain, some 10 metres in diameter has niches all around the wall on both levels, alternating between semi-circular and rectangular shapes with small Corinthian columns in front. The niches held statues, the lower ones, with water conduits, probably conveying water. At the bottom was a great stone basin, flanked by two pairs of Corinthian columns into which the water flowed. In front of this was a low wall with a number of channels that allowed the water to flow out via lions heads into small basins from where passers by could get access to it before it drained away.

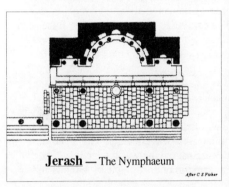

Jerash — The Nymphaeum

After C S Fisher

▶ The Temple of Artemis and area

"The whole edifice seems to have been superior in taste and magnificence to every public building of this kind in Syria..."
J.L. Burckhardt (Travels in Syria and the Holy Land, 1822)

About 100 metres north of the nymphaeum, on the left and inset from the cardo, four huge Corinthian columns with a flight of steps behind them, announce the gateway to the **Temple of Artemis.** Dedicated to the city's patron goddess, the temple was, in its time, the most important and the finest building in Gerasa, and dates from the middle of the second century AD. The actual temple stands high on a vast terrace some distance away to the west of the cardo and its ancient columns have survived the ravages of time and earthquake that have devastated so much else around.

following the sacred way

The temple complex and the sacred way that led to it really starts on the east bank of the Chrysorhoas, Wadi Jerasa, which was crossed by a bridge, only bare remnants of which remain. It is said that this bridge stood in the last century and was actually photographed. To appreciate this and the description which follows, leave the cardo to the right (east) at this point and walk across to the edge of the hill overlooking the wadi and the new town.

At the west end of the bridge (down below) a triple arched gateway gave way onto a wide colonnaded street which climbed to the top. Seven columns from the southern side of the street still remain. The end of this monumental street opened into a wide square (where you are standing), which then led into the cardo and faced the temple's propylaeum.

a church closed the way

Later centuries saw this precinct fall prey to earthquakes, and in the 6th century some smart builder saw the possibilities of transforming it. As a result, you are standing by (or on) the remains of a church rather than those of the original "sacred way" to the Temple of Artemis: in 565, according to an inscription, the Byzantines converted this open area into a church, called today the **Viaduct** or **Propylaeum Church.** This makes it all seems rather baffling to the visitor today.

The church thus built was a basilica; the paved street becoming the nave while the side colonnades became the aisles. The arches at the eastern end, then fallen, were rebuilt into an apse with the end closed by a wall. The whole was then roofed over. Part of what had been the square at the end of the street was converted into an atrium surrounded by columns. The original paving was retained.

Let's now return to my description of the Temple of Artemis and its environs.

up to the propylaeum

From the square at the end of the former colonnaded street the sacred way traverses the cardo and commences the actual approach to the temple. We now walk this way (west). The four columns which were 16 metres high and nearly 1.5 metres in diameter were flanked on either side by an additional number of smaller columns, and these delineated the eastern perimeter of the temple complex.

From here, and through a huge gateway, a long flight of steps broken into seven sections of seven steps, led up to a terrace with an altar in the centre. This terrace is c14 metres above the level of the cardo, and from it you get a wonderful view of the temple above and ahead.

many more flights of steps

From this terrace three flights of nine steps, over one hundred metres wide and the entire width of the terrace, climbed a further six metres to the **temple temenos**, the courtyard that preceded the temple.

The courtyard measures 120 by 160 metres and was encircled by a wall and a columned portico. On the south side are remains of the double row of columns that formed the colonnade. Both the northern and southern sides comprised of 36 columns, while the eastern and western sides had 26. There were entrances on the north and south sides, and between the wall and the columns were various rooms and offices.

Some 20 metres in front of the temple is the foundation of an altar dating from the 2nd century. Nearby is an arch and some ruins which belong to a ceramics factory that functioned here during Byzantine and Omayyad times.

at last!

The **Temple of Artemis** itself is positioned on a vast podium over 22 metres wide, 40 metres long and 4.5 metres high. It was surrounded by a row of columns, 13 metres high and 1.5 metres thick. Eleven of these columns stood on the north and south sides while the west side had six. On the east side, the entrance portico had a double row of six, eleven of which still stand although some are tilting! This podium was approached by a double flight of steps, long gone, but replaced by some "new" ones to provide easy visitor access, although they do spoil the appearance somewhat.

sanctuary of the priests

From the portico the *cella* was reached by the ultimate flight of steps – this time only four – and entered through a door nine metres high and five metres wide. The inside was unadorned, but had marble-faced niches. The focal point of the *cella* was at the western end, where a raised platform set beneath arches housed the likeness of Artemis, the patron goddess of Gerasa. Only the priests were allowed entrance into this *cella*, the lay worshippers required to remain in the temenos.

pillage and destruction

In Byzantine times, when the temple was no more in use, houses and ceramic kilns were built in the courtyard, and much of the building materials from the temple were taken away to be used in constructing churches. This practice continued into the Omayyad era. In the 12th century the Arabs converted the temple into a fort, which was eventually captured and wrecked by Baldwin II, Crusader King of Jerusalem.

If you are here in the spring the entire area around the temple is green, richly patterned with yellow and red wild flowers. Try getting a view from a northerly position.

From the temple you can explore the west part of the city or return to the cardo and continue north, exploring the western area later. For the sake of good order this guide will continue north.

► **The Mosque**

Returning to the cardo and continuing north, between the Propylaeum Church and the West Baths, on the east side of the cardo, is the Omayyad Mosque. All that is left of this structure is the rubble of fallen arches and columns.

newly found

Excavated in the early 1980s, this is the only Omayyad mosque found in Jerash. Dating from the 7th or 8th century it was constructed using a colonnaded forecourt of an earlier Roman edifice. The prayer hall, measuring about 6.5 by 13.5 metres, was enclosed by columns on which the roof rested. The *mihrab*, which you can see on the south wall, was derived from a niche in the original Roman construction. The paved hall had its main entrance on the western wall.

► **The North Tetrapylon**

A little more than 100 metres further north along the cardo is the **north tetrapylon** and the **north decumanus** which it marks. This edifice is quite unlike the southern one. It consists of four pillars which were lined by arches, which in turn supported a domed roof. The north and south arches had free-standing Corinthian columns and lions head fountains on the bases.

The entire structure was dedicated to Julia Domna, the daughter of the High Priest of Homs, who in 187 became wife of Septimus Severus, later Roman Emperor.

► **The Western Baths**

From the tetrapylon a path to the right leads to the very ruined **West Baths.** These can also be reached by a path from the Omayyad mosque. Although some parts have been restored, they are still in a pretty ruinous state.

not much left to see

The baths, as usual in Roman baths, had two main chambers, the *frigidarium* in the centre, and the *caldarium* to the west (closest to the Cardo). This latter had a domed roof. To the north and south of the *caldarium* were four smaller rooms, two each side, and around this section is a U-shaped *peristyle* with but a few columns surviving.

On the east were three identical rooms, *apodyteria* or changing rooms, with the entrances to the baths flanking them. At the northern and southern extremities were two other chambers which like the *caldarium* had domed roofs. These domed roofs over a rectangular room may be the earliest instances of this type of architecture in the region. The entire 2nd century building, one of the largest in the city, was 75 metres long and 50 metres wide and is one of the two main public baths of ancient Gerasa (the other one being the Eastern Baths, across the wadi).

▸ The North Gate

rustic charm

The remaining 200 metres or so of the cardo northwards is from the original, as constructed in the first century, that is before the southern end was widened and the Ionic columns replaced by Corinthian ones. It is therefore somewhat narrower and has less grandeur to it, although a certain rustic charm prevails due, possibly, to the trees that now grow along most of its length. It is surprising that after walking this far many visitors are disinclined to complete the full length of the street. Don't be one of them.

potential for finds

No excavations have yet been made along this final stretch, so we do not know if any major construction stood alongside. One or two features indicate that this could be the case.

The ruined **North Gate** marks the end of this monumental thoroughfare, built in 115 under Claudius Severus, legate of the Emperor Trajan, who also built the road from Pella in the Jordan Valley to Gerasa.

not-so-straight Roman road

Of rather unusual design, the shape of this gate was planned to accommodate the differing angles of the outside and inside roads. Whilst the cardo did not run in a true north-south axis, the ensuing road to Pella ran directly north. This meant that both sides of the gate are not parallel, the north side veering out at an approximate 20 degree angle. Thus when passing through this gate one had to make a turn to line up with the road's continuation. The two bastions at each side of the gate were built in late Byzantine times.

Return now to the north tetrapylon to begin the exploration of the western city.

▸ The North Decumanus and Theatre

Turning west at the North Tetrapylon you enter the **north decumanus** which traversed the northern part of the city from east to west, in the direction of the North West gate.

re-used columns

This nine metre wide thoroughfare was bordered with Ionic columns most probably re-used from the cardo when its Ionic pillars were replaced with the more majestic Corinthian. The street was built in the late second century, as a replacement for the simple one that had previously existed.

This excavated section of the north decumanus is short, and comparatively recent. G. Lankester Harding writing in the late 1950s reports: *"From the North Tetrapylon a street runs west, flanked by columns of the Ionic order, the tops of three of which can be seen sticking up out of the fields"*. The excavated section is only some 60-70 metres long, and after it you leave the flagstones and climb up a dirt path that bears around to the right until you reach five massive Corinthian columns. Together with a sixth (now gone), these adorned the thoroughfare's north side and protrude way above the path. The **North Theatre** is on the left. The position of this theatre vis-à-vis the decumanus can be confusing.

deeply submerged

Until the early 1980s the excavated stretch of the decumanus remained unearthed and the path you are now standing on is to the north of its line. Pass between the columns (heading towards the theatre) and look down to the left and you will see that these excavations have exposed a further stretch of the street, and to what depth it has been buried, giving the present access route to the theatre the appearance of a ramp!

remains of steps

Crossing the ramp and looking down to the left and right, particularly the right, you can see the remains of a monumental flight of steps. This led up from the decumanus to the theatre's portico. At the top of the steps stood four Corinthian columns, only a single one still stands.

visualising it

So together with this explanation let me draw you a word picture of how it all looked: the theatre-goer would walk up the broad Ionic columned decumanus from the tetrapylon. At the approach to the theatre the street became more grand with six 12 metre high Corinthian columns lining the street's north side, creating a "plaza" effect. The theatre-goer would then mount the monumental 15 metre wide stairway into the theatre's foyer which was announced by four more lofty columns of the Corinthian order. Even London's finest playhouse could not match this ancient opulence!

first an odeon

This theatre was built in the second part of the 2nd century AD and was originally quite small, perhaps deserving the name odeon rather than theatre. With a capacity of c1600 spectators it was considerably smaller than the great theatre in the south of the city.

The best way to get into the seating area is from the south side, where the external *vomitoria* were sited. From the top a grand view over the northern part of the city can be obtained.

recent excavation

The North Theatre and its vicinity was excavated during 1982/3 by archaeologists from Britain, the USA, and Australia, and at the time of writing is undergoing extensive restoration work.

church discovered

Just west of the North Theatre is a church that was only unearthed during the excavation of the adjacent theatre in the early 1980s. It has been called the **Church of Bishop Isaiah**, as an inscription bearing this name was found on a mosaic in front of the main apse. It is sited on an elevated embankment, and provides a very good vista of the neighbouring construction. Probably erected in the early 6th century, it is a three apse basilica some 28 metres long. The central 8 metre wide nave was separated from the side aisles by a row of columns, and all ended in an apse.

Apart from the apses, which were paved with stone, the whole church floor was covered with mosaics, but you will not see any sign of these now. The church was in use till the middle of the 8th century, when much of it was destroyed by earthquake. After that various parts seem to have been repaired, and it found intermittent uses, specifically in the 14th and 15th centuries. Deserted afterwards, it was buried until these times.

▸ Churches in the Western Part of the City

A group of churches lies to the west and south west of the Temple of Artemis, and although you can reach them by working your way around the back of the North Theatre and then northwards via the temple, my description will approach them from the south tetrapylon.

original arches

Return along the cardo till you reach this point and the **south decumanus**. This major cross street dates from the late first century, but a less important one existed prior to that time. It was colonnaded on both sides, and in the restored section many of these columns are in place. To the east the decumanus crossed the river by a bridge and in the construction of the modern one remains of the Roman structure were used.

You can wander down east to the perimeter fence to glance at the bridge below. Our route to the churches goes to the west.

an Omayyad house

Some 100 metres from the south tetrapylon you come to an excavated area on the north side (right). Unearthed during a major project in the early 1980s these are the remains of a large dwelling that has been dubbed the **Omayyad House**.

The structure has been dated to AD 660, a few years after a major earthquake when the Omayyads rebuilt and resettled parts of the city. The house comprised a courtyard with rooms to the east and west. The floors may have been covered by mosaics as bits and pieces of these have been found.

▸ Churches of St George, St John the Baptist and SS Cosmas and Damian

Three in a row

Continuing west along this decumanus a sign points north west to the Church of St George. Here, adjoining one another are actually three churches. (The churches can also be reached along a track south from the Temple of Artemis.)

The first one (southerly), the **Church of St. George** is of a basilica design with a central apse. The nave and aisles were separated by large columns on either side. Entry to the building was by three doors that led off the *atrium*. The church dates from about 530, and was still being used for worship in the 8th century.

the largest of them

The centre church, dedicated to **St John the Baptist,** is the largest of the group and also dates from c530. It is built as a circle inside a square with four semi-circular *exedra* in the corners. North of the apse was a room, probably a baptistry, that opened into the adjacent church. In the centre were four columns, recycled from earlier years. The floor of the nave was covered with mosaic, though little remains of it now. Entry was via doors from the *atrium* on the western side.

best mosaic

The northerly church is that of **St Cosmas and St Damian.** It cannot be entered, but you can view the interior from the high wall above to the north. Entry is prohibited because it houses one of the best surviving mosaics in Jerash. It is of similar design to the Church of St George, but has an alcove along the north wall with three Corinthian columns between it and the north aisle. The apse, with the baptistry on the south, had another small room to the north.

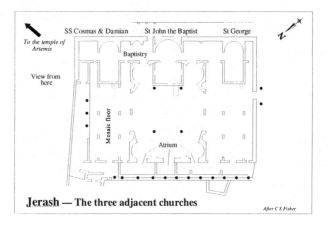

Jerash — The three adjacent churches

After C S Fisher

mosaic restored

The mosaic floor, two thirds of which still remains, was lifted in 1937 and after some restoration work was relaid on a firm base. The mosaic consists of differing geometric patterns and motifs of birds and animals. Two of the church's patrons, Theodore and Georgia, are also pictured; the head of Theodore has been much restored. At the top is an inscription dedicating the building to the saints, who were brothers, and dating it to 533. There are also likenesses of other patrons such as Dagistheus, an officer of Justinian.

liturgy once a day

The reason for building three adjoining churches was most likely an Eastern Orthodox tradition that only permitted the liturgy to be said once a day from any one altar.

The *atrium* is common to all three of these churches and had a portico of 14 Corinthian columns, a few of which are standing. The first two churches can be entered via this atrium (on the west side). A good view of all three can be obtained from the high wall to the north of the complex.

▶ The Synagogue Church

About 150 metres north of the three churches and west of the Temple of Artemis is what is known as **The Synagogue Church**. Built around 530 it acquired its name because it was built partly over a 3rd century synagogue. Little remains to be seen here, and it can be missed by those with little time.

Jews of Gerasa

It is not known for sure when Jews began to live in Gerasa, but after its conquest by Alexander Yannai in 84 BC many must have moved to the city. After the city became part of the Roman Empire resulting in the expansion of its commercial links, it can be assumed that the Jewish presence strengthened.

reverse orientation

As the synagogue was east of Jerusalem the orientation of the building was east to west in order that the worshippers could face the holy city as is the Jewish custom. (Most people are used to synagogues facing east to Jerusalem). The synagogue was built with a nave which was flanked by side aisles, with a *bema* (a raised platform where the officiants stood) at the eastern end. There was an *atrium* to the west which had Corinthian columns, bits and pieces of which are really all that is left.

covered with mosaics now covered!

The floor was covered by mosaics, some of them picturing various animals entering Noah's Ark, remnants of which have survived, but cannot be seen now. Jewish artefacts including a candelabrum were discovered under the foundations. Whether or not the presence of this building signifies a Jewish Quarter remains conjecture. When the church was built the whole place had to be replanned in order to accommodate the arrangement of a Byzantine church in which the worshippers faced east.

▸ Other churches

Directly west of the three churches, no more than 100 metres distant, is the not-much-to-be-seen rubble of the **Church of Bishop Genesius**, so called because it was built during that clergyman's tenure.

ultimate church?

This could have been the last church to be built in Gerasa as an inscription found on the mosaic floor dates it to 611, just prior to the Sasanian invasion. Although it has not been thoroughly excavated it was of basilica design with the nave delineated from the aisles by rows of columns from which arches supported the roof. The single apse bulged out and there were no side rooms. Most of the floor was covered in mosaics.

scant remains

Just inside the ramparts in the south west is the late 6th century **Mortuary Church** and **The Church of St Peter and St Paul** which is dated to 540. An inscription records that the church was dedicated to the Evangelists after whom the place is named. At neither of these two sites is there much to see.

▸ Other sites of Jerash

Across the wadi

Everything I have described so far has been in the fenced off area on the west side if the stream. Very little remains on the east as the modern town has all but swallowed what there was. However, two places are worth a visit if your schedule permits.

local colour

Near the bus station, a bustling area for most of the day and an ideal place to see the local life, are the **East Baths**. The presence of such a large public building on this side of the wadi can only indicate that there must have been a large residential neighbourhood here, for these *thermae* were considerably larger than those in the west. Not too much has been discovered about them but their very presence in such a busy atmosphere may help you to conjure up in your mind the throngs that must have crowded the city in Roman times.

hardly worth a visit

High on a hill in the very east of the modern city is the **Church of Procopius**. The scant remains are mainly made up of column drums and bases. The church was a basilica, and two rows of six Corinthian columns separated the nave from the aisles. The floor was mosaic and an inscription on it records that the church was built in 526, by a certain Procopius, a Byzantine officer.

large pools

North of the north gate is a road that leads to **Birkatayn** which is Arabic for two pools. These pools were fed from a nearby spring. The pools, which are really a single one divided, measure about 90 by 40 metres with a depth of some 3 metres.

pagan porn!

Just to the south west of the pool and overlooking it, is a small theatre, built into the hill. This is known as the **Festival Theatre** and was the site of a pagan water festival which consisted, among other things, of abandoned nude bathing between the sexes. The theatre has been dated to the early third century.

The pillars situated some 100 metres further north of the Birkatayn mark the tomb of a certain Germanus, quite clearly a man of substance.

▸ AJLUN CASTLE (QALA'AT AL-RABDAH)

Easily approachable from Jerash or Irbid, the Arab castle of **Qala'at al-Rabdah** is something with a difference as it is the only purely Arab built castle in Jordan.

How to get there

easy access

From Jerash: The road west is well signposted. The 12 km drive is through very pleasing countryside and climbs for most of the way. (It continues down to the Jordan Valley). At the village of Ajlun take the right turn towards Irbid and the castle.

From Irbid: Take the road south signposted to Ajlun.

Bus travellers will find unscheduled minibuses from both places to the village. From there its either a walk or a taxi ride.

historic mention

Of the castle a 13th century Arab traveller wrote the following:

"The castle of Ajlun...is new and small and stands on a projecting spur overlooking the Jordan Valley, visible both from Jerusalem and from the Nablus ridge. The range on which it was built is called Jabal Auf, due to a clan of the Banu Auf that lived there under the Fatamid Caliphs. They had restless Emirs who were at feud with one another because their families quarrelled. So things were until the time of Malik al-Adil Saif al-Din, [the brother of Salah al-Din] *who gave the district as a feifdom to Azz al-Din Ausama, one of his main Emirs. He immediately began to*

*build a castle to protect his governors from the Banu Auf,
but they hindered him so much that he represented to them
that he was building it merely to protect them against the
Franks* [Crusaders]. *Then they became agreeable and
helped him to build it. When it was finished he invited the
sheikhs of the Banu Auf to the castle for a feast. When they
had eaten he ordered his young slave to seize them and
lock them up. It is said that an ancient monastery once
stood on the site, inhabited by a Christian named Ajlun;
when the monastery fell into ruin, the castle took its place
and the name of the monk".*

same as Azraq

Azz al-Din Ausama built the castle in 1184 in order to prevent
further expansion of the Crusader areas east of the Jordan, which were
centred on Karak. In 1215 it was greatly enlarged by Azz al-Din
Aybak (Azzeddin Aybak), who was the Ayyubid ruler of the area and
also responsible for improvements at the castle of Azraq.

visited by ibn Batutta and Burckhardt

With the demise of the Crusader presence in the area, a settlement
grew around the stronghold, but this was unable to prevent its capture
by the Mongols in 1260. They were later driven out by the Mameluke
Sultan Baibars. The renowned Arab traveller Ibn Batutta described
the town in 1335 as *"a fine town with good markets and a strong
castle..."*. When visited by J.L. Burckhardt during his 1812 journey
through the region, he reported that about forty persons still lived
there.

The visit

In the late 1920s the castle underwent excavation and restoration
work, and what you see today is the result of that labour. Entrance is
across a wooden bridge which spans the now dry moat. Once inside,
the passage turns right then left and reaches what was the original
gate, and then leads into the castle proper. Get yourself right up to the
top for a real bird's eye view of all the surrounding area. Whether you
can see as far as Jerusalem, I don't really know — I certainly cannot
— but it's a fine panorama nevertheless!

Qala'at al-Rabdah is a popular place for outings, and on Fridays
and holidays tends to be crowded.

fine air

Ajlun is an amiable spot in summer, its elevation providing crisp
mountain air. Two tourist class hotels are situated here, and for
details see the appropriate section of this book.

10. The Desert Castles

INTRODUCTION

In the desert east of Amman are the remains of numerous palaces and forts which have come to be known as the **Desert Castles, or Palaces.** Although most are of Omayyad origin, the castles of Hallabat and Azraq are rebuildings of earlier strongholds.

pleasure palaces

The Omayyads, whose caliphate ruled the Islamic world from 661 to 750, had their capital at Damascus. But while they resided in the lavish splendour of that city, they still considered their roots as being in the desert, from where they originated. They built a large number of palaces or retreats in the deserts of Syria and Jordan. To these palaces they would retire in order to indulge in the pleasures of hunting, hawking and perhaps other delights that the spiritual and temporal rulers of the Muslim world should not be seen to enjoy.

easier access

The grand palaces they built in Syria's remote desert region east of Damascus, Qasr al-Heir, al-Sharqi and al-Gharbi, are rarely frequented by visitors today, but those in the Jordanian desert, because of their easier access, are more well known.

rewarding excursion

Driving through a monotonous stretch of desert is not the most thrilling way to spend one's time, but these palaces and forts make such a drive worthwhile. If possible, they should not be missed.

Until the 1970s this was not too easy, as the driving was in the main over tracks. Now, most of the notable castles are easily accessible from Amman over fairly good asphalted roads, and this route is often referred to as the "Desert Loop" because all the significant ones can be seen on a circular tour. Unless you particularly want to spend a night at Azraq, all can be visited in one not over-long day. I cannot recommend visiting all these places without your own transport, but Azraq can be reached by bus or service taxi. Otherwise, the best method may be a combination of minibuses, hitchhiking and walking.

At the time of writing, none of these sites charge an entrance fee. The custodians may ask you for a dinar, but unless they can produce a ticket, you don't have to pay. The itinerary described follows the route clockwise, but you can of course choose your own direction, either clockwise or anti-clockwise.

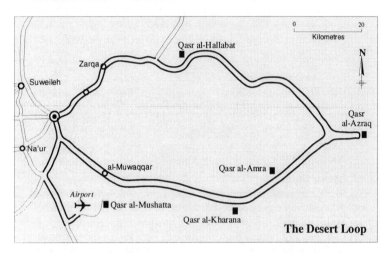

The Desert Loop

▶ QASR AL-HALLABAT

How to get there

Situated about 60 km northwest of Amman, **Qasr al-Hallabat** is reached by taking the Zarqa road. Just before the entrance to Zarqa a road forks to Mafraq, Azraq and Jerash. Take this road and then follow all subsequent signs to Azraq. You will pass on the way a free enterprise area and an enormous parking lot for oil tankers which ply the route to and from Iraq along this road.

A brown road sign to the left points the direction to the palace. After turning left the road loops around left again, doubling back the way you came. On the way it passes on the left Hammam al-Sarakh (see below) and a small Bedouin encampment. Qasr al-Hallabat is about 3 km further on, also on the left.

By bus: Take one from Zarqa to Azraq, alighting at the turn off mentioned above, then either walk or hitch.

custodian at entrance

The fenced-off area is approached by a track. It is signposted. At the gate a guardian will allow you to enter with your vehicle. If he is not there, the gate slides open. From here, the remains of the edifice can be seen ahead, a couple of hundred metres away, on a hill.

History

Roman fort

The very ruined Qasr al-Hallabat started life as a Roman fort. It was built by Caracalla in the early 2nd century as one of the positions that defended the *Via Nova Traiana*, the road laid by Trajan to link Damascus with Aila, now Aqaba, on the Red Sea. A Latin inscription found there records that it was enlarged between 212 and 215, and corner towers, parts of which still stand, were constructed. Another inscription, this time in Greek, indicates that it was restored by the Byzantines in the late 5th or early 6th century for use as a monastery.

caliph rebuilds in style

The fort seems to have been abandoned by the Byzantines around 614 during the invasions of Sasanian Persians under Chosroes II. Afterwards it may have been used for while as a monastery. In the early 8th century an Omayyad caliph, most likely Walid II, virtually rebuilt the place. Although the reconstruction followed the same basic layout as the original, it was decorated in sumptuous fashion. Most of the floors were covered with mosaics, while other decorations such as plaster frescoes, carved wood, fancy glass windows and friezes were added. Don't expect to see any of this!

The visit

corner towers

Although a modest amount of restoration work has been undertaken the general condition of the qasr is ruinous, but you will be able to obtain a good appreciation of the palace. Comprising of a building roughly 45 metres square, parts of the walls are still standing on every side except the south. Towers stood in all four corners, and some of these are visible. I suggest you walk around the ruin before entering in order to gain a better impression of its size and see some of the black and white stone decoration on those outer walls which still stand.

fallen masonry

The entrance, once imposing, is through a decorative arch, still in place. Immediately you are confronted by the rubble of the fallen building, carved stone, door lintels and other embellishments, but the excavators have cleared a passage that enables exploration of some of the rooms.

When the Omayyads rebuilt the palace they used much of the stone from the previous Byzantine structure, but not in its original context. As the walls were plastered over, any inscriptions were hidden. Now most of that plaster has gone and you will therefore notice many stones with Greek inscriptions on the walls in several rooms. One room in particular has an impressive array of inscribed masonry lying on the floor. These pieces may not have belonged to this room but gathered here by the excavators.

frescoes long gone

Odd patches of the plaster remain, but not enough to show that they were decorated, in places, with living likeness frescoes so beloved by the Omayyad rulers in defiance of Islam's teachings! The floors were of fine mosaic, and many of the designs were similar to the wall frescoes. The qasr stood two storeys high, and though you can mount steps to the second the actual upper level no longer exists.

The separate edifice with the arch on the east side is the mosque, with parts of three walls still standing. It was surrounded on three of its sides by arched porticos. The *mihrab* on the south wall (the one facing Mecca from this location), is still visible. The mosque clearly appears to have undergone some renovation.

ample water

Here, as in most of their desert palaces, the Omayyads went to great lengths to ensure a water supply. The water that was collected on the roof was conveyed by a system of conduits into cisterns. Additionally, water was brought from a nearby wadi where it was collected by dams and reservoirs.

Good views of the surrounding countryside, which today is agricultural, can be admired from the hill.

► Hammam al-Sarakh

Hammam al-Sarakh which you passed on the way was the hammam (bath house) for the palace. As befitted the luxury of Qasr al-Hallabat, they were extremely elegant baths, but of this elegance you will see nothing!

once-lavish ornamentation

They were extravagantly ornamented with mosaics and plaster frescoes, and contained the usual three bathrooms, hot, tepid and cold. This small domed building was until about 30 years ago in a totally ruined state, but it has since been excavated and partially restored by the Jordanian Department of Antiquities. Although the decoration has now gone, in the recent past patches of colour could be discerned on the walls.

Outside there is a well, some 18 metres deep; as there is no protection around it be careful!

► QASR AL-AZRAQ (Azraq Castle)

How to get there

Return now to the Azraq road, and continue through the desert until that town is reached (52 km). You have come here to see the famous castle, all other reasons for visiting this place having been removed in a undertaking of environmental irresponsibility (see below). The castle is situated on the road north so turn left at the T junction at the entrance to the town.

By bus: Minibuses run without a schedule to Azraq from either the Abdali bus station in Amman, or from Zarqa.

Iraq and Saudia

The (former oasis) town of Al-Azraq is situated in the narrow "neck" of Jordan, with Iraq to the north and Saudi Arabia to the south. It rests at the northern end of Wadi Sirhan, the broad valley which spreads away southeast into the Saudi desert.

The fortress is easy to find: after you turn left follow the road for a couple of kilometres. You can't miss the sombre looking black basalt citadel sited rather oddly now, on the left of the road between houses and shops.

History

solitary water source

As the only water in the entire eastern desert is found here, **Wahat al-Azraq**, the Oasis of Azraq, the largest in the eastern desert, was in ancient times an important stopping place for the many caravans which traversed Wadi Sirhan on their journey to Syria. Here they found immense pools of water, fed by springs, that were full all year round.

haven of migrating birds

These water sources, together with the surrounding marshes made al-Azraq a very important stopover not only for the camel trains but also for flocks of migratory birds flying between Africa and Europe. Once nearly 300 different types of fowl could be counted here. It was a unique place in the Middle East, and an important ornithological location. In addition, it possessed all the other attributes of a well-watered oasis.

fishermen in the desert!

Surprisingly, because of al-Azraq's once bountiful water, fishing for carp and catfish was a small but practised industry for a number of the region's inhabitants.

drinking the well dry

Sadly, this desert haven which existed for thousands of years is no more! The pressing requirements of the growing city of Amman have taken precedence over nature, and 15 years ago the government began to pump all the water in excess of Azraq's needs away to satisfy the capital's requirements. As a result the oasis has disappeared, and all that is left is a very dreary desert town with a few palm trees, a stopping place for the many truckers who drive through on their way to Saudi Arabia and the Gulf. Turkish signs in the roadside eateries, advertising Turkish food, cater to the numerous drivers from that country.

The migrating birds that for millennia stopped off at Azraq have moved further west to northern Israel where the waters of Lake Tiberias and Lake Huleh are constant. Someone told me recently that, realising a mistake was made, the Jordanian government with United Nations help is trying to rehabilitate the oasis! Unfortunately, such ill-conceived enterprises are all too common place in the Third World, where the rush for development overrides all other considerations.

flow from Syria

It is interesting to note that this water now pumped to Amman originates in Syria, itself not over abundant in that commodity. The course begins in the Jabal Arab (Druse) mountain range and, seeping through the permcable rock, feeds into aquifers, eventually discharging at the springs of al-Azraq.

The task of a guide book writer is always made more difficult when he has to write about a charmless place: fortunately in Azraq there is a saving grace in the form of its castle, and most visitors will be well rewarded by this in their short visit.

ancient hunting ground

Much of al-Azraq's history is bound up with the fact that the place had abundant water. Palaeolithic man certainly roamed these stretches, as artefacts dating back over 200,000 years have been discovered. It is also clear that in subsequent ages primitive man lived and hunted here. Fauna must also have been plentiful.

4th century castle

Azraq's black basalt fort was most likely built around AD 300. Inscriptions in Greek and Latin dedicate it to the emperors Diocletian (reigned 284-305) and Maximilian who reigned after him. Perched on the very edge of the Roman Empire it was used — like the two smaller forts mentioned below — to control movement along Wadi Sirhan, a major route from the Arabian peninsular. It was utilised by the Omayyads as both a fort and a hunting lodge. The Omayyad Caliph Walid, who was fond of

Qasr al-Azraq

hunting, would have found in Azraq an ideal location to pursue his sport.

military barracks

The castle in its present configuration is Ayyubid, and an inscription above the main entrance gives the date of 634 AH which conforms with 1237. It was occupied by the Ottomans in the 16th C and used as a military barracks. After that we know nothing of the building, but it was in a sufficient state of preservation for T.E. Lawrence to have made it his headquarters during the Arab Revolt of 1917.

The visit

intact walls

Despite the ravages of time and an earthquake in the late 1920s, the walls are still intact, and surround the citadel completely. The fort occupies an area of about 80 by 70 metres, and you enter from the south through a gatehouse that protrudes from the line of the wall. Above it is the inscription in Arabic mentioned above which states that the fort was built (rebuilt) in 634 AH by Azz al-Din Aybak (Azzeddin Aybak), who was the Ayyubid ruler of the area. The stronghold was defended by protruding towers in each corner, and interval towers in the wall's middle.

Lawrence slept here

Above the gatehouse you can climb up to the room that was used by T.E. Lawrence in 1917 as his headquarters. Do not expect to see any Lawrence memorabilia there! The modest room with blackened walls and slit windows looks today a very gloomy abode for anyone, let alone the legendary British officer! Once upon a time there were two storeys above the walls, but hardly anything of the upper now remains.

three ton door

Along the west wall (to your left as you step into the courtyard), is an interval tower larger than the others which includes a number of rooms. Just past the actual tower is an opening and through it is an impressive single slab stone door that with some effort still swings on the original stone pivots. It is said to weigh over three tons! You can enter the tower and explore the rooms through the stone door. Up the steps on the outside is a vaulted room with the complete vaulting still intact.

On the north side of the castle compound are a series of vaulted rooms, with their stone arches still in place. The large one on the left was the refectory; to the right of it are two kitchens. Further east, past the short stone wall, were the stables where five arches still remain. You can see along the far wall of these stables the feeder troughs, and the stones to which the animals were tethered. The cord is not original!

once a church

Facing these stables towards the centre of the courtyard is a mosque dating from the Ayyubid era, its *mirhab* flanked by columns and arches. It appears to have been a church in Byzantine times.

Facing the entrance to the mosque, closer to the walls, is a deep well, that until the draining of the oasis 15 years ago still contained water. The other rooms on the east side were used as barracks.

▸ FORTS OF QASR 'UWAINID AND QASR ASEIKHIN

only for the hardy

There are two more Roman forts in the Azraq vicinity, but as they are so badly ruined and require a four wheel drive desert vehicle to be reached, they are rarely visited.

Qasr 'Uwainid is some 15 kilometres southwest of Azraq, just north of the Shaumari Wildlife Reserve (see below).

This ruined fort overlooks Wadi 'Uwainid and some inscriptions found on a fallen lintel date it from around AD 200. It continued to be used until the early fourth century, and was then abandoned.

Qasr Aseikhin lies 12 kilometres northeast of Azraq, and is situated on a hilltop. The fort can be seen from quite some distance. This is a small fort, with some of its walls still standing, measuring some 25 metres square. It appears to date from the first century AD. It was in use until the 7th century.

▸ SHAUMARI WILDLIFE RESERVE

Rather less than successful, the **Shaumari Wildlife Reserve** may still be worth a visit. Fifteen kilometres southwest of Azraq, off the road that goes into Saudi Arabia, the reserve was a bid to re-introduce wildlife into the region that had long since gone. These included ostriches, oryx, and ibex. You may catch a glimpse of these animals roaming free but they will be few in number.

The undertaking was started in 1975, and given Jordan's limited resources and more pressing needs, is still a step in the right direction.

▸ QASR AL-AMRA

"...we came to Kusair al Amra, the little hunting lodge of Harith, the Shepherd King, a patron of the poets; it stood beautifully against its background..."

Revolt in the Desert, T.E. Lawrence

How to get there

From Azraq: return on the road you came for about 10 km till you come to a major junction with a road turning left (SE), and signposted to Amman and Aqaba. This is the Sahab-Azraq road and is the one heavy trucks take between Aqaba and Iraq, as it leads off the Amman-Aqaba desert highway just south of the capital.

By bus: To the best of my knowledge no minibuses ply this route, and if you want to visit the places along the way you will have to hitchhike. This should not be too much of a problem.

At the time of writing this transit route is not in operation due to UN sanctions against Iraq, and traffic along it is more sparse than once. About 20 km from the junction on the left is **Qasr al-Amra**, and although small it is one of the most beautiful and best preserved of the Omayyad desert palaces.

History

Situated in Wadi Butm, a wide valley where once fauna was abundant, Qasr al-Amra was a hunting lodge and a splendid bath house.

prolific builder

The 'Amra was built between 705 and 715 by Caliph Walid I who was responsible for a great number of Omayyad architectural achievements, including the splendid Great Mosque of Damascus.

Qasr al-Amra

frescoes galore

The palace consisted of a large hall with side rooms, plus a complete bath complex and surrounding wall. Most of the interior walls are covered by brilliant frescoes, and there are fragments of mosaics and other decorations.

The qasr was discovered by Alois Musil at the end of the 19th century, and its (until recent times) isolated location has contributed to the building's avoidance of gross vandalism. The frescoes did not fare so well, and time, grime, and people have all added to their deterioration. They are, though, still remarkable and rank among the best preserved secular frescoes of the period. In 1972 they were cleaned and restored by a party of experts from the Madrid Archaeological Museum.

The visit

The entrance is from the north and opens directly into a large hall that is the main part of the qasr and may have been an audience room. This triple-aisle hall is roofed by three cradle vaults which rest on arches. At the far end (S), is a vaulted recess with small vaulted rooms on either side.

Walid's wild tastes!

This hall is covered in frescoes, walls and ceiling. You may need time for your eyes to adjust to the dark interior to see them clearly. On the west wall (to your right as you enter) are women engaged in athletics and others either naked or almost so in bathing scenes, an indication of Walid's interests! The illustrations on the east wall are difficult to make out, but consist of hunting scenes with men on horses. The ones on the north east wall, just to the left of the entrance are easier to discern, and these are also of hunting scenes.

Islam's foes depicted

At the south end of the west wall (right of the entrance and at the end) is the most famous fresco in the building. It depicts three of the enemies of the Omayyads and Islam: the Byzantine Emperor; Roderick, king of the Spanish Visgoths; the Sasanian ruler, Chosroes; and the king (Negus) of Abyssinia. These are all identified by their names in Greek and Kufic Arabic. At my last visit

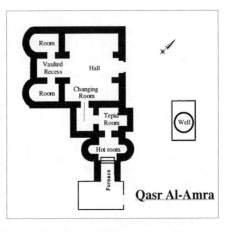

my companion looked in vain for these kings, and they may not be as clear to all as they are to me but they are there, although the faces are obscure!

Two other portraits also appear, but the names are not legible. They may be the emperor of China and a Khan from central Asia. As Roderick became ruler of the Spanish Visgoths in 710, and was killed by Walid I in 711, this picture helps in dating the qasr.

musicians and craftsmen

Other frescoes adorn the bases of the arches, where one of note shows a girl dancing to the accompaniment of a musician.

The vaulted ceilings are divided into 32 panels that each depict a craftsman. You will find a potter, blacksmith, carpenter, stonemason, tree feller, etc. These are among the clearest of the paintings.

forbidden images

On the wall of the southern recess is a picture of the Caliph enthroned and surrounded by attendants. The side rooms had mosaic floors, and the walls floral frescoes, and as these rooms are dark a flashlight will be useful. One of the surprising features of the murals in this qasr is that they contain representations of human figures, something abhorred by Islam; but then the palace was isolated, away from the public view.

clean caliph

From the hall a door on the east wall leads to the baths which comprised of a changing-cum-cold room, a tepid room and a hot room. These rooms, too, are decorated with a variety of frescoes, the ones in the tepid room being of naked women. The hot room with alcoves at each end has an interesting domed ceiling painted with the signs of the Zodiac of the northern hemisphere. It is the oldest existing stellar dome yet discovered. The painting is in a bad state of repair.

Outside, on the north side, is the Qasr's water source, a well that may be 40 metres deep, a cistern and a contraption for lifting the water with a circular area for a donkey or other beast to walk and operate it.

A few hundred metres from the palace, in the hills to the north east, are the scant remains of a building that could have been either a fort for protecting the qasr, or perhaps a caravanserai.

▸ QASR AL-KHARANA

"There was a brilliant moon and we marched till it was pale in the morning, passing the lone palace of Kharaneh...too careless to turn aside and see its strangeness."

Revolt in the Desert, T.E. Lawrence

How to get there

The road continues southwest and then bends west, and after 16 kilometres **Qasr al-Kharana** can be seen just off the road to the left. Apart from the fort at Azraq, which dates from Roman times, Qasr al-Kharana is the only place on our route which looks like a castle and has a defensive appearance to it.

The Qasr stands on a slight elevation above Wadi Janab, a valley that joins Wadi Sirhan further east.

History

Kufic dating

There is some opinion that suggests this qasr may be pre-Islamic, perhaps of Sasanian origin, and much of its style has a Mesopotamian flavour about it. Its Muslim origins rest mainly on a Kufic inscription over one of the doorways and gives a date of 92 AH which is the beginning of the Muslim era. This corresponds to the year 711.

Byzantine blocks

Prior to its construction (whether by the Sasanians or Muslims), a Byzantine or earlier structure most likely stood here, as fragments of early Byzantine pottery and some stone blocks with incomplete Greek inscriptions have been found.

unknown origins and purpose

If it was built by the Omayyads the purpose is not very clear. It does not fit the category of a hunting lodge, and in any case with Qasr al-Amra so close there would be no need for another here. The sheer number of rooms, 61 in all, together with the presence of the large courtyard, give the building the appearance of a caravanserai, and many believe this was in fact its purpose. It could also have been a defensive position, as although not on a major desert route, a number of tracks that must have been well-used in those days converge in the vicinity.

For whatever reason it was erected, this fine structure must have been of considerable significance in its time.

The visit

On two levels

The building is about 36 metres square, and has two storeys. There are round towers in each corner with a semi-round one in the centre of each wall. The outside is composed of limestone, and below the top is a decorative band of diagonal blocks that give a "herring bone" appearance. A double band of this decoration appears on the towers and the entranceway.

only one way in

The sole entrance is on the south side. This is flanked by partially rounded protrusions. Above the door is a window and a line of fancy recesses. Inside is a passage which has on either side a large arched and vaulted room. These are generally thought to have been stables.

The passage opens into a courtyard, and on both sides are stairs leading to the upper storey. On the ground floor there is one large entrance on each side leading to a series of rooms that open from one to another. They all vary in size and are quite plain.

arched rooms

On the upper storey the rooms are vaulted and have the original stonework decoration. A few of the rooms have half-domes at the ends, with decorative columns and squinches across the corners. The large room on the west side has the Kufic inscription giving the date (see above). The entire structure is in remarkably good condition, although the fact that there are patches of concrete indicate that restoration and shoring work has been carried out.

water puzzle

Although there is a cistern in the courtyard there is no well. This cistern must have been filled, therefore, by rainwater which was taken from the roof in the short but often heavy rainy season. It is probable that a well or other source of water was available in the nearby wadi.

▶ QASR AL-TUBA

Qasr al-Tuba is the only desert palace that retains the aura of isolation and remoteness which was common to them all until roads made them accessible. It can only be reached with a four wheel drive desert vehicle, a good map, and a compass. If you fancy going there, make it a special trip.

desert track

Situated some 50 km south of Qasr al-Kharana and accessed by a desert track, you can also reach it from Qatranah, 150 km south of Amman on the Aqaba highway. Here you turn east on what is initially a paved road, but which soon peters out into a track. It is about 35 km along the track.

huge but unfinished

Qasr al-Tuba, had it been completed, would have been the largest of the Omayyad desert palaces. It is thought to have been built by Walid II around 744 and, as it stood on a well-used caravan route that led into Wadi Sirhan, it is believed to have been a caravanserai as well as a desert retreat.

stone and mud

The area of the Qasr was some 140 by 70 metres, and was planned as two identical halves, north and south. Only the northern part was anything like finished, the southern one hardly getting off the ground. Built of stone and mud bricks, the northern part consisted of some large, high vaulted rooms with connecting courtyards and corridors. There were some finely carved door jambs and lintels, but of these hardly anything is left on site. The pieces that have survived the centuries are now on view in the Amman museum.

For the enthusiast

In the desert north west of Tuba are the very bare remains of a few more castles. If you are very keen on ruins — or want to experience the ambience of the desert — you could, with the aid of a guide and the right equipment, spend a couple of nights under the stars. If you fancy this, an agency that rents desert vehicles will be able to help.

▸ Al-Muaqqar

Another very ruined castle, **al-Muaqqar** would also not be worth visiting had it not been along the Sahab-Azraq road. Sited on a hilltop, between houses, of the village of the same name it has a commanding view over the surrounding landscape. As recently as the 1940s some parts of the qasr still stood, but today there is practically nothing. From what is left it is difficult to ascertain the layout of the place, and when it was built.

If you fancy a glance, turn left when you reach Mushatta, and follow the narrow road up into the village. Ask anyone for the qasr or the *khirbet* (ruins).

► QASR AL-MUSHATTA

Even if you have not had time to visit all the other Omayyad palaces
you should find little excuse for not visiting **Qasr al-Mushatta** as it
is situated right by Queen Alia International Airport.

How to get there

If you are visiting at the end of your circular desert tour, turn south at
the end of the Sahab-Azraq road. Take the perimeter road that skirts
the airport from the south, it is signposted, follow it around (passing
the various checkpoints that most modern airports now have), and you
will eventually reach the qasr which is situated to the north east. All
these checkpoints have instructions to allow tourists through in order
to visit this ruin, but you should take your passport with you.

From Amman follow the road south to the airport and proceed as
above. There are no buses from the airport to the site.

History

solid construction

The ruined castle has a very unusual and attractive appearance. Of all
the sites on this desert tour Qasr al-Mushatta covers the largest area,
with a surrounding wall 145 metres long on each side.   Built   by
Walid II it was, like Walid's other huge qasr, Tuba, never finished,
and soon after his death the Omayyad dynasty was overthrown by the
Baghdad-based Abbasids.

present for the Kaiser

The only entrance is on the south side, and the facade was once
covered with the finest carvings of floral, animal and geometric motifs.
That is until 1903! In that year the Ottoman Sultan Abdul Hamid
gave the entire facade to Kaiser Wilhelm of Germany as a present. It
was taken down piece by piece and shipped to Berlin where it can be
seen today in the Pergamum Museum in that city.

The visit

burnt brick building

Wander about the vestiges of the palace. Inside the entrance were
rooms, passages and courtyards. The most important was the large
three apsed hall, entered through a triple archway no longer there.
Some marble columns are standing in the hall. A large dome covered
part of it and it was constructed of burnt brick as were other parts of
the complex. This was an unusual building material, which has made
some people speculate as to the origins of this qasr. Although the
eastern and western parts were never finished there are signs that
many more rooms were planned along the sides. To the east of the
entrance gate is a rectangle that was once a mosque. All that remains
is the *mirhab* at the south end against the wall.

11. The Route of The King's Highway

"From Kadesh Moses then sent messengers to the King of Edom... 'Please let us pass through your land...We shall go along the King's highway not turning to the right or left, until we pass through your territory.'"

(Numbers 20:14,17)

INTRODUCTION

Above the rift
The ancient road south has always followed roughly the same route, along the heights east of the Dead Sea and the Arava. Every so often the route plunges into the deep ravines that carry watercourses to the low-lying land of the Great Rift Valley of which the Dead Sea and Arava are a part.

biblical name
The route is referred to as the **King's Highway,** an expression taken from the biblical passage quoted above. Translated from the Hebrew, the original implies that this was the main route rather than the King's road. When Trajan improved on it, building his great road which connected Damascus with the Red Sea, he named it the *Via Nova Traiana*. The Arabs called it *Tariq al-Sultani*, the Sultan's Road. Nowadays the more evocative biblical title has returned and for most visitors the road is known as the King's Highway, even though it is no longer the main route.

Roman road
From earliest times this was a great caravan course, and as such was important to the economy of the Nabateans. For Trajan its importance lay in the fact that the better the road he constructed (remnants can still be seen at some places), the quicker his soldiers would be able to move from place to place.

magnificent drive

Today there are three roads south: a new one along the Dead Sea and the Arava, the easterly Desert Highway, and the King's Highway. Those in hurry will take the easterly route which cuts through the desert. But the journey is boring, with nothing to see but barren, flat desertscape. In contrast, the King's Highway traverses some magnificent scenery and passes locations of great historical interest. In spite of the slow going it is definitely the preferred route for touring, at least one way. Before World War II, when the desert road had not yet been laid, it was the only way south and even this was not paved! Thankfully, today it is well asphalted the whole distance, and the entire Highway is a very comfortable drive.

difficult for bus users

For those who do not have a vehicle I am sorry to say that a satisfactory traverse of this route, visiting all the sights, will be very difficult. Many of the minibus services along it are irregular and to connect one with another could prove to be almost impossible. This does not mean that the hardy and patient cannot do it but the above should be borne in mind. Having said that, some

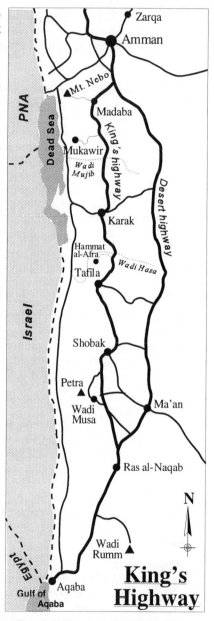

places like Madaba (see chapter 6) and Al-Karak can be reached by bus comparatively easily. Details of buses, where available, will be found in the text.

getting off the beaten track

Like most places in Jordan, the use of a vehicle will allow you to enjoy the journey without the worry of ongoing or return transport and enable detours to the off-road locations that are otherwise hard to get to.

▸ MADABA

The first stop on the Highway, some 30 km from Amman, is the town of Madaba, and this, together with the adjacent area of Mount Nebo, are described in chapter 6. To see this area properly it is preferable to cover it in a separate trip but if time does not permit, you can fit in a brief excursion to the places of chief interest on the way to Petra.

▸ MUKAWIR OR MACHAERUS PALACE

Until comparatively recently the road to **Mukawir** was no more than a track, making a difficult drive for the 20 km or so that it lies off the main road. Now this is paved and, though narrow, enables you to reach the site easily.

How to get there

archaic settlement

Leaving Madaba south on the road to al-Karak, the King's Highway continues to the village of Libb, a place that has existed since ancient times. Almost as you exit from the village a by-road turns off right (W), signposted for Mukawir.

Twisting and turning, first through farmland, and then through semi-desert, this road reaches the village of Ataruz, also known as Mukawir, and then on to the parking place that overlooks the flat-topped hill on which the palace fort of Mukawir or Machaerus is perched. You will get a fine view of the citadel before you actually reach it. **By bus:** A minibus from Madaba which also stops at Libb can take you as far as the village. From there it is a 3-4 km walk.

History

Jewish stronghold

First built by Alexander Yannai on the frontier with the Nabatean lands, Machaerus was one of the most heavily fortified strongholds in the Hasmonean domains and was used in their fight against the Romans. It is mentioned by Pliny in his *Natural History 5:16, 72* as the strongest place in Judea with the exception of Jerusalem, and Strabo in his *Geography* mentions it as an erstwhile Hasmonean citadel.

Herodian palace

Herod the Great rebuilt it into one of his strongholds-cum-palaces of which he had quite a few, the most famous being (Mount) Herodion, southwest of Bethlehem. As a much despised ruler he sensibly

147

chose locations for his palaces which offered natural defences.

sick in body (and mind)

To these palaces he would retire, away from the people who hated him, and also, by all accounts, because of the diseases which made him repulsive to look at and be with.

John the Baptist criticises

It was at Machaerus that the well-known scenario as related in Matthew, Chapter 14 was enacted: Around AD 41 Herod Antipas, a son of Herod the Great, married Herodias, his daughter-in-law, who had recently been divorced from his brother Phillip, an act forbidden in Jewish Law. John the Baptist opposed this and spoke out against it vehemently. In consequence, *"Herod had seized John (the Baptist) and bound him and put him in prison...and although he wanted to put him to death, he feared the multitude, because they regarded him as a prophet." (Matthew 14:3&5.)*

dance of the seven veils?

The crunch came when Herod made a birthday celebration attended by Salome, the young and beautiful daughter of Herodias (by her first marriage): *"But when Herod's birthday came, the daughter of Herodias danced before them and pleased Herod. Thereupon he promised with an oath to give her whatever she asked...she said, 'give me here on a platter the head of John the Baptist'. And although he was grieved the king commanded it be given...and he sent and had John beheaded in prison. And his head was brought on a platter and given to the girl..." (Matthew 14:6-11.)*

Jewish uprising

After the destruction of Jerusalem in AD 70 Jewish zealots, in revolt against Rome, took over the fortress (Josephus, Wars of the Jews, 2:285). In the year 72 the Roman Governor Bassus laid siege and eventually captured it (Josephus, Wars, 7:164). The place was then destroyed. Thus it remained until the Jordanian Department of Antiquities got to work on it a few years ago.

Israelis visit

Formerly very few visitors found their way here, as there was little to see. Now, since the restoration and the paving of the road, it is more on the traveller's itinerary. Since the rapprochement with Israel, Israelis especially come here in order to see one of the last stands of the Jews against the Romans.

take a drink and take it easy!

From the car park an ascending pathway, with well-spaced steps, takes you to the summit of the table-top mountain. It's quite a strenuous walk, sometimes made more difficult by the heat at the location. Take a bottle of water with you!

view to City of Palms

Apart from anything else the view is terrific. Below is the Dead Sea, and if the air is clear you will be able to see Herod's other great palace at Herodion. The palms of Jericho, near where Herod had yet another palace are also visible, and if you know what to look for so are the spires of Jerusalem.

Archaeologists have found many remains that point to this place as having been a luxury palace, but it may be hard for you to appreciate that. There was a huge cistern, and like any good fortress, warehouses that enabled the isolated place to withstand a lengthy siege. Remains of the baths have also been found. Restored or rebuilt, albeit with new looking tiles, is the terrace from which (the guardian will tell you in his very limited English) Salome was supposed to have performed her enticing dance.

opera in the desert!

What a location to stage a performance of Richard Strauss's *Salome*! If *Aida* can be performed at Giza why not *Salome* here?

back the same way

To continue the journey along the King's Highway you must now return to the main road at Libb. From here the road soon begins to descend into **Wadi al-Wala**, which flows for most, if not all the year. This wadi is a tributary of Wadi Mujib (see below) which eventually empties into the Dead Sea. An early Bronze Age village, evidenced by archaeological finds, once stood on the northern side of this wadi. Where the road crosses the wadi bed, trees and oleanders border the stream's bank, contrasting with the landscape you have been driving through. After ascending, the road reaches the village of Dhiban.

▶ Dhiban

Dhiban is where the Mesha Stone or Stele was found in 1868 (see box below) and, as ancient Dibon, was the capital of King Mesha of Moab (line 28 of the Stone). There is little to see here, the place having long been consigned to history. Excavations at the *tell* show Dibon was settled as far back as the Early Bronze age, c3000 BC. Its zenith was probably in the time of King Mesha, which was the middle of the 7th C BC. The different layers uncovered clearly show subsequent occupation by the Nabateans, Romans, Byzantines and the Arabs. In the east of the *tell* a section of the city wall has been found, impressive for its solidity.

The Mesha Stone

149

The Moabite or Mesha Stone

One of the most famous "finds" in Jordan has been the **Moabite** or **Mesha Stone**. This stele was found in 1868 by one F.A. Klein, a Prussian missionary who reported it to the French Consulate in Jerusalem. In the meantime, local Bedouin tried to destroy it by fire, believing that the foreign interest indicated that the stone was full of bad spirits. Being made from basalt, it fragmented into pieces. Fortunately a copy had been made and from that, together with the pieces, it was reconstructed.

The stone was discovered at Dhiban, between Madaba and Al-Karak and was a stele erected by Mesha, a king of Moab. It was about one metre high and 75 cm wide and was rounded at the top. On it he records his dealings with the kings of Israel. It was inscribed in Moabite, which was very similar to Hebrew. Mesha consecrated the stone to the god Chemosh because of Moabite deliverance from Israelite rule.

The importance of this text is that it is the only extra-Biblical record of the period. This is the same period as related in II Kings Ch.3 and you might want to compare the stele's text with that. In the Bible, Mesha is described not only as a king but also as a sheep master who paid tribute to Israel of 100,000 lambs and the wool of 100,000 rams. Choose for yourself, the remarkable historical document or the Bible!

The reconstructed stone is now in the Louvre, Paris and a replica stands in the Israel Museum, Jerusalem.

▶ WADI MUJIB

Takes your breath away

About 8 kilometres south of Dhiban the road reaches the top of **Wadi Mujib**, the biblical **Arnon**. This is one of the finest scenic sights in Jordan, indeed in the whole region! Breathtaking may be an overused word in describing panoramic views, but it truly fits here!

The chasm is a full four kilometres wide at the top, and is over 400 metres deep. There is a viewing point with car park just before the road descends, and from there you can marvel at the view. Take your fill here as on the way down you will need to keep your eyes firmly on the road! From the top you can clearly pick out the route of the black asphalt road as it snakes its way down to the bottom, contrasted against the pale-hued rock of the canyon. Once a nightmare for drivers, the modern well-engineered road makes the descent at a comfortable gradient. Watch out for oncoming vehicles especially trucks, as they tend to swing out on the hairpin turns.

winter torrents

Wadi Mujib starts in the desert area east of al-Karak. First flowing from south to north it turns west and traverses a distance of about 80 kilometres before emptying into the Dead Sea. After the River Jordan it is the longest watercourse in the region, east or west of the Jordan. In the season the waters can become a torrent.

Translation of the Mesha Stone (line by line)

1. I am Mesha, son of Chemosh-Yat king of Moab, the
2. Dibonite. My father was king over Moab for thirty years and I became king
3. after my father, I built this high place for Chemosh in (Qarho), a high place
4. of salvation, because he delivered me from all assaults, and because he let me see my desire upon all my adversaries. Omri
5. King of Israel, had oppressed Moab many days, for Chemosh was angry with his land.
6. His son succeeded him, and he too said, I will oppress Moab. In my days he said it;
7. but I saw my desire upon him and his house, and Israel perished utterly for ever. Omri had taken possession of the land of
8. Medeba, and dwelt there his days and much of his son's days, forty years; but
9. Chemosh dwelt in it in my days. I rebuilt Baal-Meon, and I made a reservoir in it; and I rebuilt
10. Kiriathaim. Then the men of Gad had settled in the land of Atarot from of old and the king of
11. Israel had fortified Ataroth for himself; but I fought against the town and took it; and I slew all the inhabitants of
12. the town, a spectacle for Chemosh and Moab. I brought back from there the lion figure of David, and dragged
13. it before Chemosh at Kerioth; and I settled in it the men of (Saron) and the men
14. of (Maharit). Next Chemosh said to me, Go take Nebo from Israel. So I
15. went by night, and fought against it from break of dawn till noon; and I
16. Took it and slew all in it, seven thousand men and women, both natives and aliens,
17. and female slaves; for I had devoted it to Ashtar-Chemosh. I took from thence the vessels
18. of Yahweh and dragged them before Chemosh. Then the king of Israel had fortified
19. Jahaz, and occupied it while warring against me; but Chemosh drove him out before me.
20. I took from Moab 200 men, his whole division, and I led it up against Jahaz and captured it,
21. annexing it to Dibon. I carried out repairs at (Qarho) on the parkland walls as well as the walls
22. of the acropolis; and I repaired its gates and I repaired its towers; and
23. I repaired the King's residence, and I made banks for the reservoir at the spring inside
24. the town. But there was no cistern inside the town at (Qarho) so I said to all people, Each of you make for yourselves
25. a cistern in his house. I had ditches dug for (Qarho) with Israelite prisoners.
26. I carried out repairs at Aroer, and I mended the highway at the Arnon.
27. I rebuilt Beit-Bamoth, for it had been destroyed; and I rebuilt Bexer, for it was in ruins,
28. with fifty men of Dibon, because all Dibon had become subject (to me). So did I become king
29. (over) hundreds in the town which I annexed to the land. Then I rebuilt
30. Medeba also, and Beith-Diblathaim. And as for Beth Baal-Meon I led (my shepherds) up there
31. (in order to tend the) sheep of the district. Then in Horonaim there had settled.............
32. ...., and Chemosh said to me, Go down, fight against Horonaim. So I went down (and
33. fought against the town and took it), and Chemosh (dwelt) there in my days. As for ...., from there ....
34. .... so did I ....

During the time of the Israelite exodus the Arnon was the border between the Moabite and Amorite lands (Numbers 22:36). When the Israelites fought for the land they were told, *"Arise, set out, and pass through the valley of Arnon. Look! I have given Sihon the Amorite king of Heshbon, and his land into your hand..." (Deuteronomy 2:24).* It was allotted to the tribes of Reuben and Gad: *"So we took possession of this land at that time. From Aroer which is by the valley of Arnon...and I gave (it) to the Reubenites and to the Gadites." (Deuteronomy 3:12)*

history carved in stone

The Ammonite town of Aroer, which was taken by the Israelites (Joshua 12:2), was situated on the north side of the Arnon. At various times in the biblical narrative this town assumed some importance, and in the time of King Mesha of Moab in the mid 7th century BC it must have been destroyed as Mesha repaired the town (line 26 of the Mesha Stone). The fords, or ways across (Hebrew, *messilot*) the wadi near Aroer were also repaired (line 26) indicating that for some time communication between the lands north and south of the wadi must have been difficult. Eventually Aroer was destroyed by Tiglath-Pileser III around 730 BC. Excavations have been carried out at an archaeological site in the wadi at Khirbet Arair.

remains of Roman bridge

In later times the Hasmoneans, after conquering the territory, made the Arnon the border between the Jewish and Nabatean kingdoms (Josephus, Antiquities of the Jews 13:254-255). When the great Roman road was built a Roman bridge spanned the river, and bare remnants of this can still be noticed.

Things here were very different in the past, as according to the medieval Arab geographer al-Idrisi the canyon was rich in wild fauna, and the waters abundant with fish.

The bottom of the gorge is now crossed by a modern bridge.

▸ Al-Rabbah

After crossing the wadi the road ascends to the plateau again, and c22 km further on reaches the village of **al-Rabbah,** the biblical **Rabbath Moab** which was conquered by Alexander Yannai, but later given to the Nabateans by Hyrcanus II.

on the Haj route

The place was called Rabathmoba by the Greek geographer Ptolemy in the second century AD. Later, Eusebius referred to it as **Aeropolis**, a Roman provincial town and some relics of this period can be seen as you pass along the main road, looking quite incongruous in these settings. They include columns that were part of the Roman main street, and the facade of a temple. The town continued to exist after the Muslim conquest and was mentioned in the 14th century as a place on the road south from Damascus, on the *haj* route.

see it driving through

In 1812 when J.L. Burckhardt passed this way he wrote *"The ruins of Rabba are about half an hour in circuit, and are situated upon a low hill, which commands the whole plain...On the west side is a temple, of which one wall and several niches remain...Near them is a gate belonging to another building... Distant from these ruins about 30 yards stand two Corinthian columns of middling size... There are many remains of private habitations, but none entire."* (Travels in Syria and the Holy Land, 1822.)

The present-day village has been built over many of these relics, and you will not need longer than a few moments to see them.

► AL-KARAK (Kerak)

How to get there

Although **al-Karak** is situated on a hilltop, you will make a sharp descent to reach it. Some 12 km south of al-Rabbah, the town's elevated position is preceded by Wadi al-Karak which makes its way down to the Dead Sea 16 km west. The road drops into this valley before climbing up the other side to the town. It is on this descent that you will get a first class view of the castle, perched high on a precipitous ridge.

Al-Karak marks, roughly, the half-way point on the King's Highway, and is the only place where you can stay the night before reaching Petra (see chapter on Amenities). The town and castle are built on top of a very steep walled elevation, 950 metres above sea level. It is because of this that it acquired its ancient names, all of which began with *kir*, the Hebrew (and possibly Moabite) word for a high steep cliff, wall or palisade.

By bus: Al-Karak can be reached from Amman along the Desert Road. Getting there along the King's Highway is difficult as you will have to go by local bus from one place to another using infrequent and unreliable services.

History

In the Bible al-Karak is known variously as *Kir-Hareseth, Kir Heres,* and *Kir of Moab.* It was the Moabite stronghold of King Mesha, and II Kings, chapter 3 describes how the joint armies of Israel, Judah and Edom were unsuccessful in taking the town despite a long siege (see box on the Mesha Stone). Isaiah foretold its destruction (Isaiah 15:1, 16:7 & 11).

The 6th century BC saw invasion by the Assyrians and later, when the Moabite people lost their identity as the Nabateans took over the area, Kir-Moab came to be called Karakmoba, an Aramaic form of the Hebrew version of the name. Ptolemy, the classical geographer, referred to the town as Characmoba, the Greek *charach* having a similar sound and translation.

firmly on the map

On the Madaba mosaic map al-Karak is depicted as a walled fortress.

Inside the walls are colonnaded streets and two churches. In Byzantine times it was a prosperous town and the seat of an archbishop. However, the town is best known for its Crusader associations and this is what you will have come to see.

La Pierre du Desert

In 1115 Baldwin I, king of the Crusader kingdom of Jerusalem, founded the Seigneury of Mont-Real and built a castle there (today, Shobak, see below). When a certain Payem le Bouteiller became lord he transferred his quarters to al-Karak, and in 1140 built the huge castle on the foundations of the ancient citadel. He called it **La Pierre du Desert,** known also as the Krak de Moabites. It became the capital of Crusader "Oultre Jourdain", a name revived during the British Mandate this century.

In 1177 Renauld de Chatillon, because of his marriage to Payem's heir, became master of al-Karak. Besides being a plunderer of the local caravans, which had a right to pass unhindered through the territory, and a general despot, he was – even by Crusader standards – a particularly bloodthirsty individual.

gruesome enemy disposal

If you are one of the people who still believe that the Crusaders were an upstanding Christian order, let me tell you about de Chatillon's ways of disposing of his enemies. He would have his prisoners thrown from the castle wall to be dashed to pieces on the rocks below. However, to ensure that they survived long enough to feel the impacts and were not knocked unconscious on the way down, he would have their heads enclosed in a wooden protective box!

Salah al-Din's revenge

In 1183 Salah al-Din (Saladdin) besieged the fortress but failed to take it. In 1187 Renauld de Chatillon participated in the Battle of Hittin, west of the Sea of Galilee in which the Crusader armies were routed by the great Muslim warrior. Chatillon was captured and although normally a very generous man with his vanquished, because of his despicable deeds, Salah al-Din had him put to death..

Although La Pierre du Desert had still not fallen, being defended by de Chatillon's widow Etiennette, the defeat at Hittin spelt the beginning of the end for the Crusaders, and the castle was soon forced to surrender.

decline of al-Karak

Salah al-Din's younger brother, al-Adil, then became ruler of the al-Karak area and after Salah's death extended his rule to Damascus in 1196 and Cairo a few years later. In 1264 the Mameluke Sultan, al-Malik al-Zaher Baibars rebuilt the castle's damaged ramparts but it was never of much importance again. The present name, al-Karak, is first recorded by Arab geographers around 1225.

In 1840 Ibrahim Pasha, son of Muhammad Ali, in his attempt to dominate Syria, captured the citadel and destroyed much of the fortifications. In 1893 and 1910 al-Karak was the centre of rebellions against the Ottoman Turks.

persistent Christian presence

Throughout all this a Christian population had endured in al-Karak, being the majority until the 14th century. In the last part of the 19th century the local unrest prompted many of them to leave and resettle in Madaba. A sizeable Christian minority remains.

In the immediate years following the First World War, al-Karak became the capital of a short-lived administration bearing the strange-sounding name "The Arab Government of Moab". Today al-Karak is the centre of the Governorate of the same name, and this had a population of 193,000 in 1991. In spite of all this history, most of what remains comprises the castle which, although spectacular, is so ruined inside that a visit does not take too long but is still thoroughly worthwhile.

The visit

Al-Karak (Kerak) is a busy town and those who arrive by car will quickly realise this from the traffic that clogs the narrow streets. Although today al-Karak is a Muslim town, as mentioned above a small but spirited Christian community still testifies to its Christian past.

You will want to make straight away for the castle, and this is situated in the south west part of the town. As there is a one way traffic system in most of the old town watch the street directions, but it is not too difficult to find. Just before the castle is the Government Rest House, which provides accommodation as well as restaurant services (see chapter on Amenities). If you do eat here, the restaurant offers a magnificent view towards the Dead Sea.

▸ The Castle

The huge mass of the castle is at the end of the street and the entrance is on the right. There is a 1 JD entrance fee.

unassailable from the east

On entering you will immediately get the feeling of being inside a citadel of considerable strength, as most Crusader castles are. You are now on the east side of the castle and over the battlements is the sheer drop to the valley below. Obviously the castle could never be taken from this side. A long sloping flight of stairs leads down to a lower terrace where the walls and their battlements are more in evidence. To the back of this terrace is the **museum** which is housed in a huge vault. In the museum are various artefacts from the Neolithic, Bronze and Iron Ages. Other objects from Byzantine and subsequent periods can also be viewed.

At the south end of this terrace is the dungeon (al-Habis). It is said that this place was used by the Turks in WW I when they imprisoned and tortured local chiefs who they suspected of disloyalty.

Near the beginning of the terrace, steps climb to the upper level, where there are many underground chambers. It's a pity that the Tourist Authority has not erected signs describing their purpose as all the chambers are now so cleared of debris that they tend to look rather sterile.

plain but solid builders

As there is little above ground still standing it is difficult to get an impression of how austere the place must have been. The Crusaders did not build their castles for beauty, but for military purposes. There was no need to waste time and money on frills and decorative bits and pieces, although the Great Hall at the Krak des Chevaliers in Syria is an exception.

From the upper level, if you walk across to the west side you will get a view towards the Dead Sea.

▶ Tower of Baibars

In the northwest corner of the town near the Italian Hospital is a bastion known as The Tower of Baibars. An inscription records that it was built by that Mameluke Sultan. Behind it was a tunnel some 75 metres long that reached the town walls.

detour to the Dead Sea

From al-Karak a new road goes down to the Dead Sea. Overlooking Wadi al-Karak for most of the way, its vistas are quite amazing. If you are on your way to Petra it is off the route, though those with 2 hours to spare could take it, there and back. The part of the Dead Sea it reaches at the southern end is not very interesting, but you could drive back to Amman this way (see chapters on Planning your Itinerary and Dead Sea).

▶ Mu'tah and Mazar

Back on the King's Highway c10 km south of al-Karak you will pass through the village of **Mu'tah**. There is nothing to see there, but it has historical interest. It was here, around 632, that the first engagement between Islamic and Byzantine forces occurred. Three of the first Muslim leaders, Zaid ibn Harith, Jaafar ibn Abu Talib and Abdullah ibn Ruaha perished in the fierce battle with a superior Byzantine army.

early martyrs

These three men are accorded a place among the earliest martyrs of Islam. They were buried at **Mazar**, the next village, about 6 km further on where there is a modern mosque constructed over the site of a 12th century mosque which housed the tomb of Jaafar ibn Abu Talib.

Both Mazar and Dhat Ras (below) can be reached from al-Karak by local minibus service, but it should be stressed that these services do not have a rigid schedule.

▶ Dhat Ras

About 5 km from Mazar and off the road to the east, the village of **Dhat**

Ras is sited on top of a hill. It is generally believed that here once stood one of the most important Nabatean towns of the area. There are remains of a temple and, though renovated during the Roman era, it was originally Nabatean – perhaps from the 2nd C AD. This is a lovely region, with fertile land nearby. It was here that the rich grazing lands of Moab, so alluded to in the Bible, began. In later years when the Byzantines built many of their towns over the remains of former ones it is apparent that they did so here. Besides remains which point to a town of Byzantium, there are remnants of what must have been a huge church.

▸ Wadi Hasa

From the plateau the road soon starts its descent into **Wadi Hasa**, known as the Zered in the scriptures (Numbers 21:12 and Deuteronomy 2:13). The terrain becomes more rugged, and the limestone of the plateau gives way to sandstone rock. The drive into the wadi is imposing, with very good views. Along the valley floor the perennial river is bordered with the usual oleanders. In biblical times the River Zered delineated Moab from Edom. The deep canyon is about 45 kilometres long, and empties into the southern tip of the Dead Sea.

When J.L. Burckhardt passed this way in 1812 he wrote, *"There was more water in the rivulet than in any I had passed south of Zerka; the water was quite tepid, caused by a hot spring, which empties itself into the Ahsa from a side valley up the wady..."* *(Travels in the Holy Land).*

▸ Khirbet al-Tannur

As the road climbs out of the wadi, high on a hill to the west is **Khirbet al-Tannur** an important Nabatean temple. Khirbet al-Tannur, or the Ruins of Tannur is a difficult place to find and even more so to reach, involving a drive over a bumpy, stony track and then a strenuous 30 minute climb. The site is rarely visited now as it has been emptied of all artefacts, and I write for interest only. The temple stands atop a hill known by the local Bedouin as Jebel Tannur. The hill is skirted by Wadi La'aban on the south and west sides. This wadi, a tributary of Wadi Hasa, plunges down and empties into the main watercourse. As Wadi La'aban is usually dry, the road to the·site crosses it by a ford.

excavated by rabbi

Khirbet al-Tannur is the only Nabatean temple to have been fully excavated. This was done mainly in the mid 1930s by Dr. Nelson Glueck, a rabbi and a noted Holy Land archaeologist. Most of the temple has crumbled and what is left in the main are the foundations. All the statues and carvings have been removed to a museum in Amman.

The temple of Tannur dates from the around the first century BC or AD. A striking facade, adorned with columns and pilasters is on the west side, and in the centre is an entrance preceded by some steps. Over this was a huge bust of a veiled goddess. Niches on the wall held other busts of deities. Inside the entrance is a courtyard, with the main altar in the centre. This altar, a square podium 2 metres high and 3 metres square, had a facade decorated with pilasters and an arch. In niches stood more statues of deities, but only one was found still in place, that of a bearded man with a small bull standing by him. On the top half of the altar the pilasters were adorned with floral designs and heads of female deities. To one side steps led up to the altar surface where the sacrifices were offered.

tremendous feat

Today, in its very ruined state, Khirbet al-Tannur does not stand out strikingly against the desert landscape. Yet once this gleaming, white limestone building must have been clearly visible to all who travelled along the historic road that passes nearby. Why the Nabateans chose such an inaccessible site for an important temple is difficult to know. The levelling of the hill's summit, and the transport of huge blocks of stone must have required a massive undertaking that we, in a mechanised age, can only wonder at.

Because of its isolation the temple was never taken over by subsequent peoples. The Byzantines, for example, were very fond of building their churches over the ruins of pagan temples and shrines. Even the local Bedouin kept clear of it, perhaps believing that some mystical power resided here, and this may have been why it was not totally looted.

▸ Hammamat al-Afra

A place you can make a detour to and enjoy a unique experience is the somewhat isolated hot spring of Hammamat al-Afra.

How to get there

About 5 kilometres from the wadi a clearly signed road leads west (right). The signpost points to Hammamat Afra and Hammamat Bobita. Our route will lead to the former. There are no buses and very little traffic on this road. The drive is 12 km each way on a winding road, so if you stay there for say half an hour allow about 75 minutes for the diversion. Follow this sealed road to its end. In addition to the water in Wadi Hasa there are many fresh water springs in the area and this enables the local people to cultivate some of the land to the right.

neglected spring

The road ends rather abruptly, and on an incline ahead of you, you will see some disused changing rooms. Until 10-15 years ago many people came here, and I really do not know why the place is now virtually abandoned. As the signposts pointing here are new it would seem that the Ministry of Tourism has plans for development. Perhaps by the time you visit some of these plans will be underway. The conditions described are from late 1995.

To get to the spring, park your car and walk down the slope that is to the right.

avoid bare feet

Hammamat al-Afra is one of the springs alluded to by Burckhardt in the passage from his journal quoted above. The flowing water in the wadi is not deep, but it is really hot. As the stream bed is stony, a pair of rubber mules makes entering it easier. The hot water emanates from a subterranean spring situated, today, beneath a concrete pool built on the opposite bank. The spring constantly gushes up into this pool and the overflow enters the wadi through the pipe at the top. Be careful as the water in the pool, which is about 1.5 metres deep, is really steamy, hotter than the water in the stream.

Unlike some hot springs this one is not sulphurous, and there is no chemical odour. Although the surrounding area is not too clean the water is, so you can use the pool even though the water appears cloudy. There may be a few local youths around enjoying the place, but more likely you will be alone.

Return to the main road to continue south.

▸ Tafilah

The ascent from Wadi Hasa continues until the road emerges onto a plain. It was on this plain that T.E. Lawrence fought the battle of Tafilah, one of his important clashes with the Ottomans.

no entry ahead!

As the road begins another descent into a valley towards the town, you come to a major crossroads where there is a one way system in and out of the town. The road from the east leads to the Desert Highway; the road straight ahead is the up road from Tafilah, and the road to the right – the one we take – leads down to the town. This road descends quite steeply, turning to the left after 3-4 km. From here you can see Tafilah nestling in the valley below, surrounded by the olive groves for which the region is renowned.

well sited

Tafilah has a rather wonderful setting, curled in the valley hollow and spreading up the hillslopes. From afar it is reminiscent of a Tuscany village, but when you actually drive through the similarity soon vanishes!

The Crusaders had a presence here. It formed part of their line of fortifications along the Highway. All that is left of this now is a rectangular building about midway through the village on the west side.

Until the 1960s the paved road only reached as far as Tafilah, and from here on to Petra was over a track.

by bus

As noted before, irregular local minibuses ply the main road, and Tafilah can be reached by one from al-Karak.

▸ Shobak Castle

There is little of interest for the next c55 km until you reach , the road, after climbing out of the valley at Tafilah, continuing south on the edge of a flat plateau.

How to get there

At **Shobak** there are crossroads, with the road from the east bringing the Desert Highway traffic bound for Petra. Take the Petra road, and after no more than a kilometre a road to the right (W) with a signpost leads to Shobak Castle. The castle lies about 3-4 kilometres from the main road and is reached along the narrow asphalted lane that twists and turns the whole way. You cannot see the castle from the highway.

Until recently it was in a very ruined state, with much of what remained from former years being further reduced by an earthquake in 1927. Because of the condition few people visited the place, being content with a view from the approach road. Since 1991 much restoration work has been done, and it is now definitely worth visiting.

By bus: There are irregular buses from Tafilah to Shobak and you can walk or hitch to the castle.

History

First built by Baldwin I in 1115 when he established the Seigneury of Mont-Réal, it served initially as the main residence of the Seigneur, Payem le Bouteiller. Later it became a key link in the Crusader chain of castles that ran from Antioch in the north to the Red Sea.

Besieged unsuccessfully by Salah al-Din in 1187, he finally captured it in 1189. The Mamelukes rebuilt the damaged structure in the 13th and 14th centuries and this caused J.L. Burckhardt to think the castle was of Muslim origin. He wrote:

"In the morning I went to the castle of Shobak...also called Kerek el Shobak...The castle is of Saracen construction, and is one of the largest south of Damascus".

In describing the castle he continued:

"The greater part of the wall and several of the bastions and towers are still entire. The ruins of a well built church are now transformed into a public inn..."

He adds that the castle area was being used as a village, and about one hundred people lived there. At various times during the Ottoman period the castle was occupied by soldiers.

The visit

The entrance is on the west side. To the north of this is a tower and near the top is a Kufic inscription from Mameluke times. In the castle and seen above the entrance is the Crusader church dating from the original time of construction in 1115. Later, the Muslims transformed it into a mosque. Climbing up to the church you can see on the east side what was one of the water cisterns. On the summit of the fortress are the remains of nine towers. What is left of the 14th century hammam can also be seen here.

caves for the slaves

If you look towards the valley in the north east there are caves and caverns where the Crusaders' servants and slaves were quartered. The tower on the north side was particularly high, and signal flares lit on it could be seen as far away as al-Karak. Also the main living areas were on the summit, including the redoubt, keep and refectory. Some parts of these have been restored, a process which is ongoing. Originally the stronghold comprised of three storeys, and covered an area of about 20,000 square metres.

the delights of spring

Situated as it is on a high hill with commanding views on every side it is easy to see how defensible it was. Like so much of Jordan, in the spring when the hillsides are covered with greenery and wild flowers, the whole locality is delightful. But if your visit occurs towards the end of the year, you will be compensated by a more dramatic aspect of the once fearsome citadel.

There is a guardian who speaks fairly good English, and he will be pleased to show you around. In 1995 he told me that very few tourists reach there – perhaps 20-25 a day. This may now increase as word gets about that the castle has been much restored and is worth the detour.

on to Petra

Return to the main road and continue along the Highway for about another 26 km and your journey will end as you arrive at the bustling village (or town) of Wadi Musa, which guards the entrance to the hidden city of Petra.

12. Petra

"Here was the land of Edom, in which Mount Hor looks down upon the wonderfully tinted rocks of the 'Valley of Moses', and the no less wonderful ruins of Petra,...once capital of Arabia Petraea, its tombs and temples carved out of precipitous sandstone cliffs in an arid gorge now uninhabitable, and long seldom visited through fear of its Bedouin guardians..."

A.R. Hope Moncrieff, 1922

INTRODUCTION

The special mystique of Petra

For most people touring Jordan, Petra is the *raison de visiter*. And quite rightly so. In spite of some of the misgivings mentioned below it will not disappoint. For here is a truly outstanding site of antiquity. Petra possesses a different grandeur to that of ancient cities like Palmyra or Jerash, but it is so imbued with an indefinable air of mystery, made all the more awesome by its unique setting, that it exceeds even those tremendous sites in its fascination.

the price of fame

In these days of modern mass travel and ease of communication, Petra is no longer the remote, isolated location it once was. It must be understood that for Jordanians, who are short of natural resources, Petra has become a real money earner, with ever more hotels being built along with the other accoutrements of tourism. What was until the late 1960s still a tranquil, away-from-it-all locale, is now a veritable tourist spot (I hesitate to say "trap").

In spite of this, your visit to Petra will certainly rank high on your list of never-to-be-forgotten experiences; even more so if you choose your season carefully, start early in the morning and are physically able to get to some of the remoter parts of the site.

once virtually inaccessible

Until comparatively recently Petra was only visited by those who could undertake an arduous journey and had the means to do so. Gerald Lankester Harding, the noted Middle East archaeologist, writing in his book *The Antiquities of Jordan*, states that when he travelled there in 1932 from Jerusalem via Amman, apart from a brief stretch of road outside Jerusalem, there was not a "yard of surfaced road the whole way".

the paving of the King's Highway

When I first visited Petra, as a young man in the mid '60s, The King's Highway was only paved as far as Mu'tah, although there was paved access via the Desert Road and Ma'an. Just outside Petra at Elji, then a small sleepy village, one had to report to the police post and (if I remember correctly) pay a very small fee.

There were only two possibilities of accommodation: either at the Rest House, which was much smaller than it is today, or the Nazzal Hotel, partly a camp, partly housed in the rock tombs of al-Habees, near to where the rest area is today. Petra had very few visitors and you could almost have the place to yourself; certainly you encountered isolation and solitude, qualities which tend to enhance the beauty of Petra.

tea and Coca Cola

By the time of my next visit in the late '70s the luxurious Forum Hotel had sprouted, and the King's Highway had been paved the whole way. Inside the site, where once the local Bedouin sold you only sage-scented tea and Arab coffee, Coca Cola and bottled water had made their appearance alongside.

Almost every time I visit Petra more and more hotels have appeared, and during several visits in 1995 it seemed like the whole of Wadi Musa was one vast building site. But remember, Wadi Musa is outside the enclave which is Petra, and once you have entered the Siq gorge, the booming tourist town disappears as completely as if it doesn't exist.

escalating admission charge

I have also seen the admission price escalate from 1 JD in 1991 to its present immoderate level (see below). Whither in the future? That's up to the Jordanian government. Too much expansion could harm the goose!

Bedouin village

As you may have gathered from the above, Petra is the name of the historical mountain-locked city, not of today's living settlement which lies outside it. This is now called Wadi Musa, although previously it was known as Elji. It has been a Bedouin settlement for centuries.

Two tribes of Bedouin have long made their home in or around the village. The Bdul live in the surrounding area and until recently were semi-nomadic (a minority still are). Most of them now dwell in a nearby village, and are fully settled. In the past they would live, according to the seasons, in tents, caves or rock-hewn houses which you can still see on the road to Beidha. The second tribe, the Ligatyneh, inhabited Elji, and still own much of the land in Wadi Musa.

where Moses struck the rock?

The wadi, and subsequently the settlement, gets its name from a spring high up at the entrance to the village. Called **Ayoun Nabi Musa**, it is one of two springs named after Moses in Jordan. Did Moses strike the rock causing water to gush out here? I'll leave that for you to speculate! The local Bedouin believe so.

The spring is housed in a small building to the right of the village's entrance as you drive in along the King's Highway. It cannot be missed; there are two white domes on top. The building is not a religious one.

HOW TO GET THERE

For those coming by car there is a choice of the King's Highway or the Desert Road. Most will elect for the former because of the wealth of places to visit en route. The Desert Road, although considerably faster, offers nothing but stretches of monotonous parched landscape.

If you are driving from Aqaba, take the road north, and just after Ras al-Naqab a signposted road leads off from the left. The drive is quite scenic, especially the approach to Wadi Musa.

bus service

From Amman: For those travelling by bus, there are a variety of alternatives: JETT offer a daily service leaving their terminal at 6.30am. The journey is via the Desert Road and takes three hours. You can book a one-way ticket or a day trip that includes return fare, a guided tour and lunch. (Entrance fee is not included.)

The return bus leaves Petra at 16.00. A day tour does not give you much time, and involves 6 hours of travelling, but is obviously better than nothing. The cost for fare only is JD5.50 each way, day tour JD30.

Ordinary (cheaper) buses also leave Amman from the Wahadat bus station, but these services have no fixed schedule so you must check first. Service taxis may also be available from the same bus station, but also on an unscheduled basis.

From Aqaba: JETT also have a return service from Aqaba to Petra which operates 3 or 4 times a week. For details of this check with JETT in either Aqaba or Wadi Musa. If you are going to travel by bus I recommend the comfortable JETT service, but you must book a day or two in advance

If you are travelling by bus throughout the country, you will probably want to continue from Petra down to Aqaba rather than return to Amman, and this will present no problem.

How long to spend there?

Many visitors only spend one day at Petra, some even arrive in the morning and leave the same evening or next morning. If this is all the time you have available it is still worthwhile, but it will only allow you to see the so-called "main" features. To really see and enjoy Petra in its entirety, a minimum of two full days are needed. If you are an avid climber and want to reach some of the remoter peaks, then allow three days.

climatic considerations

Remember, the time of the year will affect the amount you can do in a day. In the early spring and late autumn it is possible to spend the whole day touring with just a lunch break. In the hot months, late May through to October, you will need to rest at least between 12 noon and 3pm.

Before I go into further details of the site, itineraries and other things you will want to know, the historical background to this intriguing place should be examined.

HISTORY

Ancient caravan route

Petra lies hidden in the mountains to the east of Wadi Arava (see Chapter 2, Geography) which rise to over 1000 metres. Further to the east a second ridge towers above 1600 metres. Between the two lies the ancient caravan route which made Petra the important city it once was. For not only was there passage north and south along this route, but a course through to the west and into Palestine was also possible.

trade and prosperity

Trains of camels bringing merchandise from southern and eastern Arabia replenished themselves at Petra and would then continue north towards Damascus along the route that was – and still is – called the King's Highway, or venture west to Gaza and from there take a coastal route into Egypt. This made Petra one of the most important intersections on the trade routes of the ancient world, and the source of Nabatean power and prosperity.

I am, though, jumping forward, as the history of the site goes back much further.

Palaeolithic finds

Palaeolithic man undoubtedly lived in the Petra area, as artefacts from this period have been found. There were also Neolithic settlements and one, Seyl Aqlat (al-Beidha), dating from around 7000 BC, has been thoroughly excavated (see Tour 9).

The next important stage does not occur until c1500 BC. Here we have to turn to the Bible to follow the course of events, although other ancient sources are also informative. The Old Testament most commonly calls the area Edom, but the appellations *Seir* and *Mount Seir* are also used. Mount Seir, or Jabal al-Shara, is the main mountain range of Edom that extends the entire length of the Edomites' homeland, from Wadi al-Hasa, south. Historically, and in extra-biblical texts, Seir is the earliest name used. In one of the 14th C BC Tell Al-Amarna (in Egypt) documents the name Seir is found, whereas the first mention of Edom does not appear until the end of the 13th C BC.

red lentils or red rocks?

According to the Old Testament, the Edomites were the descendants of Esau who was also called Edom (Genesis 36:1). Esau married a Hittite woman (Genesis 26:34), and from Akkadian and Egyptian written sources we know that Hittite tribes settled in the land east of the Jordan. Decide for yourself whether Edom, which means red, got its name from the reddish colour rock which prevails there or from the biblical account that Esau was called Edom because of his hunger for red lentils:

> *"And Esau said to Jacob, 'Please let me have a swallow of that red stuff there, for I am famished.' Therefore his name was called Edom (red)." (Genesis 25:30)*

King of Edom turns away Moses

The next important mention of Edom is during the Exodus of the Hebrews from Egypt. Whilst in the desert west of Wadi Arava, Moses sent messengers to secure from the King of Edom safe passage for the Israelites through his territory:

> *"From Kadesh Moses sent messengers to the King of Edom... 'Please let us pass through your land.... We shall go along the King's highway ... until we pass through your territory.' Edom, however, said to him, 'you shall not pass through us lest I come out with a sword against you'... Thus Edom refused to allow Israel to pass through his territory..."   (Numbers 20:14-21)*

If true, these events would have occurred around 1200 BC and began a lengthy confrontation between Israel and the peoples to the east of the Jordan which has only been settled during the writing of this guide!

King David's terrible vengeance

In succeeding centuries Edom, and indeed the other peoples who lived east of the Jordan, the Ammonites and Moabites, were regularly invaded and slaughtered by the Israelites and later Judah. After David became king around 1000 BC he set out to conquer all the nations around Israel:

> *"So David made a name (for himself) when he returned from killing 18,000 Edomites in the Valley of Salt." (II Samuel 8:13)*

Dispensing with the Edomite monarchy, David installed his own governors and garrison, and turned most of the Edomites into his slaves. In the words of I Chronicles 18:13, *"Then he (David) put garrisons in Edom, and all the Edomites became servants to David..."*. David's chief motivation for this action must have been his desire to control the trade routes along the King's Highway, and also the port on the Red Sea.

the riches of Solomon

Israelite rule continued throughout the reigns of David and Solomon. We know that the trade in Solomon's time was so vast that he built a new port, Etzion-Geber, to cope with it: *"King Solomon also built a fleet of ships in Etzion Geber, which is near Elot on the shore of the Red Sea in the land of Edom" (I Kings 9:26)*. The site of this port may lie between the present towns of Aqaba and Eilat, or (some modern researchers say), it is the tiny island off the coast of Sinai, called Jazirat Faroun by the Arabs and Isle de Graye by the Crusaders (see chapter on Aqaba).

visit of the Queen of Sheba

We are sure that very large caravans came up from South Arabia even this far back in time, and their only passage lay through Petra:

> *"Now when the Queen of Sheba heard of the fame of Solomon, she came to Jerusalem...She had a very large retinue, with camels carrying spices, and a large amount of gold and precious stones;"* (II Chronicles 9:1)

The land of Sheba, or Saba, is today part of Yemen.

Hadad briefly frees Edom

Edom was eventually freed from Israel by Hadad who was of the Edomite royal line, and may have been the grandson of the king who David deposed.

During Jehoshaphat's reign in Judah (Israel had been divided), it would appear that Edom was probably reconquered, as II Chronicles 17:11 talks of "Arabians" bringing Jehoshaphat tributes of animals, and there was most likely a governor as in David's time (I Kings 22:47).

Jehoshaphat was succeeded by Jehoram as king of Judah. During this time Edom rebelled: *"In his (Jehoram's) days Edom revolted from under the hand of Judah, and made a king over themselves"(II Kings 8:20)*. Although an attempt was made to bring the Edomites back in line it seems to have failed, although the biblical text is not too clear here.

massacre at Sela (the Rock)

Edom managed to stay independent for some 60 or so years until the time that Amaziah became King of Judah. Now, (according to the scriptures), another massacre took place some 300 years after David's bloodbath. In the account of this action the name *Sela,* Hebrew for rock, is mentioned:

> *"He (Amaziah) killed of Edom in the Valley of Salt 10,000 and took Sela by war..."* *(II Kings 14:7)* and *"Now Amaziah strengthened himself and led his people forth, and went to the Valley of Salt, and struck down 10,000 of the sons of Seir. The sons of Judah also captured 10,000 alive and brought them to the top of the cliff and threw them down so that they were all dashed to pieces."* *(II Chronicles 25:11-12)*

For a long time this "Rock" was incorrectly identified with Umm al Biyara (see Tour 7), the flat-topped mountain which overshadows every part of Petra. The error was compounded by the fact that the place name Sela (Hebrew for rock), when translated into Greek, is Petra.

definitely the wrong Rock

Excavations conducted in the 1960s by Crystal-M. Bennett have disproved any linkage between Umm al Biyara and the biblical Sela. Although the excavations indeed uncovered an Edomite settlement atop the mount it was only a small one, and certainly not one that would have had to be taken "by war". Further, Amaziah reigned from about 796 to 781 BC (early 8th C BC) whereas this settlement dates from the 7th C at the earliest. It was deserted in the 6th C after being devastated by fire.

Archaeologists are not certain where the Sela referred to may be. The Edomite capital was at Bozrah — not the place of the same name in the Syrian Hauran but Busairah near Tafila (c100kms north of Petra) — very close to the southern end of the Dead Sea. As the biblical text refers to the "Valley of Salt" this looks a more likely location.

brief domination by Judah

Uzziah completed the domination of Edom: *"He built Eloth and restored it to Judah" (II Kings 14:22)*. But again Judah's domination did not last long. While Ahaz was King of Judah *"... Rezin king of*

Syria recovered Eloth for Syria* and cleared out the Judeans..."
(* Note from NASB states that in this case the ancient Hebrew text
means Edom.)

In the 7th C BC Edom, like Judah, became an Assyrian vassal
state.

The advent of the Nabateans

All this was but a prelude to the coming of the Nabateans, the
people with whom Petra is firmly associated, and the architects of the
wonderful city of our visit. Any history of Petra must therefore also
be a history of these people.

The Nabateans were a nomadic Arab tribe. It appears that their
original home was the northwestern Arabian Peninsula, as remains of
their early civilisation have been uncovered there. As the area was on
the trans-Arabian caravan routes it is quite possible that one of their
earlier exploits was the raiding of these. At that time they led a
typically Bedouin lifestyle, living in tents, moving about on camels
and getting their food from their flocks or by hunting.

Nabateans supplant Edomites

It is not too certain how the Nabateans replaced the Edomites as
the population of Southern Jordan. We do know that by the 6th C BC
nomadic tribes, apparently Nabateans, had begun to infiltrate into the
region and into the land just north, Moab. These people were known
in Assyrian texts as Nabaitu. In the middle of the 7th C BC they
appear in these Assyrian texts as enemies of the king, Ashur-Bani-Pal,
the first mention of them in history. As the Assyrians were constantly
warring with them and imposing heavy burdens it seems probable that
their exodus to TransJordan was the result of these incidents.

descendants of Nebaioth?

Whether these people can be equated with the descendants of
Nebaioth, the first son of Ishmael (Genesis 25:13), is a matter for
conjecture. They were an Arab tribe, and the Arabs trace their
ancestry from Abraham's son by Hagar so, according to your
inclinations, there could be a case.

In the beginning they lived alongside the Edomites and Moabites
learning much from these more settled peoples. By the fourth century
they were firmly established in all parts of Edom, parts of Moab, the
Arava, and in areas of the Negev (particularly Avdat where there are
many fascinating remains of their agricultural enterprise). In addition
they controlled territory along the eastern coast of the Red Sea.

the Edomites move on

As the influx increased, the Edomites began to move out, mainly
to southern Judea, which became known in Hellenic times as Idumea,
a corruption of Edom. Nevertheless some may have been absorbed by
the migrating Nabateans due to intermarriage and general assimilation.
As the Nabateans were a Semitic people descended vaguely from the

same line as the Edomites, this would not have presented any difficulties.

Little is known of this period of Nabatean settlement but it is safe to assume that they established themselves in Petra as indicated by an early Nabatean village which has been unearthed atop Umm al-Biyara, in addition to the earlier Edomite settlement.

The first firm date in Nabatean history comes to us from the Sicilian historian, Diodorus Siculus and is dated around 59 BC.

the account of Diodorus Siculus (Diodorus of Sicily)

In Diodorus' first mention of the Nabateans he writes "...in the land of the Nabateans is a Rock (Petra) which is exceedingly strong since it has but one approach, and using this ascent they mount it a few at the time and thus store their possessions in safety." (Diodorus Siculus, II 48.6.)

The historian then refers to events that occurred in 312 BC, taking his information from Seleucid records. He records that Antigonus Cyclops (382-301 BC), ruler of Syria, sent a force under Athanaeus "to the region of the Arabs who are called Nabataei".

frankincense, myrrh and silver

Diodorus relates how this force, during the hours of darkness and while the younger men were away from the settlement, attacked and pillaged the Rock seizing quantities of frankincense, myrrh and much silver.   News of this assault quickly reached the absent men. Subsequently the Nabateans chased and stormed the invaders' camp, killing all but a handful of them, and recovering all their goods.

The Nabateans were very irritated over this incident, and sent a letter to Antigonus detailing the episode and protesting about it. Antigonus replied blaming the whole affair on his general.

The "Rock" referred to was Umm al-Biyara and Diodorus, writing in Greek, used the Greek word Petra. Thereafter, the Greek word for rock became the name for the whole emerging city.

bribed to retreat

Later, the Hellene ruler tried again to take the Nabatean stronghold by dispatching a force under his son, Demetrius. But after the first raid the Nabateans had posted lookouts to guard against such a second attempt. Demetrius found it impossible to take the redoubt, and eventually retreated having been plied with bribe gifts by the Nabateans.

From Diodorus' account we can build up a picture of Nabatean life in the late 4th C. They must have still been tent dwellers and not yet engaged in agriculture, for Diodorus tells us that "they neither sow corn nor plant fruit trees or build houses". That they were already reaping the rewards of the rich caravan trade is also clear by the type of goods that were seized in the first raid (this was, no doubt, the reason for Antigonus' interest in the place).

advent of Petra as a city

In spite of the fact that there was no real city at Petra at that time (Diodorus stated that they did not build houses) it is clear (from Antigonus' interest) that the area was already an important trade route, carrying a hugely profitable quantity of commerce from Southern Arabia and beyond. When Petra actually became the Nabatean capital is difficult to determine. In fact we do not know exactly when it developed into something that could even be called a city. Suffice it to say that the Nabatean transition from nomads to master city builders was a gradual one. Certainly by c170 BC a city of importance had been established there and this was mainly in the lower-lying areas between the heights.

Petra's Nabatean name

Of course Petra was not the Nabatean name for the capital. The Jewish historian Josephus tells us it was called Rekem, and this name, Reqmu in Nabatean, was confirmed a few decades ago by the discovery of engraved stones at the site itself (see page 187).

History next mentions Nabatea and the Nabateans c169 BC when we have the first record of a Nabatean king, Aretas I, referred to in 2 Maccabees 5:8 as the "tyrant of the Arabs". It was to him that Jason, the high priest of Jerusalem, went after he was driven from office.

making the desert bloom

The Nabateans proved themselves to be very capable people. For not only did they carve cities out of the mountain rock, but their ability to turn wasteland into agricultural service must also be recorded. Edomites had already developed water conservation techniques, something vital in this parched land. The Nabateans improved on this by building better dams, cisterns in the wadis (seasonal water courses) and turning them into reservoirs. Aqueducts led the water to the places it was required. Avdat in the Negev is a good example of how they managed to grow crops in the desert.

quiet prosperity

After the account of Diodorus, except for the mention in Maccabees, we do not hear of Petra by name again until the first century BC, in the writings of the geographer Strabo (54 BC to AD 25). After stating that the Nabatean domains stretched as far as Arabia Felix (the southeastern part of the peninsula), he continues that their metropolis is Petra (Rock), *"...for it lies on a site which is otherwise smooth and level, but is fortified all round by rock, the outside parts of the site being precipitous and sheer..." (Strabo, Geography 16.4.21).* In the same work Strabo cites that a companion of his, Athenodorus, a philosopher who had visited the city *"used to describe the government with admiration... and they in every way kept peace..."*. In spite of this it is safe to assume that much was happening there. The caravans, the source of Nabatean wealth and power, were increasing in number and the merchandise was coming from further afield. Trade with China and India was certainly being conducted with goods from these lands being unloaded at ports in the (now) Persian Gulf, the ports of Southern Arabia or even via the Bab al-Mandab to Aqaba.

Language of the Nabateans

The Nabatean language was either a form of Arabic or a mixture of both Arabic and Aramaic, the *lingua franca* of the entire region. For literary and communications purposes they appear to have used Aramaic.

They used a very distinctive alphabet and form of writing. It comprised of letters that were similar to ancient Hebrew, but more elongated, and connected often by ligatures at the bottom (Hebrew letters are not connected). The Nabatean script was the forerunner of Kufic and Arabic. Later, like most other peoples in the region, they also used Greek, and inscriptions have been found using a mixture of the two languages.

In all cases the route to the prosperous markets of Gaza, Damascus and Aleppo, as well as onwards to Europe, lay via Petra; for besides being the route crossroads, most of the journey until there traversed only inhospitable desert. At Petra the caravaners found plenty of fresh water which was essential for their continuation north or west.

conflict with Hasmoneans ends peace

Under successive kings the Nabatean kingdom was vastly extended. Obadas I became King around 96 BC. Soon hostilities began between the Hasmonean Jews and the Nabateans. Alexander Yannai (the Hasmonean ruler) captured 12 cities in Moab in breach of an agreement between the two nations c92 BC (Josephus, Antiquities of the Jews 13:395-7). At a battle near Gadar in Gilead, Obodas defeated Yannai and Hasmonean expansion east of the Jordan was checked (Josephus, Antiquities of the Jews 13:372 & Wars of the Jews 1:90). This Nabatean victory paved the way for Nabatean occupation of the Hauran, today in southern Syria.

Antiochus loses his head

In 87 BC Rabel I came to the throne. At the same time the Seleucid ruler of Syria, Antiochus XII Dionysus, decided to invade Nabatea. Initially the Nabateans withdrew into the desert, but when the

Seleucids pursued them "the Arab king" (as Josephus calls him) assailed them with some 10,000 cavalry. Antiochus fell and was decapitated.

Greek culture

It is probable that along with Antiochus, Rabel was also killed in this battle, as Aretas III became the Nabatean king in the same year, 87 BC. Known as the "Philhellene" he brought his kingdom into close contact with Hellenistic culture.

Nabatean prosperity is attested to by the development of Petra, with its extraordinary rock cut tombs, its magnificent facades and portals, and huge religious edifices.

control of the caravan routes

This vast wealth was amassed by the Nabateans because by then they held almost complete control of the land along the entire trans-Arabian trade routes. The routes traversed the desert to the Nabatean port of Leuke Kome, an entrepot on the Red Sea coast at the mouth of Wadi al-Hamd. As mentioned earlier, at Petra the caravan route split in two directions — one north towards Damascus and beyond and the other west to Gaza and Rhinocolura, today el-Arish, from where the cargoes could either continue to Alexandria or, at this stage in history, be shipped direct to Italy. Strabo records this in his *Geography*: *"Now the loads of aromatics are conveyed from Leuce Come to Petra, and thence to Rhinocolura, which is in Phoenicia near Aegypt, and thence to the other peoples..." (16.4.24)*. The Nabateans had even established a colony in Italy at Puteoli, which was at the time a port for Rome.

war and peace with the Hasmoneans

Conflict with the Hasmonean Jews continued as both nations vied for control of southern Syria and the route to Damascus. With the Hauran already under his control Aretas III occupied Damascus in 85 BC (this first occupation did not last long). Shortly afterwards he battled Alexander Yannai, defeating him near Lydda. After the death of Yannai his queen, Salome Alexander, became the Hasmonean ruler, and Aretas made a peace with her.

Petra remains impregnable

In 64 BC Pompey annexed Syria, and a year later made Judea a Roman dependency. Before the annexation of Syria and Judea, Pompey had set out on a punitive expedition to Petra, but was forced to abandon it when unrest in Judea required his attention (Josephus, Antiquities of the Jews 14:46ff). In 62 BC, Scaurus the governor of Syria had another go. The impregnable nature of the Nabatean capital proved too much for him, and he withdrew. Thus the Nabateans were able to hang on to their independence for almost another 150 years, though they were decidedly subject to Rome's desires and approvals.

Nabatean sandwich

The next few Nabatean kings found themselves placed in a sensitive position, sandwiched between the Romans and the Parthians (who were threatening Roman Syria from the east), and between Antony and Octavian (later the first Roman emperor, Caesar Augustus), in Egypt. Indeed, in 47 BC the Nabatean king Malchus I sent cavalry to Alexandria to aid Octavian (Bellum Alexandrium 1:1).

the king who loved his people

Aretas IV came to the throne in 9 BC. He was known as *Rehav Amah,* or *Philopatris,* lover of his people. His reign was a long one, lasting until AD 40. During his tenure the prosperity and economic well-being of Nabatea, and of Petra in particular, reached its zenith.

Nabateans again in Damascus

By the beginning of the 1st C AD Damascus was again under Nabatean control, and was so at the time of the events of Paul as recorded in Acts Chapter 9. Paul relates, *"In Damascus the ethnarch under Aretas the king was guarding the city...in order to seize me." (II Corinthians 11:32).* (It might be added that the "Arabia" Paul went to after his Damascus experience was most likely Nabatea.)

Malichus succeeded to the throne in AD 40. During his reign Roman control became tighter, and Nabatean rule in Damascus was terminated, though they continued to hold parts of southern Syria, including Bostra (Bosra). Malichus' tenure saw the diminishing of Nabatean power.

end of Nabatean independence

The last royal Nabatean ruler was Rabbel II who became king in AD 71. In 106 Cornelius Palma, on the orders of Trajan, annexed Nabatea and it became part of the Roman province of Arabia, the capital of which was Bostra.

a boost from the Romans

With the construction of the *Via Nova Traiana,* which ran from Bostra to Aila (Aqaba) via Petra, Romans soon began to settle in Petra and the city underwent something of a renaissance. The colonnaded cardo was built and, though small compared to, say, that of Apamea or the Great Colonnade of Palmyra (both in today's Syria), was still impressive. The Romans were careful to preserve the traditions of the Nabateans, and their building intruded on the way of life as little as possible.

decline of the hidden city

Whereas Petra continued as a hub of trade for another century or so, changing patterns and routes, and in particular the rise of Palmyra in eastern Syria, foreshadowed its demise. The fall was gradual but by the close of the third century Petra was no longer a city of any significance. Indeed, without the flow of camel trains the city was nothing, locked as it was in a fortress of mountains. Many of the inhabitants moved away, probably to other Nabatean cities further north which would have had an existence without the caravans.

Christian Petra

As elsewhere in the Middle East, Christianity came to Petra with Byzantium. In the 4th C Petra became a Bishopric, and there were apparently many churches. An inscription in Greek in the Urn Tomb (see Tour No 2) dated 446 confirms that the tomb had been converted into a church.

Petra vanishes for 1000 years

At the time of the Islamic conquest in the 7th C, a few people were still living in Petra, but when Islamic power shifted from Damascus to Baghdad and Petra was no longer on the route to Mecca, the place soon faded from history, although the Crusaders did build a castle there (see Tour 5) and one or two forts.

From the end of the Crusader period right up until the year 1812 Petra was lost in obscurity. Its location was unknown to the world apart from a handful of knowledgeable Arabs who kept it a tight secret.

Burckhardt's rediscovery of Petra

John Lewis Burckhardt, a Swiss who was educated at Leipzig and Göttingen, was intent on a life of exploration in an era when much of Asia and Africa was beginning to be discovered. In 1807 he met Sir Joseph Banks of the Association for Promoting the Discovery of the Interior Parts of Africa, and for the rest of his short life he conducted explorations on behalf of this British society.

master of Arabic - and of disguise

After spending a little time learning Arabic he travelled to Malta where he further studied that language and gathered information to enable him to pass as a Muslim merchant from the Indian sub-continent. His purpose was to go to Syria and absorb himself fully in the Islamic and Arab lifestyle. Burckhardt knew that only as an Arab could he hope to travel freely in the areas he proposed to visit. The next two years were spent mainly in Aleppo, perfecting his disguise. He became so proficient in Arabic and Koranic studies that when adopting an appearance and mode of dress that was thoroughly Islamic, he was able to play the part he had planned flawlessly. In 1810 Burckhardt made journeys within Syria, exploring and recording his visits to hardly-known sites such as Palmyra, Baalbeck, Apamea and the Hauran.

from a rock to a hard place?

The existence of the Nabateans and their city, Petra, had long been known of from the works of Josephus and the classical writers but its location was much in doubt. A good idea of early 19th C thinking on this matter can be garnered from William Martin Leake's preface to Burckhardt's journal, *Travels in Syria and the Holy Land*, published in 1822 in association with the above mentioned society. In it he hypothesizes that Kerak (al-Karak), a city built on the top of a cliff or rock, was the original Nabatean capital of Petra and only later did they move to the city in Wadi Musa, a site that was also suited to the name Petra. Subsequent research and scholarship does not substantiate this.

Burckhardt sets out

In the summer of 1812 Burckhardt set out to journey from Damascus to Cairo, from where he planned to start his exploration of Africa. His route was through present day Jordan, passing Amman, Kerak, and Shobak. Around the Shobak area he began to hear stories of an archaic site full of ancient remains. He made up his mind to try to visit the place, which was hidden in the mountains. Burckhardt does not mention that he suspected in any way at this stage that the place spoken about was the ancient Nabatean capital. He recorded:

> *"August 22nd.-- I was particularly desirous of visiting Wady Mousa, of the antiquities of which I had heard the country people speak in terms of great admiration;" (Travels in Syria and the Holy Land, p.418)*

sacrifice at Aaron's tomb

Burckhardt knew that the locals were suspicious of foreigners visiting such places, believing — not without foundation — that they were only on the lookout for treasure to loot. He therefore pretended that he had made a vow to slaughter a goat *"at the tomb of Haroun (Aaron), whose tomb I knew was situated at the extremity of the valley...to this my guide had nothing to oppose; the dread of drawing upon himself, by resistance, the wrath of Haroun..." (As above p.419.)*

But his line of persuasion proved more difficult for Burckhardt than he anticipated, as his guide told him that other Arabs who made similar vows thought it quite enough to kill the animal within *sight* of the tomb, which is perched on a high mountain top. But Burckhardt insisted that *his* vow was to slaughter the goat at the very tomb itself!

abandoned Christian village

After passing Ain Musa he first came to a little village, Badabde, which had been abandoned a few years earlier by its inhabitants who were Greek Orthodox Christians. A little further on as he entered the wadi (Musa) he came to the village of Elji, which was until the 1960s still called by that name. (It has now acquired the name of the wadi itself, and is known as Wadi Musa). Burckhardt commented: *"This place contains between two and three hundred houses, and is enclosed by a stone wall...It is most picturesquely situated...".*

With the local guide he set off, westwards, along the wadi. *"In following the rivulet of Eldji westwards the valley soon narrows...and it is here that the antiquities of Wady Mousa begin. "*

Burckhardt was unable to explore in detail the works he saw here. He knew what kind of people were around him: *"I was without protection in the midst of a desert where no traveller had ever been seen; and a close examination of these works of the infidels, as they are called, would have excited suspicions that I was a magician in search of treasures... ".*

first sighting of the Siq Gorge

He did, though, mention that he saw many tombs, some still with ornaments. As the valley narrowed it appeared to be enclosed by high rock, *"I perceived a chasm about fifteen or twenty feet in breadth, through which the rivulet flows westwards in winter; in summer its waters are lost in the sand and gravel before they reach the opening, which is called El Syk".*

Thus Burckhardt discovered the hidden city, and recorded much of what he saw, yet according to his journal he spent less than a day there. A man of undoubted learning and keen intellect, his explorer's instincts did not let him down. On the day after his discovery he wrote,

" ...it appears very probable that the ruins of Wady Mousa are those of the ancient Petra...Of this I am persuaded, from all the information I procured, that there is no other ruin between the extremities of the Dead sea and the Red sea, of sufficient importance to answer to that city." (as above p.431).

By the way, Burckhardt never did get to Aaron's tomb; by the time he reached the plain at the base of the mountain on which it stands he was so tired that, like the pilgrims his guide had told about, he slew the goat there and then!

discovery of Abu Simbel

Eventually Burckhardt continued on to Cairo. From there his other adventures included the momentous discovery of the Temple of Abu Simbel in Nubia, and he was probably the first non Muslim to enter Mecca for many centuries. He never actually renounced being a Christian, but his study of and close association with Islam had a great effect on him.

a Muslim burial for a great Sheikh

In October 1817, while in Cairo, the young John Lewis contracted dysentery. By the end of that month he was dead. He had expressed a desire to be interred in a Muslim cemetery in that city, and so he was, under the name he had used so successfully during his travels, Sheikh Ibrahim ibn Abdullah.

in the footsteps of Burckhardt

Burckhardt's journal, which he had written under the most secretive of conditions, was published in 1822. Prior to that others had already learned of his discoveries and in 1818 a C.L Irby and J. Mangles, two British Navy officers, accompanied by Messrs W. Banks and Legh spent some days exploring the site. Although it was not approached, it appears that these people were the first to see El Deir (Tour No 4). An account of this journey, penned by Irby and Mangles, was published in 1868 by the same house that published Burckhardt's manuscript.

In 1826 two Frenchmen, the Marquis Léon de Laborde, accompanied by an engraver, M Linant, came to visit Petra. This incursion resulted in some splendid etchings. The Marquis eventually became the Director General of the Archives Français. His travels were detailed in his book *Voyage de l'Arabie Pétrée* in 1830.

fine drawings from last century

In 1829 the famous artist and Royal Academician, David Roberts, made the journey which resulted not only in the most beautiful drawings of Petra, but of the Holy Land too, particularly Jerusalem. (These are now generally available as prints and make fine souvenirs!)

After his visit in 1840, Henry Layard, the discoverer of Nineveh, wrote:

"The rocks of friable limestone, worn by the weather into forms of endless variety, some of which could scarcely be distinguished from the remains of ancient buildings; the solitary columns rising here and there among the shapeless heaps of masonry; the gigantic flights of steps, cut in the rock, leading to the tombs; the absence of all vegetation to relieve the solemn monotony of the bare brown soil; the mountains rising abruptly on all sides; the silence and solitude, scarcely disturbed by the wild Arab lurking among the fragments of pediments, fallen cornices, and architraves which encumber the narrow valley, render the ruins of Petra unlike those of any other ancient city in the world."

C.M. Doughty, author of *Travels in Arabia Deserta*, found his way here in 1876 but was decidedly the odd man out of these pioneer explorers – he disliked the place!

profusion of serious writings

Most early books on Petra were narratives of the travels of the authors. However, in the first years of the 20th century many scholarly books, the results of much research, saw the light. In 1904 the German archaeologists, Brünnow and Domaszewski published a detailed survey in German. Drs Libbey and Hoskins published in 1905 *The Jordan Valley and Petra*, and in 1907 Alois Musil's *Arabia*

Petraea was printed, although this was based on work done some 10 years previously. The year 1908 saw the publication of G. Dalman's German work, *Petra und Felsheiligtunner* and in 1912 his *Neue Petra Forschlungen* appeared.

Since then archaeological activities have been numerous and almost continuous, and a host of Petra's secrets have been revealed.

Gods of the Nabateans

The Nabateans had two "main" deities: **Dushara** and **Allat**.

Dushara was adopted from the Edomite god Dhu-esh-Shera, also called Dusares. This deity was depicted as a block of rock or stone. Dushara or Dhu-esh Shera means He of Shera, Shera being the mountains around Petra. In the Old Testament they are called Seir. This god had its shrines on mountain tops and other "high places". Allat is also known as al-Uzza, a goddess usually linked with water and springs. Allat translates "the Goddess" while al-Uzza means "the Great One". This divinity was also venerated by the Arabs in the Arabian peninsula.

Other, though lesser, deities, included **Ara**, a mother goddess; **Atargatis**, a fish goddess; and **Gad**, the god of luck. **Hadad**, the Semitic storm god, was also high on the list of divinities. Later, when the Nabateans fell under Hellenic influence, Dushara became equated with Dionysus, Hadad with Zeus or Jupiter (Roman influence), and Gad with Tyche.

Some Nabatean kings, starting with **Obodas I**, were also deified.

VISITING THE ANCIENT CITY

Petra is described below in eleven tours as follows:

1. Site entrance to the theatre via the Siq and the Treasury
2. The Royal Tombs
3. Central City, Colonnaded Street, and Qasr al-Bint
4. Rest Area to al-Deir
5. Al-Habees
6. Theatre to Zibb 'Attuf and along Wadi Farasa to Qasr al-Bint
7. Ascent of Umm al-Biyara
8. Wadi Siyagh
9. Al-Beidha and Siq al-Barid
10. Al-Madras
11. Jabal Haroun

179

What you will need

♦ First and foremost, as you will be doing a great deal of walking and climbing, some over quite difficult terrain, **strong, comfortable walking shoes** are a must. Good strong trainers may be suitable, but if rough climbing is planned something more substantial is preferable.

♦ Clothing should be light and loose. Although some visitors wear shorts, you will find that cotton, or cotton and polyester, trousers are just as cool and probably more comfortable as the sun is strong and for those not used to it, exposed parts can burn easily without you noticing.

♦ Wear a **hat**!

♦ Carry as little as possible, but make sure you have at least **one litre of water per person**, more can be obtained at the rest area and some of the Bedouin tents across the site. You can also buy food there, but you might want to take a snack along with you.

♦ If you intend to do any scramble climbing you will need your hands free, so take a small rucksack for carrying your things.

♦ Because of the limitations of the maps printed in this book, you may also need a more detailed one. These are on sale at the visitors' information centre.

♦ A good **pocket compass** is indispensable, as is **this book**!

Entrance fees

The entrance fee is high, especially if you only want to spend a day there. JD20 for a single day, JD25 for a two day ticket, and JD30 for a three day visit! In 1991 the fee was a lowly JD1 per day and in 1994 still reasonable, despite a five-fold increase to JD5 per day. But the hefty jump to the present excessive level in less than one year is very difficult to justify! It is not due to any devaluation of the Jordanian dinar which has not fluctuated a great deal in the past couple of years.

priceless Petra

Obviously no "value for money" tag can be put on a visit to such a unique spot, but the authorities might reconsider their apparent conclusion that tourists have unlimited resources to draw upon.

ITINERARIES

Most people spend one or two days touring Petra. How much you can see during that time depends on physical fitness and the amount of time you occupy examining the various monuments. Some places, like tour No.11 to Jabal Haroun, can only be undertaken by staying a third day, so it will be left out of my proposed itineraries, although it is described below for those who want to undertake it.

▸ **Basic one day Itinerary**

As with most large historical sites, there is a "standard" tour of Petra, the one done by most one-day trippers of average energy. This is what I have called the basic itinerary.

* Tour 1:   Site entrance to the theatre.
* Tour 2:   Royal Tombs.
* Tour 3:   Central city to Qasr al-Bint, and rest area (lunch).
* Tour 4:   Al-Deir

Option:

* Tour 8:   Wadi Siyagh, – can be inserted between tours 3 and 4.

▸ **One day itinerary to see as much as possible**

* Tour 1:   Site entrance to the theatre.
* Tour 6:   Zibb 'Attuf/Wadi Farasa to Qasr al-Bint (lunch break can be taken now or after tour 8 if you do it).
* Tour 4:   Al-Deir.
* Tour 3:   (In reverse) Qasr al-Bint and central city.
* Tour 2:   Royal tombs.

Option:

* Tour 8:   Wadi al-Siyagh – can be inserted between tours 6 and 4 if time and energy permits.

▸ **Two day itinerary to see as much as possible.**

Day one–

* Tour 1:   Site entrance to the theatre.
* Tour 6:   Zibb 'Attuf/Wadi Farasa to Qasr al-Bint
* Tour 5:   Ascent of al-Habees (lunch).
* Tour 4:   Al-Deir.
* Tour 3:   (In reverse) Qasr al-Bint and central city. This will bring you to beneath the area of the Royal Tombs, but leave exploration of these for the second day and return to the site entrance .

Day two–

* Tour 9:   (Early morning start) Siq al-Barid. Then return to the Petra site entrance and ride by horse to the Siq entrance then walk to theatre.
* Tour 2:   Royal tombs.
* Tour 8:   Wadi Siyagh.
* Tour 7:   Ascent of Umm Biyara
* Tour 10   Al-Madras.

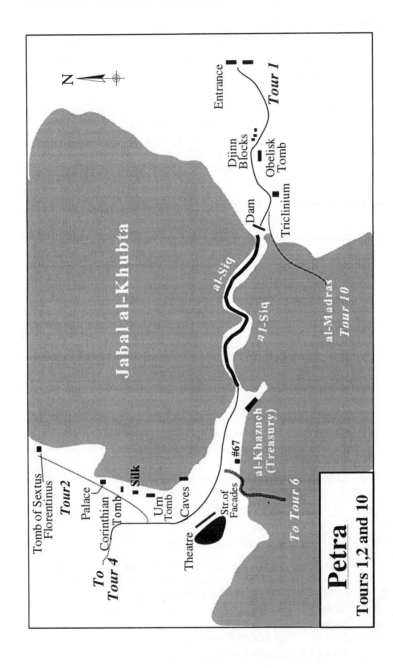

Petra
Tours 1,2 and 10

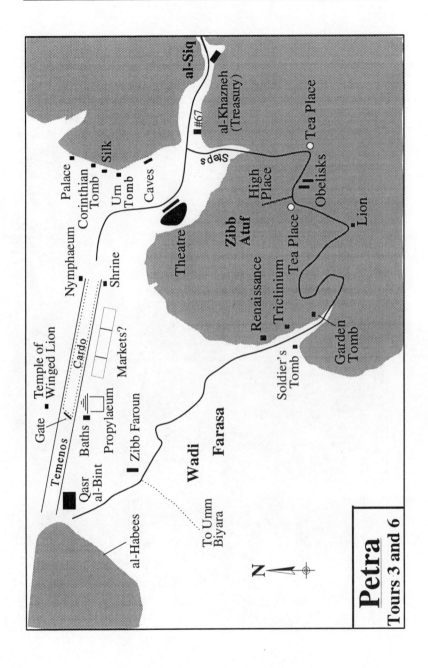

Petra
Tours 3 and 6

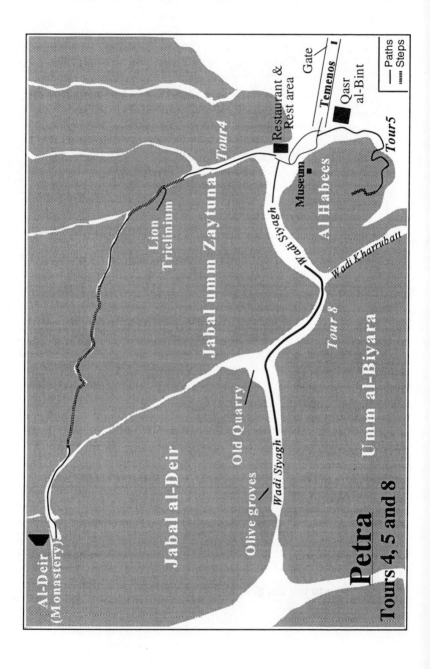

Petra

Tours 4, 5 and 8

▸ THE TOURS OF PETRA

> *"But rose-red as if the blush of dawn*
> *That first beheld them were not yet withdrawn;*
> *The hues of youth upon a brow of woe,*
> *Which Man deemed old two thousand years ago,*
> *Match me such marvels, save in eastern clime,*
> *The rose red city, half as old as time"*
> *J.W. Burgon, Petra 1845*

As you can see above, I have divided the Petra site into 11 routes. At the beginning of each I have estimated how long it will take. In doing so I have allowed time for photographing, resting and just stopping to admire the view. Additionally, I have, in a few words, described how easy or difficult the route is.

▸ **Tour No 1 – Site entrance to the theatre**

MAIN FEATURES: **Bab-al-Siq — Djinn blocks — Obelisk Tomb — the Dam — Siq Canyon — the Treasury (al-Khasneh) — Street of Facades — the Theatre** TIME: **Depending how much time you spend gazing at the Treasury, 1.5-2 hours** TERRAIN: **easy walk on flat ground.**

Starting the tour

The entrance to the antiquities is just to the south east of the Rest House. After paying and entering you will, almost immediately, be confronted by Bedouin horse and donkey owners eager to persuade you to ride the first part of the tour, that is as far as the entrance to al-Siq, a distance of around one and a half km. But on your first day I recommend you walk, as not only will you save around JD3, but there are a number of things to see on the way which you might not notice too well on horseback — the horse leaders will not stop on the way. Until late 1995 the horses used to continue through the Siq gorge as far as the Treasury, but this has now been stopped as they constituted a nuisance to walkers. However, small horse-drawn traps are allowed through to the Treasury for people with walking difficulties.

gateway to the Siq gorge

The stretch of the valley to the Siq gateway is fairly wide and is called *Bab al-Siq*, Gateway to the Siq. The actual wadi, Wadi Musa, is on your left. There are two pathways on the right; one for walkers and the other for the horses and donkeys. The paths follow the wadi's course which is below on the left. The rocks here are a creamy yellow, so if you expected a rosy hue you will be disappointed. In the past I often trod this section virtually alone, but nowadays it's not so easy! If you do prefer quiet, try starting out soon after dawn - there will certainly be few people about then.

spirits of stone

The first monuments you see are on the right. These comprise an array of three enormous stone blocks known as **Djinn Blocks**, djinn being the Arabic word for spirit or ghost (the word *genie* is a derivative). The blocks are generally believed to have been graves and are isolated from the rock from which they were cut. Of the three, the last is the most interesting, being decorated with pilasters topped by step-like grooves.

four huge obelisks

A little further along, across the wadi on the left (south), you come to the first rock-hewn facade, two tombs one on top of the other. The fact that they are not exactly aligned makes some doubt whether they have anything to do with each other. The whole structure has been given the name the **Obelisk Tomb** because the upper section has four huge obelisks. In between the two centre blocks is an alcove with a surround which once contained an image of sorts. Inside is a large chamber that has two tombs on each side wall and one at the rear.

The lower structure with a carved facade and four attached columns is in the form of a *triclinium* with benches around the three sides, the grave being in the centre. One can surmise that people sat on these benches during some sort of funeral ritual. The chambers on each side of the facade were most probably tombs.

The valley winds on with the cliffs gradually assuming a more pinkish tone, and then veers quite sharply to the right. Just before the bend, on the left (S) there is an area with many trees. From there a path leads to the sanctuary of **al-Madras**, but more of that later.

violent flooding halted

Now as you wheel right you can see the entrance to the **Siq canyon**, with a recently built dam in front of it. To the right is a ravine with a roughly-hewn **Nabatean tunnel** at the end. The dam was constructed in 1963 to prevent flood waters from Wadi Musa rushing down the gorge. Until then the wadi's torrent flowed through its natural course, the Siq. This was especially dangerous when heavy rain fell high in the mountains, perhaps unknown to those in Petra. Flash floods often resulted in which gushing water would suddenly pour in torrents into the wadi, sweeping away all before it.

Nabatean dam

In just such a flood in 1963, 23 visitors were drowned and the dam was built to prevent it happening again. Vestiges of a similar dam built by the Nabateans already existed. The early dam (as does the modern one) diverted the flood waters from the Siq into the ravine and tunnel and thereafter towards Wadi Mataha on the north side of Jabal al-Khubtha, and then into the city.

Petra's name discovered

Construction of the new dam yielded many fascinating finds. The most important was an inscription on one of the obelisks found carved in the rock opposite the Siq. It referred to someone who "lived at Rekem (the Nabatean name for Petra, see page 171) but died at Jerash, and was buried there". This was when the ancient Nabatean or Semitic name for Petra was first confirmed.

ticket inspection

In front of the Siq entrance is a Bedouin souvenir shop, and you may also find officials there who check your entrance tickets.

Just inside the canyon, high up on both sides, especially on the left, you can see the remains of the spring of a monumental or **triumphal arch**. Burckhardt saw a little more: *"About 50 paces below the entrance to the Syk a bridge of one arch thrown over the top of the chasm is still entire;"* The span must have been very shaky as towards the end of the 19th C it was no more.

the truly stupendous Siq gorge

The Siq, a narrow gorge that slices through the southern edge of **Jabal al-Khubtha**, is one of most enthralling entranceways to any city anywhere in the world. About 1.5 km in length — and in some places barely 2 metres wide — its perpendicular sides soar to over 100 metres, often obscuring both sky and light. This is the natural course of Wadi Musa, and must be the consequence of a geological fault from the distant geological past. Although it runs in a general east/west course, it constantly twists and spirals so you cannot see more than 20 paces ahead at any time. Even sound from one bend to another reaches you in muted tones.

multi-coloured rocks

Along its winding route are many votive niches which have been carved into the rock. The colours in the seams of the stone are magnificent here, varying from deep reds and browns slashed with tinges of purple, to the sandier tones of bronze, yellow and ochre. In spring many of the crags are full of fresh greenery and brightly coloured oleander, especially in the nooks open to the sunlight.

remains of Roman road

In two places on the left you will be able to spot remnants of a Roman road which was raised above the level of any flood water that flowed through. Step up onto the first stretch and you will see a votive niche on the gorge face opposite. On the second stretch is a free standing stone block, under a tree. A few worn steps lead up to its front. It is thought to be a shrine or betil. The carved front of an entablature with a frieze is supported by two pilasters. Below the frieze are square blocks that symbolise the Nabatean god Dushara, a god often depicted as a stone block. This piece of carved rock was only discovered in 1977 after a load of debris had been cleared.

the moment of anticipation approaches

Your transition through the gorge may prove to be the most dramatic part of your visit to Petra. If you are able to take my advice and go early in the morning, the tranquillity and serenity will make it even more so.

The walk along al-Siq takes about half an hour, and as the end is approached it becomes extremely deep and dark. The towering walls of the gorge seem to hem you in, creating an almost claustrophobic sensation. Suddenly, a ribbon of light appears ahead and, as the canyon is at its darkest, the moment most visitors have been waiting for arrives, the facade of **al-Khasneh** slowly peels back.

▸ AL-KHASNEH (THE TREASURY)

"We went on in ecstasies until suddenly between the narrow opening of the rocks we saw the most beautiful sight I have ever seen; imagine a temple cut out of the solid rock, the charming facade supported on great Corinthian columns standing clear, soaring upwards to the very top of the cliff in the most exquisite proportions, and carved with groups of figures almost as fresh as when the chisel left them. All this in the rose red rock with the sun just touching it and making it look almost transparent."
Gertrude Bell, letter to her father, 1900

J.L. Burckhardt, in his book, describes his arrival thus: *"...an excavated mausoleum came into view, the situation and beauty of which are calculated to make an extraordinary impression upon the traveller..."* Less poetic, perhaps, than Gertrude Bell's letter quoted above, but perfectly accurate nonetheless! This, the most famous of Petra's monuments, does not disappoint. Even if you arrive early, before the sun's rays illumine the stone facade, the first sight of this monument is unforgettable.

the best time of day— a difficult choice

But there is no doubt that to see it at its best, the time of day is important. Until a few years ago when Petra was less frequented, an early morning start was not necessary. Nowadays, one has to balance the crowds with the right time of day to arrive at the Khasneh. Too early, and it sits in deep shadow, too late and the colours are lost. The best time to view this exceptional edifice is between 9.00 and 10.00am in the winter months and an hour later from April on. In peak season this hour will be the most crowded and you may find that the splendid sight of the sun striking the facade will be marred by the hordes of visitors in front of it (as well as the constant flow down the Siq).

I cannot help you with this; bearing in mind my advice below, you must decide for yourself. (Of course in the off-season there are fewer visitors.)

sunset over the red rock

But the Khasneh in late afternoon can also be enchanting, as the sinking sun adds an extra warm glow to the carved cliff face. Even if you make a morning excursion, you should try to see it again at sunset if you have the time.

photographic tips

This later time of day is also the best for taking photographs, as the high contrast of the dazzling morning light tends to "burn out" the detail of the facade. As the film in your camera does not adjust to light the same way as the eye does, the resulting colour on photos taken in late afternoon will be an even warmer shade of pink than the naked eye perceives. Under-exposing will accentuate this effect; try a shot at -5 and one at -1. In spite of Burgon's delightful poem, this is the most truly "rose red" edifice in Petra!

Pharaoh's urn

The common name for this awe-inspiring monument is the *Khasneh al-Faroun,* meaning Pharaoh's Treasury, though the local Bedouin have also used the appellation *al-Jarrah,* the Urn, after the large carved urn over the centre of the facade. Burckhardt gives the name as *"Kaszr Faraoun"* Pharaoh's castle, and says the locals thought it once a residence of a prince.

The urn is also the reason why it is called Pharaoh's Treasury. After the demise of the Nabatean kingdom, other desert nomads migrated into the area. They assumed that only someone great, like a pharaoh, could have fashioned such a place and that the urn was where he hid his treasure. Many bullets have been fired at this urn in the hope of splitting it open. Although they may have succeeded in damaging it, they had little hope of splitting it open: it's solid rock all the way through! The urn has also lent its name to the wadi in front of al-Khasneh, Wadi al-Jarrah.

marvellous sculpturing

The Khasneh is deeply chiselled out of the living, pink rock, and it appears as if it is actually supporting the rock above. This illusion is created because the two huge blocks on either side at the top are attached to it. The double storey facade is richly adorned with columns, statues and sculptures, especially about the friezes. Situated in a set-back position which shelters it from the elements, the marvellous sculpturing is still in a remarkable condition. The dimensions of the facade are incredible — it spans some 28 metres in width and ascends to a height of 40 metres at the top of the urn, which itself is nearly 4 metres tall!

mystery of its origins

There is no firm evidence as to who built this structure and when, or even what its purpose was. The use of Corinthian-like capitals on the columns shows a Hellenistic attitude, perhaps from the time of King Aretas III who was known as the "Philhellene". However, carvings of winged sphinxes on the upper level frieze show an Egyptian influence.

The time of its construction varies among scholars from the middle of the first century BC till the end of the first AD. The usage was most likely as a temple to one of the gods mentioned below, for the layout is similar to that of Egyptian temples. There is a possibility that it could have been a tomb, but this is not very likely. The figure in the centre of the upper level, below the urn, is said to be the Egyptian goddess, Isis, but other theories say it could be Petra's patron god or the deity al-Uzza.

collapse of column

The portico has 6 Corinthian columns. The first pictures of the rock-cut edifice show that the third one from the left (looking at it) had collapsed, but it was re-erected in 1960 by the Jordanian Department of Antiquities. It is interesting to note that, had this been a supporting instead of a carved column, the whole facade might have fallen. At each end of the portico are chambers approached by steps. The entrances have decorated friezes and pilasters. Above these entrances is a circular window.

The main chamber, which is approached by steps, is quite large, some 12 metres square and high. Three doors open off it, one at the rear, presumably to the sanctuary, and two with ornamented surrounds.

tombs galore!

From al-Khasneh the wadi continues round to the right, slightly north west, widening gradually. The lofty red walls of the canyon, along with the massive faces of al-Khubtha on your right, are dotted with tombs and sepulchres of varying sizes and at differing heights. The facades present a variety of embellishments, corner pilasters, triangular pediments, and typical Nabatean "crowstep" banding. As Burckhardt noted, some of the facades are considerably larger than their interior hewn rooms. This area is called the **Outer Siq.**

Number 67

At the point where the wadi becomes noticeably wider there is a series of sepulchres, the most outstanding of which bears the humdrum name of "Number 67". (The German researcher, Brünnow, numbered all the monuments at Petra, and those that lack a more definite title are known by these numbers). Number 67 is easily recognisable by the elaborate frieze over the entrance which is flanked by two columns. The double-storeyed monument has no ready access to the upper portion, and this part remained unexplored until an experienced mountaineer managed to gain entry by working his way over the facade.

Number 813

Almost facing number 67 is a series of unimportant tombs numbered from 821 to 830. High above them and slightly to the NE you can see number 813, the fine Tomb of Uneishu who was a minister of a certain Queen Sheqilat.

Number 70

Further down is Number 70 which stands out at an angle (just before the steps that lead up the mountain). This tomb face has very striking colours and had defined detail, now badly deteriorated. At the top is the typical Nabatean "crowstep" strip.

The wadi now continues to the theatre and into the heart of Petra, but to the left (by the Bedouin tent) are rock-hewn steps that lead up to the **Zibb 'Attuf High Place** (see Tour 6).

along the Street of Facades

Between the steps that ascend the 'Attuf ridge and the theatre, a distance of some 250 metres, there are so many facades that it has been given the name "The Street of Facades". These frontages are of houses as well as tombs, and number about 40. They are arranged on 4 levels, and constitute a most curious sight. A very dramatic view of them will be obtained when, later, you climb the 'Attuf Ridge along route number 6. Note how many of them have a double band of crowstep carvings at the top. It would appear that this sort of embellishment, originally Assyrian, was a standard feature of Nabatean architecture. This rather crowded array of houses or tombs is interrupted by the Roman theatre.

► THE ROMAN THEATRE

The theatre, the first quite "foreign" structure we have come to, is Roman. As Petra's imperial period began at the beginning of the 2nd C AD, it probably dates from then.

3000 capacity stadium

Houses or tombs were most likely situated on the hillside prior to the theatre's construction. As the entire hill would have required excavating in order to accommodate the rear part of the auditorium, these would have been destroyed in the process. Comprising 34 tiers chiselled from the soft, dull-coloured sandstone, the theatre was able to seat upwards of 3000 spectators. In the 1960s the Jordanian Department of Antiquities discovered remains of the stage and this has now been partly reconstructed. Facing the theatre are some unimportant tombs and an easy scramble into them gives a good picture-taking vantage point for the theatre.

From the theatre the Outer Siq widens to become a broad valley. The sides of Jabal al-Khubtha recede around to the right, and the main path continues north before bending around to the left (W) towards the **colonnaded street**. To the right (E), another path leads up to the tombs known as the **Royal Tombs**, the focus of Tour 2 below. There are three main tombs, all carved out of the west side of al-Khubtha, the **Urn Tomb**, the **Corinthian Tomb**, and the **Palace Tomb**.

> ► **Tour No 2 – The area of the Royal Tombs**

MAIN FEATURES: **Urn Tomb — Silk Tomb — Corinthian Tomb — Palace Tomb — Roman Tomb** TIME: **1-1.5 hours** TERRAIN: **Many steps to climb, but not difficult.**

> *"The finest sepulchres in Wady Mousa are in the east in front of this open space, where I counted upwards of fifty close to each other. High up in the cliff I particularly observed one large sepulchre, adorned with Corinthian pilasters."*
> *J.L. Burckhardt, Travels in Syria and the Holy Land, 1822*

► **THE ROYAL TOMBS**

The western face of al-Khubtha is dotted with tombs, and the ones towards the north, the grandest of them, are known as the royal tombs. Even if they do not all qualify for that regal title, they look as though they should. (To the south are another series, less grandiose and of no particular significance, but adding their share to Petra's allure by their presence.)

The carved rock face, in rich tones of reddish-brown, is magnificent. In spring, bright patches of green sprout from the crevices and more colour is provided by splashes of wild flowers in the foreground.

The tombs are reached by a flight of steps about 75 metres past the theatre (N), between two Bedouin refreshment places.

grand prison or King's tomb?

The first tomb at the top of the steps, a massive edifice, is titled the **Urn Tomb**. At a more elevated level than the others, you enter it up another stepped climb. The Urn Tomb is one of Petra's grandest monuments, with only the Khasneh and al-Deir more imposing. There are two tiers of arched vaults beneath it, and local Bedouin believe them to be a prison, with the edifice atop being the court. There is absolutely no evidence for this belief, and the structure is almost certainly a tomb. It probably dates from cAD 70, and one theory is that it may have been the tomb of Malchus II who died at that time.

A very stately courtyard, about 22 metres wide, has cloisters at each side that are separated from it by colonnades which are hewn out of the rock. The facade, a very simple affair, has four massive Doric-like columns also carved from the tinted sandstone rock.

tombs within the tomb

High up on the facade are three openings. At one time it was thought they were windows to an upper chamber. In fact each one has its own small chamber cut into the rock. The outer ones were just simple graves while the centre one has a well-worn bust of a person wearing what looks like a toga, probably the likeness of the individual interred there.

converted into a church

The main room of the Urn Tomb, measuring 20 by 18 metres, is undecorated. The interior was remodelled in AD 447 when the building was converted into a church by Bishop Jason. An inscription in Greek, painted in red on the left of the rear wall, is the source of this information.

From the courtyard there is a magnificent panorama in the direction of Umm Biyara which includes the length of the Colonnaded Street to Qasr al-Bint. The view is at its best first thing in the morning – but then one would need to spend days here in order to always be at the right place at the right time!

The urn that gave this tomb its name is at the top of the pediment. As so many places in Petra have such items on the frontages, why, in this case, it became the name for the tomb is anyone's guess.

silky stone

North of the Urn Tomb you pass a row of sepulchres that are of little importance until the **Silk Tomb** is reached. Set deep into the side of al-Khubta it is the one with an entrance and a narrower "window" above it. The crowstep battlements are higher than the adjacent tomb, which is not named. The reason for its name is immediately clear – the delicate pattern of the multi-coloured veins in the rock lend the facade the appearance of being wrapped in smooth silk.

ravaged by the elements

The next monument of note along this western face of al-Khubtha is the so-called **Corinthian Tomb**. (Between the Silk Tomb and this are a couple of unimportant ones.) It received this name because of the Corinthian-like columns which make it look very similar to the

Khasneh, albeit without that edifice's perfection; unlike the Khasneh it stands in a very exposed position, and consequently the elements have eroded the facade so badly that the similarity is less apparent. The entrances are all of different sizes and styles.

Inside the central and very damaged entrance is a room some 10 by 12 metres, and through the other doorways are much smaller chambers. Obviously, because of its size it must have been an important tomb.

the largest and the last

The last, and largest of the Royal Tombs, almost joined to the Corinthian, is the **Palace Tomb,** also called the Three Tiered Tomb. Fronted by the widest facade in Petra, it is, reputedly, a copy of some Roman palace. Most of the uppermost tier, which was erected with masonry as there was not enough rock above for carving, has disintegrated. The middle tier has 18 Corinthian-like columns (this may have been the tomb that Burckhardt noticed from the valley, see quote above).

Four entrances are surrounded by pilasters on which arched pediments rest. Inside these portals are four chambers, the largest being about 10 by 7 metres.

▸ THE ROMAN TOMB

One more monument of interest lies some 300 metres further on round the western face of the mountain. A track leads to it. **The Tomb of Sextus Florentinus**, unlike the preceding ones, is cut into the rock at a low level, and faces north. Over the entrance is an inscription in Latin which translates:

> *"To Lucius...Ninius, son of Lucius Papirius Sextius Florentinus, Triumvir for coining gold and silver, military tribune of Legion I Minerva, Quaestor of the Province of Achaia, Tribune of the Plebs, Legate of Legion VIIII Hispania, Proconsul of the Province of Narbonensis, Legate of Augustus, Propraetor of the Province of Arabia, most dutiful father, in accordance with his own will."*

In documents that were found in a cave in Nahal Hever in the Judean Desert, Yigal Yadin of the Hebrew University of Jerusalem, discovered the name Sextus Florentinus, and suggested that he was the Governor of the Roman Province of Arabia around 127.

eagle of Rome

The facade is a mixture of Nabatean and Roman influences. Above the entrance, resting on Nabatean style capitals is a semicircular pediment which has a very weathered relief of a medusa and the hydra. Atop this pediment, with outstretched wings, is the imperial Roman eagle.

Instead of returning via the steps you originally climbed to reach these tombs, take the path west in front of the Urn Tomb and follow it straight in the direction of the wadi (Musa). You can then cross it to the Colonnaded Street.

> ▸ **Tour No 3** – **Central City, Colonnaded Street and Qasr al-Bint**

MAIN FEATURES: **Colonnaded Street — Triumphal Arch — Qasr al-Bint**. TIME: **35-60 minutes** TERRAIN: **Easy walking**

▸ THE CENTRAL CITY AND THE COLONNADED STREET

So far, with the exception of the detour to visit the Royal Tombs, the route has been along Wadi Musa. At the point where the path turned off towards those tombs, the wadi bends round to the left (W) and meets Wadi Mataha coming from the north west. This is the start of the Roman Colonnaded Street. Wadi Musa runs parallel to this on the north side.

imagination required

Very little remains of the main city. The baths, temples, houses and other offices of a Roman city are now mere blocks of sandstone, with perhaps here and there just enough to make something look real. If you have seen the colonnaded cardos of other Roman cities such as Jerash you will find this one disappointing. Quite short and with only a few pillars re-erected, your walk along this Roman street can be quite bland or as interesting as your imagination lets it be. The magnificent backdrop of the Royal Tombs helps!

double-colonnaded street

The street was double colonnaded along its entire length with a portico on each side. There were probably one or two bridges which spanned the wadi at different points. Excavations have shown that although what we see today was a Roman affair, there existed earlier an unpaved Nabatean street.

On the right near the confluence of the two wadis, by a big tree, stood a semi-circular **nymphaeum**. Facing, on the left of the street, well-placed in the hillside, are the remnants of **two pillars**, flanked by a wall. Hardly noticeable to most visitors, these are most likely vestiges of a votive shrine.

plenty of shopping

A little further on, wide steps lead up to what was the main **market**, the entrance to which had two columns, now fallen. Adjacent to this (W) are two further enclosures that seem likely to have been

195

The Urn Tomb

either further market places or other public places such as a **forum**. The frontages of these areas facing the colonnaded street had small shops or stores, and their remains can be seen. It is strange today, in this mountain-locked enclave trodden now only by the curious, to conjure up images of bustling markets and streets thronged with shoppers.

Back on the right side, and past the nymphaeum is a Byzantine structure, and beyond that are remains which were possibly a palace, though for the ordinary visitor there is hardly anything to see. It appears that a bridge crossed the wadi at this point.

temple to an unknown god

At the end of the Great Colonnade is a **monumental gateway** but just before it on the left (S), steps lead up the bank. At the top is another short incline with fallen pillars. These steps were the *propylaea* to a *temenos* of a large temple on the hill behind. There is no definite information as to which deity this temple was dedicated. Excavations are continuing at this location. Standing here you can see the pillar known as **Zibb Faroun** over to the SSW (see the end of Tour No.6).

newly excavated baths

To the west of this temple are the ruins of **Roman baths** only recently excavated. These consisted of three chambers, one circular and the other two square. Around the wall of the circular chamber are 8 short columns with niches between them. Each chamber was topped by a dome with an opening for light in its centre. Although these rooms are currently below ground level, it is probable that this was not so at the time of use.

gateway of many names

The monumental gateway marked the end of the Great Colonnaded Street and opened onto the *temenos* of the temple (Qasr al-Bint) a little further west. This gate is called, variously, **Temenos Gate, Triumphal Arch, Roman Arch,** or just **Monumental Arch.** It is one of the few erected (as against rock-carved) monuments still standing in Petra. It was built towards the end of the 2nd C AD. The gateway consists of the main, central opening, flanked by smaller ones on either side, and is decorated with both Hellenistic and Nabatean motifs. On both the north and south sides the gate was bounded by towers, and you can see remnants of these. The southern tower is the most interesting, as it contains a vestibule that led into the baths, although this is now blocked.

view to the temple of winged lions

Standing on a hill to the north of the gate, and across the wadi, is **the Temple of the Winged Lions**, a Nabatean structure dating from either the end of the final century BC or the beginning of the first AD. You can just pick out the remains of the steps that climbed the bank. In those times a bridge spanned Wadi Musa and a path led to the *propylaeum.* The temple was excavated in the early 1970s, and it was the column blocks, decorated with winged lions that gave it the name.

temple forecourt

As noted above, the gateway led on to the *temenos* of the great temple at the foot of al-Habees which is known today as **Qasr al-Bint** (see below). The south side of the *temenos,* which is a rectangle, is shown to have had two rows of benches where spectators sat to watch the religious events that took place there. On these seats near the temple a block of sandstone was discovered in 1964 which turned out to be the base of a statue of Aretas IV (8 BC-AD 40). The block was inscribed in Nabatean and dates from the beginning of the first century AD.

Of the north side of the *temenos* nothing remains as the flow down Wadi Musa has eroded whatever was there.

▶ QASR AL-BINT

Qasr al-Bint (al-Faroun), the castle of (Pharaoh's) daughter acquired its name from the habit of the local Bedouin to attribute so much to the great rulers of ancient Egypt. Why a pharaoh's daughter? Well no one really knows! Burckhardt simply records that it was the name given to it by the local inhabitants.

It is usual to ascribe Qasr al-Bint to the god Dusares (Dhu-esh Shera) although Margaret Murray, in her book *Petra, the Rock City of Edom* has suggested that it may have been dedicated to Al-Uzza. (See box on Gods of the Nabateans, page 172.)

2000 year old temple

Once it was thought to have been built in the Roman era, but archaeological research now places its construction in the late Nabatean period. Some evidence points to the last years of the final century BC, yet other indications, such as the statue base of Aretas IV, makes a date in the first half of the first century AD possible. What is clear, is that it is a temple.

only surviving building

Qasr al-Bint is the only building in Petra still surviving that was built, and not rock hewn. Now just a ruin, this was once a magnificent monument, described by Burckhardt as a *"stately edifice"*.

The front was on the north side and opened out onto the *temenos.* It was a vast portico with four enormous pillars, impressive remains of which still stand. This portico was part of the actual building and not an extension of it. Atop the portico was a decorated pediment. The vestibule was approached by steps, still in a fair state of preservation, which ran the entire width of the facade.

entry to the inner sanctuary

The actual entrance into the building was through a high arched portal, once with a lintel above it, in the wall at the rear of the portico. Inside this portal, and comprising the full width of the building, was the *cella* (sacred chamber) and forward of this the inner sanctuary or *adyton*. This inner sanctuary was divided into three parts: a central flight of steps (which would have led up to the edifice) flanked by two niches, both with a second storey. The back wall of this *adyton* was double with perhaps a metre between the two walls.

rich decoration

The exterior of the temple was highly decorated, and some of this decoration is still in evidence. On the south (rear) and west wall some carved stucco and plaster remains visible.

Just before the entrance steps is a large area strewn with blocks of masonry some 12 metres square and originally about 3 metres high. Excavations by P.J. Parr in the 1960s have shown this to be an external altar platform. This feature can be more readily viewed in conjunction with the temple from the heights of al-Habees (see Tour No 5).

time for a break

The area around Qasr al-Bint is the rest area. Here are a number of tented refreshment places which serve tea, cold drinks and light snacks. Across the bridge that spans Wadi Musa, on the right, is the Forum Restaurant, a high class, airconditioned facility complete with spotless toilets and washrooms! It is a sight few would expect to find in this locale — and very welcome so long as it remains the only one!

▸ MUSEUM

On the eastern side of al-Habees, the large rock that overlooks the rest area, is a small museum that displays some of the artefacts found all over Petra. The place is not too interesting.

beware the midday sun

Depending on the time of day you have arrived here you may decide to take a break from touring now. If you are visiting in the warmer months of the year, the siesta hours between noon and 2.30-3.00 may be too hot for serious activity. If it is very hot, even the proverbial mad dogs etc really should keep out of the midday sun – it can be dangerous!

> **Tour No 4 – Rest area to al-Deir**

MAIN FEATURES: **The Lion Tomb — The Hermitage — Al Deir (The Monastery).** TIME: **return trip 2-3 hours** TERRAIN: **The path there ascends almost all the way, sometimes steeply, but taken slowly, even the most senior readers will be able to make it! If possible, make this tour in the afternoon as the path will then be mostly in the shade and the Deir's facade will be sunlit.**

► THE LION TOMB

From the Forum Restaurant head north following a track that runs along Wadi al-Deir, signposted towards the **Lion Tomb** or **Triclinium.** This part of the trip is easy and in the springtime wild flowers and oleanders offer a dash of colour to the sandy way. After a short while an opening to the left leads up to the triclinium. The rock-hewn path has steps at the steepest sections. The triclinium is situated near a small wadi on the left and, thoughtfully, a signpost has been placed there.

another urn

This monument achieved its name because of the carved lions on either side of the entrance. Their state of preservation is so poor that it may be difficult to recognise them at an initial glance. The tomb is of classical design, probably from the period of Roman rule. The facade is well decorated with side pilasters and an elaborately carved frieze with a head of Medusa at each end.
The pediment is topped by – guess what? Yes, an urn!

following the sacred way

Back on the main path you soon reach the first flight of steps. These steps have been recut many times. In its time this route was, undoubtedly, a *via sacra* or processional way. The stepped path ascends through a narrow steep gorge. The incline is now quite precipitous, and every now and again a panoramic view opens up over the deep gorge. Eventually you come to a signpost which indicates **the Hermitage.** This is a cave in which crosses have been carved on the walls indicating occupation by Christians, probably in the Byzantine era.

► AL-DEIR

striking sight

Not far beyond the Hermitage, the path, after narrowing between boulders, opens out to a broad, flat terrace-like area. To the right (E) is the colossal facade of **the Deir.** Though architecturally inferior to the Khasneh, seeing it at the right time of day (in late afternoon), it is a sight only marginally less impressive.

The enormous frontage has been hewn out of the yellow sandstone mountain. It is 50 metres wide (the Khasneh measures but 28!) and 40 metres high. The urn on top alone is 10 metres high — greater than the height of five men! The simplicity of the Doric frieze, coupled with its immense size, compensates for its lack of elegance and decoration when compared to the Khasneh.

a succession of deities

Inside the 8 metre high doorway is one large chamber measuring 11.5 by 10 metres. At the rear of this chamber is a niche, with steps leading up to it, which would have held the deity the temple was dedicated to. It must have been used by Christians in the Byzantine era as crosses have been found on the walls; hence the name al-Deir, the Monastery.

Because of its size it can be assumed that this was an important temple. This is reinforced by the fact that a *via sacra* led to it and also that the vast area preceding it could have been used for congregational ceremonies.

climb to the urn

It is possible here to climb up to the urn and enjoy a remarkable view. The way up is on the left, where there are some rather worn steps which continue in steep flights to the top of the facade.

Walk over to the west side of the area, in front of the Deir on the edge of the plateau, for a dramatic vista of Wadi Arava. You should also be able to glimpse Jabal Haroun, topped by the white shrine to Aaron.

The way down is the same as you came up, but the views will be substantially different, and the trek much easier!

► Tour No 5 – Al-Habees

MAIN FEATURES: **Magnificent panoramic view over Petra**
TIME: **1-1.5 hours.** TERRAIN: **Strenuous rock climb. Only for those used to such activity.**

Al-Habees is the precipitous rock rising just behind Qasr al-Bint to its southwest. Surrounded by Wadi Siyagh to the north and west, Wadi Thughra to the south and the wide valley of the central city in the east, it appears like an island when looking at a map. Because of its commanding position over the centre of Petra it has also been called *Acropolis Hill.*

accessible from the west face

Almost at the top are the scant remains of a **Crusader fort,** but the main reason for wanting to climb is the view. From the top, or somewhere near it, the whole expanse of the main city of Petra is spread out below in a broad spectacle.

The north and east faces of al-Habees are so sheer that only a mountaineer could scale them, but from the west it is more accessible.

The way to climb

Go east around Qasr al-Bint, and take the ascending path towards Zibb Faroun (see Tour No 6). Immediately opposite the pillar (which is on your left as you approach it), two paths fork off. Take the right fork (heading west, the "main" one) and al-Habees is facing you. Continue towards the rock following the path as it skirts the rock. Above, high on the rock is the fort, but it can only be reached from further on.

watch for the (fallen?) signpost

After a while there is a rather shabby sign that points the way up to the fort. At my last visit this sign had fallen down and the writing was very weathered so keep your eyes out for it. The first part of the climb is over loose rocks, but soon rock cut steps are reached. From here its a matter of climbing, partly by steps and partly by scrambling up the rocks.

Crusader remains

Eventually the remnants of the stronghold come into view. There is not much; just enough to show that a presence was once here! This Crusader presence in Petra was, probably, the last incursion of "outsiders" into this rock city until Burckhardt's relatively recent visit.

serenity and beauty

The view from up here is stunning, extending from almost beyond the theatre down to Qasr al-Bint, and it is just possible to spot the Deir to the northwest, but you will have to look very carefully. In all probability, you will be alone up here, undisturbed by the crowds you may have encountered below, the mountain top uncluttered and serene. If you have brought lunch with you, as I recommend you do, there is no finer spot to enjoy it.

▸ The other way down

If you did not make use of a guide, and want to return from the other side, descend to where you saw the sign that pointed up to the fort and turn right (N), following the ridge around. Eventually, deep below you will see Wadi Siyagh. Somewhere to the left, near the precipice, are steps that will lead part of the way down to a path (slightly difficult to locate), which will take you to the mouth of the wadi.

Alternatively, instead of taking the steps down you can follow the path further around the rock to where it finally reaches the **museum** above the rest area.

▸ **Tour No 6** – **From the Theatre to the Zibb 'Attuf High Place and along Wadi Farasa to Qasr al-Bint**

MAIN FEATURES: **Obelisks — Zibb 'Attuf Great High Place — Wadi Farasa — Lion Monument — Garden Tomb — Roman Soldier, Broken Pediment and Renaissance Tombs — Zibb Faroun — Qasr al-Bint.** TIME: **2.5-3 hours.** TERRAIN: **The ascent is a very steep, 25-35 minute climb mostly up rock cut steps, but there are a few tricky parts. Once at the top some rock scrambling is required to reach the precipice. The descent via Wadi Farasa is easy, but long. The best time for this tour is in the morning as the ascending route will be mostly in the shade.**

Starting point

The route starts a short way before the theatre and is clearly signed. The ancient rock steps have been renovated where possible and the whole way has been rendered very safe. As you climb glance back at the view, especially of the gorge below, as you will not be descending this way if you follow the full tour. This was a processional route which led to one of Petra's — indeed the Nabatean's — most important high places of sacrifice.

When you almost reach the top the path turns sharply west (there is a Bedouin tea tent at the bend) and continues up a little way more to where it opens out into a wide area that has been levelled.

obelisks chiselled from summit

On the left (S), high above, are two **obelisks** some 7 metres high which were hewn out of the sandstone rock. These obelisks are all that remained of that summit after it was levelled. The effort in achieving this can only be imagined! Although there is no definite evidence, many scholars think that these blocks are representations of the god Dushares (see box on gods) who was often depicted in a stone block form.

phallic obsession

Curiously the Arab name for this plateau is **Zibb 'Attuf**, zibb being Arabic for a phallus. This could indicate, assuming the name has been handed down over the years, that the obelisks were manifestations of a fertility goddess. A more simple (and likely) answer would lie in the shape association, as with the Zibb Faroun pillar (see Tour No 3 and below)!

On the north side, are the very scant remains of a fort which could be either Byzantine or Crusader, although the former is more likely. Between the ruins a path, at first stepped and then requiring some scrambling over the rocks, leads to the plateau and the **Great High Place.** (There is a signpost pointing the direction just below the fort ruins.)

fabulous high place of the gods

There were numerous religious sites in the Nabatean realm, and many were in Petra. Of them all the Zibb 'Attuf High Place was, in all probability, the most hallowed, and the most important. Over 1000 metres above sea level and 200 metres above the wadi below, this altar area offers one of the finest views in all Petra, and was thus an appropriate place to celebrate sacrificial rites.

In ancient days gods were often thought to inhabit the "high places" and it is probable that this one was sacred long before the Nabatean city of Petra made it one of prominence.

drains for the blood

The plateau is about 60 by 20 metres and the sanctuary area consists of a large rectangle known as the central court. Almost in the centre of this court is a raised platform. To the west of this platform and outside the rectangle three steps lead up to the main altar. The channels for the blood run-off are clearly visible. A couple of metres to the south of this altar, and also approached by three steps is another altar, this one circular. In this one an opening in the centre allowed the sacrificial blood to drain away. Further to the south was a water cistern with channels on the north and south sides. Water was an essential element for post sacrificial cleansing.

Blood sacrifices were an integral part of almost every ancient religion, blood being the usual symbol of life. (In the biblical narrative, the blood of a lamb on the doorposts of the Hebrews' homes in Egypt spared the lives of the first born sons.) Sacrifice was also the method of entreating deities for favours and for atonement. Although there is no evidence that the Nabateans indulged in human sacrifice, the concept cannot be entirely ruled out.

see it all from here

The precipice faces north and the view down to the central city is fantastic. It is from here that the valley in which Petra lies can be best appreciated. In one broad panoramic expanse you can take in everything from the Royal Tombs to Qasr al-Bint, with al-Habees behind. Those with really sharp eyes who know what to look for will be able to pick out the urn of al-Deir: look NNW (310 degrees) between a cleft in the mountain. To the west is the flat-topped Umm Biyara, with many sepulchres at its base. Umm Biyara is higher than

Zibb 'Attuf and perhaps the site of the first settlement in Petra. To the SW is Jabal Haroun with the small white shrine at the summit which is said to be the tomb of Aaron, Moses' priestly brother. Almost due east the village of Wadi Musa slopes down the ravine, while almost facing to the NE is the Khubtha Massive. The village to the north is village of Bdul, where settled Bedouin from the area live.

visions of carnage

If you are lucky, you will be almost alone up here, the emptiness and tranquillity providing a total contrast to the hubbub below. The atmosphere carries a peculiar quality and it doesn't require very much imagination to visualise the calm being breached by the primitive and bloody rites that were enacted on this place. Often though, especially in high season, there will be so many other visitors that this eeriness will be obscured.

To descend from the High Place, return first to the area below the fort. Those with little time can now go back the way they came, but our tour takes a different route and descends into **Wadi Farasa.**

► WADI FARASA

The route down is via short flights of steps, sandy and rocky paths, and finally enters the wadi via a rather spectacular and lengthy twisting rock stairway.

Almost facing the fort, to the right, is another of those Bedouin tea places, a little smarter than most. Follow the track which leads past it south. After c50 metres a gap in the rocks to the right reveals some rock cut steps which descend through a short rock corridor and along a rough path. Continue along this for about 150 metres until another set of steps is reached. Just before these and to the right by a spreading tree, is an overhang of rock with a **Nabatean inscription** carved on the rock face underneath. You can recognise its Nabatean origin by the elongated letters. It is the longest such inscription found in Petra.

Carry on down the steps and along the path at the bottom. To the left, are some strangely shaped rounded black rocks. The route then descends and almost immediately ascends short flights of steps before proceeding downwards along a path. Further along, the route turns sharply left and goes down some more rock steps, with a sandy path at the bottom.

rainbow sands

The sand and rock along the route varies in colour from pink to red to green to brown and all the other shades that are sifted into bottles and sold by the Bedouin across the site. Then a short stretch of ascending steps passes through a narrow stone passage. Walking at an average pace it would have taken you 15-20 minutes to reach this point.

the not-so-headless lion

The path then opens out into a wide area before turning right. Here on the left, and clearly signed, is the **Lion Monument**. This 5 metre carving on the mountain face, in a very deteriorated condition, shows the animal's body in profile, its tail curling upwards, its head facing out (some say it is headless, but close examination reveals one of sorts). As there are remnants of a water channel above the head it is presumed that this was a drinking fountain, with the water flowing through a pipe so it would come out of the mouth. This route was a way up to the sacred high place, and in the summer heat the worshippers would pause and drink here on the way.

striking rock staircase

Past the lion carving very steep winding steps make their way down through a striking rock passage to the floor of Wadi Farasa. As you descend these steps notice how the rock overhangs the path in places forming a roof. The colouring of the rock strata is marvellous here, with deep purple and almost gold-like seams among the streaking.

desert garden (sometimes!)

At the bottom the route turns north along the sandy ground of the wadi bed. Ahead is the **Garden Tomb** or the **Farasa Triclinium** as it is signposted. The edifice is on a level area with a sort of "garden" terrace preceding it, although the garden aspect of it will only be appreciated in or just after the spring. The facade, Hellenistic in style, is very weathered. Four columns, two free-standing and one at each end, are topped by a badly worn entablature.

To the right of the tomb, and above it by a brick wall, is a huge cistern which was able to collect water as it cascaded down the rocks. A pipe outlet for the water can be seen at the very bottom of the wall. In spring the whole setting is extremely attractive, with much greenery punctuated by wild flowers. By high summer and autumn this will have turned to quite a dreary brown with a little patchy scrub, and the garden setting will be lost.

crumbling statuary

Past the garden triclinium the final flight of steps lead, this time gently, down to the main part of the wadi and the **Tomb of the Roman Soldier** on the left (W) with another **triclinium** facing it. A Bedouin refreshment tent is situated just before the triclinium. Set back from the path, the tomb has a straightforward classical facade with the capitals and parts of the pilasters having some typical Nabatean ornamentation. Three niches, halfway up, house very dilapidated statues. The centre one is a headless figure in a short tunic that some say could be Roman armour (hence the name of the place) while the other two are not recognisable although they appear almost naked.

Whether the figure in the central niche is the person for whom the tomb was prepared is impossible to know; suffice it to say that it must have been for a man of rank and standing, though not necessarily a Roman!

Bedouin barbecues?

The doorway is decorated with pilasters that support a pediment. Inside the tomb there are two rooms. One has arched recesses. The walls are black from the fires which Bedouin must have lit in here over the centuries.

elegant interior

Facing the tomb is the outstanding **triclinium,** possibly having a linkage with the tomb. It has no facade but this is compensated for by an elaborate interior. Many tombs in Petra have nothing to see inside; this one has. The cavernous room is about 100 square metres in area and is the only monument in Petra with a carved interior. Engraved and fluted semi-columns divide the walls into alcoves. By each alcove is a rectangular niche. The walls are further enhanced by the coloured strata of the sandstone.

The place was used for funeral rites and feasts, with the participants sitting at long tables along the three sides (hence triclinium). In the centre was a raised platform which can still be made out.

Italianesque?

The path continues its way in a north-westerly direction, and after a short distance, on the right, you will see the **Renaissance Tomb.** There is no apparent reason for this name other than that its graceful doorway has a design that may evoke to some a similarity to Italian Renaissance architecture.

artistic doorway

Facing west, and preceded by a courtyard, this is the sole monument of its style in Petra. Today much worn, the doorway must have been very handsome in its day, a work of undoubted artistry. Above the door is a segmented arch that sits on the pilasters and entablatures. The lofty facade with a low pediment follows the Petra style in that it is topped by an urn.

unfinished sepulchre

Further along the wadi where the gorge opens out, high up on the right (E) and facing to the north is the **Broken Pediment Tomb.** Because of its high position facing the way of the tour route you can only see it after walking past it and then glancing back. It is reached by a well-worn flight of steps which led to a terrace the width of the facade. It appears that this tomb was never used, as there were plans to cut a whole series of *loculi,* but only four at the back were ever actually cut. It's easy to see how it acquired its name!

Past this tomb the path opens out, and on the right, high in the cliff face are many tombs, most having the Nabatean crow-stepped ornamentation.

remains of the city walls

The path soon veers west and descends. At the bottom another sandy track turns north (right), but our route continues in a westerly direction. (If you want to curtail this tour, the path north will lead you back to the theatre area.) To your left you will see a blue sign warning that it is not advisable to leave the paths without a guide or companion. Carry on past this sign, but do not descend into the narrow wadi bed to the left. Stay on the ascending path which is to the right, keeping Umm Biyara to your left. Not too far along, the path turns left, still slightly ascending. On the right are remains of Petra's walls.

the virile pharaoh

Another short ascent will bring you to a further relic of the walls, and then to the solitary pillar known as **Zibb Faroun**. Of this pillar Burckhardt wrote in his *Travels*, *"On the rising ground...are the ruins of a temple, with one column yet standing to which the Arabs have given the name of Zib Faraoun, i.e. hasta virilis Pharaonis..."*. The partially-eroded pillar we see today appears to have been somewhat emasculated!

This pillar stands while another lies fragmented on the ground, unmoved since it fell. As mentioned earlier, the local Bedouin dubbed everything grandiose as a product of a pharaoh, but in reality nothing here has any connection with such a person. It would appear that a shrine or temple once stood on the spot, and these pillars could have been part of the entrance. As with the Zibb High Place, the temple could perhaps have been dedicated to a fertility goddess.

parting of the ways

At this point two tracks, one coming from al-Habees to the west, and another from Umm-Biyara to the south west, join our route. These are the paths you will need to take if you want to climb either of these peaks.

hidden treasure?

Qasr al-Bint al-Faroun (the Castle of Pharaoh's Daughter) is a short walk to the northwest, along the path you are on, and you will see that the area towards it is considerably higher than around that monument (the last section of the route is a descent). Some have speculated that this high ground is in fact a vast *tell* hiding deeply buried remains of the city. There is plenty of rubble about to support this. Qasr al-Bint is described in Tour No 3.

► **Tour No 7 – Ascent of Umm al-Biyara**

MAIN FEATURES: **Wadi Thugra — Umm al-Biyara (Mother of Cisterns) — fantastic views**   TIME: **3 to 4 hours.** TERRAIN: **Difficult and strenuous. Only for really fit persons.**

Don't climb alone

The climb to the flat summit of **Umm al-Biyara**, which translates Mother of Cisterns, is very worthwhile if you have the time and energy. The ascent should *only* be made in the afternoon when the eastern face is in the shade. A guide is definitely advisable, but not essential if you have a good sense of direction. I do not recommend anyone to climb alone. A guide can be procured from around the rest area.

The way there

Go east around Qasr al-Bint, and take the ascending path towards the pillar of Zibb Faroun (see Tour No 6). Just opposite the pillar on the right of the road, two tracks fork off. The right fork (W), (the main-looking one) leads to Al-Habees. Take the other track (southwest) and this will take you down into **Wadi Thughra**. Just past a clump of bushes look up to the west and you should be able to see a white sign at the base of Umm Biyara. Make your way to this sign.

The way to climb

The ascent is via a cleft in the rock found practically behind this sign. However you cannot reach it directly as fallen rocks block the way. Carry on south until you come to a tree and you will see an obvious detour route to reach the cleft.

amazing rock-hewn corridor

A little way up along the path of loose stones you reach a dramatic smooth ramp that ascends between lofty smooth rock walls. This rock hewn corridor is one of the marvels of Petra. The section here is a fairly easy ascending hike. At the beginning are the remains of an arch that once spanned this spectacular pathway. There seems no plausible reason why the Nabateans constructed such a monumental course. Although there are many ruins at the top there are no traces of any temples of importance.

Further along, the ramp bends back on itself before continuing upwards. The left side of this return ramp has a protecting wall.

a tough climb

Past the ramp the ascent becomes much more difficult as the fallen rock and erosion has all but obliterated the path. What started off as quite an easy hike now becomes a real climb with sheer drops to one side most of the way. Often you may have to use all four limbs to negotiate some stretches safely. The direction of the path is also none too easy to follow, and the services of a guide would greatly ease the progress.

It takes between 40 and 60 minutes to get to the summit which, being a wide plateau, is reached suddenly; you cannot see it until you are virtually on it. Arrival is on the south side, the terrain rising gently towards the north west which is the highest area. The plateau is covered in light brush and is treeless.

Edomite settlement at the summit

The Edomite settlement of Umm al-Biyara uncovered by Crystal-M Bennett is at the centre. Excavations in the early 1960s revealed a community that existed in the 7th and 6th centuries BC. In the area explored, houses and other units have been uncovered, all leading off one main long wall. The stone walls are built of the local stone which was very easy to break. No mortar was used to hold them. The floors were simply beaten earth.

discovery of King's seal

The finds include fragments of pottery, many domestic items and the burnt remains of looms. A seal of the King of Edom was also discovered, but without the tablet it was once attached to.

It is assumed that this small Edomite village was an agricultural settlement. It was completely incinerated down to its foundations.

family of cisterns

There are eight cisterns cut deeply out of the rock summit (hence the name Mother of Cisterns). They are assumed to be Edomite, and they show how even at that early time the local people were adept at rock cutting. Although the cisterns were all filled with debris when found, one has since been cleared revealing its considerable depth.

On the eastern side a terrace-like area right at the edge contains some Nabatean remains. As a statuette of an unidentified deity was discovered nearby it is thought these may be of a small temple.

many great views

From this side there is also a fine view over Petra, and slightly to the south a scary and dramatic drop to Wadi Thughra From the western side there is a commanding view across to Wadi Arava, and on a clear day the heights of the Negev and even Sinai may be visible. From the south west, Jabal Haroun with its shrine is very clear.

I have heard that one of the finest views from the summit of al-Biyara is the dawn breaking, but I suspect few will ever experience it!

The descent is much faster than the ascent. Do it, though, in the hours of daylight, remembering that in these latitudes there is but a fleeting twilight.

▸ Tour No 8 – Wadi al-Siyagh

MAIN FEATURES: **Wadi Kharrubatt — Quarry — Siyagh Spring**
TIME: **1-1.5 hours.** TERRAIN: **Very easy walk.**

The way to walk

After a lot of climbing, and with a little time to spare, a walk along this seasonable watercourse makes a pleasant change.

Enter **Wadi al-Siyagh** from the rest area. It is always cooler here than out in the open areas, and for most of the day the foliage gives plenty of shade. Follow the wadi in a roughly westerly direction.

ancient quarry

After about 15-20 minutes you come to a junction with **Wadi Kharrubatt,** with the latter coming from the south. Al-Siyagh bends around northerly before turning west again. Follow this, and at the point where it turns west an ancient **quarry** can be seen on the northern side.

Huge quantities of stone have been cut from this quarry and used all over Petra in past centuries. It is generally assumed to have been excavated by the Nabateans, but it could have also been used before their arrival.

figs, olives and flowing water

The watercourse, even if dry, now becomes muddy in places. Oleanders grow profusely and the wadi begins to descend. Here some areas are fenced off, with olive trees growing in the enclosures. As the wadi continues, more and more vegetation appears, including fig trees as well as olives. These are all cultivated by local Bedouin, and the environment is completely different from the surrounding semi-desert.

You can now see water flowing from **Ain Siyagh,** the Siyagh Spring, and this continues right down into the canyon whose walls tower ever higher.

As you make your way further along, the stream has to be crossed and recrossed to progress down the wadi. After a few hundred metres you will reach a deep pool of very cool flowing water. Water falls into it (depending on the time of year) from the steep canyon sides. During the wet season it becomes a torrent. The gorge narrows suddenly here and descends sharply (this is about as far as one can go), eventually emptying into the Arava.

Return the same way.

> ### Tour No 9 – Al-Beidha and Siq al-Barid

MAIN FEATURES: **Castle of "Valley of Moses" (Al-Wu'aira) — Al Beidha — Seyl Aqlat — The Painted House — Siq al-Barid** TIME: **1.5 hours.** TERRAIN: **Except for the far end of Siq al-Barid, easy walking.**

How to get there

You need transport to get to these adjacent sites located some 12 km north of the Forum Hotel on a good tarmac road. It is best to go first thing in the morning as by late afternoon the siq is in full shadow.

Follow the road from the Forum Hotel turning left (N) at the nearby junction. After a couple of kilometres, just before the road ascends to the west, are the remains of **al-Wu'aira**, a Crusader castle.

▸ VALLEY OF MOSES (Al-Wu'aira) CRUSADER CASTLE

Warning beacons

The Crusaders called it *Le Vaux Moyse*, the Valley of Moses. Built in 1127 by Baldwin II, king of Jerusalem, the castle today comprises of a building with arches, vaulted rooms and the walls. Though modest in size it was far larger than both the forts on al-Habees and Zibb 'Attuf. From here a beacon could be seen at the great Castle of Shobak (Mont-Réal) (see page 160), so it might have been used as an early warning station in the Crusader chain of castles and forts along the King's Highway.

From here, continue to Seyl Aqlat as described below.

▸ SEYL AQLAT

How to get there

From the Crusader castle the road continues, passing through a Bedouin village, till it reaches its end. There, turn left onto the track and Siq al-Barid is a few hundred metres ahead. Park out of the way.

A track leads from this parking area south to **Al-Beidha**, about 1.5 kilometres away. Follow the path south and just over a rise there is a fork. Take the left one and very shortly you will come to the excavations inside a fenced off area.

The site

recent important find

The early neolithic village of Seyl Aqlat is one of the most famous and important archaeological finds of the area in the last 50 years. The site dates from c7000 BC, and is contemporary with pre-pottery Jericho. The location was discovered in 1956 by Diana Kirkbride with help from the local Bedouin. The excavations began a couple of years later and have been very revealing.

Seven levels have been excavated, although the last two did not reveal any permanent type of dwellings. The digs show so many levels of building that it is very difficult to obtain a discernible picture of the layout. Like so many of these archaeological sites, you need a trained eye to realise the details.

round houses

Of the first 5 levels it appears that each level lasted for around 60-70 years. It also appears that at the earlier levels the houses were circular, and some of these are discernable. Later buildings acquired a more rectangular shape, but the corners remained rounded. At an even later time, as was discovered on level 2, the buildings consisted of a corridor with rooms on either side, which may have been dwellings or workshops. These houses were built of mud and stone as you can see by standing on the northern edge. Later on some may have been made only of stone, as on the west side there is a building of this type. The houses were partly subterranean and may have been roofed with mud and branches, although this is not known for sure.

early hunting man

The inhabitants were mainly hunters and nomads, but when they learned how to plant grasses and develop hybrids they began a more settled existence. Around the top of the diggings are **querns**. These were used for grinding corn and storage purposes.

Finds here include bone tools, flints that were worked into cutting tools, arrowheads and other tools. Man had not yet learned how to fashion pottery although some very crude clay items have been found.

destroyed by fire

Fire finally destroyed the place, and after c6500 BC it was not settled again, although the Nabateans used the area for agriculture, terracing it in places. The area around this site is often used by Bedouin who still live in tents and one camp is usually sited on the rise to the east on the way back to the parking area.

Return to where you parked your car at Siq al-Barid to explore the gorge.

► SIQ AL-BARID

Siq al-Barid, or Little Petra as it is often called, is a gorge divided into three sections.

Entry is via a very narrow rock passage preceded by an iron gate. Before this entry, on the right is a fine **classical temple**. Inside the gorge are two monuments of main interest. The first is a modest hypogeum (tomb) with a portico *in antis*. Of the two pillars, one is so badly worn that it looks quite odd.

naked figures and cherubs

The second monument is often termed the **Painted House**. This is also a sepulchre and you reach it by climbing a flight of rock-cut steps. Inside, the walls show remains of stucco and it was painted with naked figures, winged cupids chasing different birds and bunches of grapes. All this is in a very deteriorated condition as the building has been used by shepherds and the like over the centuries. In addition to these two edifices, there are a number of caves which may have been storerooms, and many cisterns.

a boulder blocks the way

At the far end of the gorge, a long flight of rock steps leads up to a flat area. The first part of this ascent is quite straightforward, but later a boulder blocks the way, and can only be got around with difficulty. Once round it you will be rewarded by a fine view. There are supposed to be steps down from this end but I do not know anyone who has used them. The gorge is well endowed with greenery, and the pink oleanders lend their usual dash of colour. It is generally quiet and deserted here.

► Tour No 10 – Al-Madras

MAIN FEATURES: **Al-Madras excavations**   TIME: **60-75 minutes.**
TERRAIN: **Some rock stair climbing is required.**

How to get there

Al-Madras is a "suburb" of Petra brimming with a variety of monuments. It is located high on the mountain to the south of the Siq entrance. Some 50 metres before the dam, on the left, is a blue sign pointing to the suburb. Just to the right of the sign is a pathway that runs behind a stone wall towards the cliffs. After crossing some shrub to a rocky area you will see some stone piles which mark the way. Keep west, following the stone piles until you come to the rock-cut steps leading to al-Madras. There are four flights of Nabatean steps before you reach it.

Dushara, god of Madrasa

The site abounds with rock cut tombs, cisterns, votive niches etc. We know the area had the name Madras in Nabatean times from an inscription mentioning *Dushara, god of Madrasa* which was discovered here. The translation of the word Madras poses a problem. In conventional Arabic *madrasa* means school, but there may be a different meaning in Nabatean.

This is a very attractive location, particularly at sunset, and makes a pleasant end to the day — assuming there is still energy left!

> ▸ **Tour No 11 – Jabal Haroun**

MAIN FEATURES: **Tomb of Aaron — the views.** TIME: **At least six hours.** TERRAIN: **This is a long hike and an exhausting climb. Only for experienced climbers.**

▸ AARON'S TOMB

It is possible to climb Jabal Haroun, the mountain with the "tomb" of Aaron, though the views are similar to those from Umm al-Biyara. **A guide is essential to ascend this mountain**, and it will take about 6 hours for a return trip from the rest area. It is a steep exhausting hike and climb, only for the experienced climber.

7th century tomb

The tomb at the top was erected by Muslims in the first years of the Islamic conquest. It was restored by Qalaun, the Mameluke Sultan in the late 13th C. At one time, before Qalaun's restoration, some Byzantine monks lived there.

This mountain was identified with the Mount Hor of the Bible in the early years of Christianity, but since the Edomites barred the Hebrews' way through this area (Numbers 20:14-21), I cannot see how this can be anything other than an apocryphal site. The views to the Arava and Negev are superb.

13. Wadi Rumm

"We were riding for Rumm...a place which stirred my thoughts, as even the unsentimental Howeitat had told me it was lovely..."

T. E. Lawrence, *Seven Pillars of Wisdom, 1926*

INTRODUCTION

And lovely it still is; but certainly not at first sight when you will be surrounded and accosted by the local Bedouin, now greedy for the tourist dollar. To fully appreciate this piece of magnificent desert scenery, the finest in the entire Middle East, you must penetrate deep into the valley, and wait till evening —

"We entered Rumm at last, while the crimson sunset burned on its stupendous cliffs and slanted ladders of hazy fire down the walled avenue." (*Seven Pillars of Wisdom*)

awesome and magnificent

The region of Wadi Rumm embraces a series of valleys in southern Jordan, running roughly north to south, which are the result of some great geological disturbance millions of years ago. Traces of fossilised marine life have been found, signifying that it was once covered by ocean. The valley is about 120 kilometres long, dotted with lofty mountains, many of which carry the title *Umm*, or Mother (of). In some places these are so close together that they rise up like sheer canyon sides, and the valley's extraordinary rock formations are endlessly fascinating. No words of mine can ever describe the awesome magnificence of this place, and in truth only Lawrence, briefly quoted above, has got anywhere near an adequate word picture. I can but refer you to his *Seven Pillars of Wisdom*, chapter 62.

film location

Wadi Rumm itself is the largest of the valleys, always associated with Lawrence, and where most of the biopic of his life was shot. Its breadth is some two kilometres and it is edged by high, rust coloured mountains.

215

changing hues

The colours are the outstanding feature, but you will have to spend a long time here to see them all, as they constantly alter, transforming the purple hues of dawn to stark rusts at noon, to warm orange-reds at sunset and to an eerie black at night.

Few tents are left now, as most Bedouin have adapted to a more sedentary way of life in the villages around. As you would expect, there is little flora, and what there is consists mainly of a coarse grass growing in clumps. What remains of the fauna is now hardly ever seen, unless you find your way to the very outlying parts of the valley.

How to get there

From Aqaba: Wadi Rumm is about an hour's drive from Aqaba: 40 km to the Rumm junction, and then another c30 km along a narrow, but paved road.

From Petra: If you are leaving Wadi Musa for Aqaba early in the morning you will be able to visit Wadi Rumm on the way. The alternatives are either to go there on your way north from Aqaba (but this may leave little time), or make a special journey while staying in Aqaba.

lunar landscape

From Wadi Musa take the signposted route to Aqaba, and after about 30 minutes the road joins the main Amman-Aqaba highway. Continuing south for a further c15 km, you reach Ras al-Naqab. It is here that the plateau comes to a rather abrupt end, and at a height of 1200 metres the view south is quite dramatic, with an almost moon-like aspect to it. The tones of the brown and red hills surrounded by very light reddish sand are especially enhanced at sunrise and sunset, but still wonderful at any time of day. This is one of the finest visual treats in Jordan. There is a rest house here where you can stop for a drink and have an opportunity to enjoy the vista at leisure. The road now winds very steeply to the plain below, a drop of some 600 metres, before sloping gently to sea level at Aqaba. A further c25 km will bring you to the signposted Rumm junction to the east.

once a day bus

For those travelling by public transport there is an early morning bus from Aqaba to Rumm and a late afternoon one back again. As times change, check these first.

take photo mister!

Your first sight of Rumm will not be very exciting: a rest house, where you have to pay a small entrance fee (which includes a drink), with a large parking area; swarms of Bedouin children with camels asking 1 or 2 JD just to photograph them; a village of breeze blocks and huts; and a line of battered jeeps waiting to take you into the valley — at a price!

The nicest and most evocative thing you'll notice is the small fort, complete with tower, which stands out from everything else. A soldier of the Desert Patrol guards the entrance, a force first set up by the (then) Emir Abdullah to keep order in the "untamed" desert region. The soldier will be dressed in the typical Patrol uniform of a full length tunic, *kefiyeh* headdress, bandoliers of bullets and, of course, the curved dagger.

no stars under the stars

You can stay overnight in tents at the Rest House, but facilities are rather spartan — a mattress on the floor — so you will need your own sleeping bag. The washroom is simple but adequate, and you can prepare your own food or eat at the restaurant.

Choosing a tour

Camel or Jeep tours can be booked through the rest house office at government fixed prices, or you can go to the village and negotiate yourself. If you intend to stay only for the day you are better off to choose a jeep tour, as it is only really worthwhile taking a camel if you can spend at least one night camping out; this will add quite a bit on top of the already high price for the camel and guide.

At my last visit in 1995, I negotiated a price for four people to take a 2½ -3 hour jeep tour. At JD 45 it was cheaper than the regulated price, but still expensive when you consider that many Jordanians do not earn that in a month! If you are travelling alone or with one other person, try getting together with other tourists to reduce the price. Too much haggling over price is pointless as you are a captive customer and the locals know how to take advantage of it; such a tour is a must if you have come this far!

Visiting the wadi

ancient graffiti

Besides the beauty of the landscape there are a great number of places where you can see **Nabatean and Thamudic inscriptions** and drawings. The Thamuds are an Arabian tribe, mentioned in the Koran, who first appeared between the 5th century BC and the 7th AD. It seems they were a literate people as most tribesmen were able to write their own names, many of which are still used by Arabs to this day. Their script is unusual, being somewhat akin to that used in Ethiopia.

Jordan's highest

Jabal Rumm, Jordan's loftiest mountain, reaches a height of 1754 metres. A huge sandstone lump that rises nearly 700 metres from the wadi bed, Jabal Rumm sits on a massive base of granite which is 33 metres thick in places.

Between the rest house and the base of the Jabal are the ruins of a **Nabatean temple**, dating from the first century BC. Its rectangular courtyard had rooms on three sides. The east side was open and approached by steps. The walls of the courtyard were plastered, and had engaged pillars. An altar stood in the centre, and during excavations a statue of a goddess was discovered.

Lawrence drank here!

Throughout the wadi there are a number of springs, and one about 2 kilometres south of the rest house bears the unlikely title, **Lawrence's Well**. A track from the southern extremity of the valley leads towards Aqaba, but this route is not for you or me!

For those who wish to explore Wadi Rumm more thoroughly or spend time climbing I can but refer them to excellent books by experts in this field (see bibliography).

14. Aqaba

INTRODUCTION

If ever there was a misnomer, it's the Red Sea, for it is the bluest ocean I have ever seen!

shining sea

Shimmering in almost perpetual sunshine, Aqaba lies at the northernmost end of the eastern arm of that sea, the **Gulf of Aqaba.** (The western arm is the Gulf of Suez.) Four countries border the shores here: Saudi Arabia, Jordan, Israel and Egypt. It also marks the end of an ancient sea route that brought ships around the Arabian peninsular with merchandise from as far away as India and even China.

Only one other town borders the Red Sea at this point — the Israeli resort/port town of Eilat. A little further south on the Egyptian side you can see the resort of Taba touching the shoreline, but this is no more than a hotel complex. On the east side, 12 kilometres to the south is the Saudi border.

sole port

Aqaba is Jordan's only outlet to the sea, and is therefore a very busy port. Nearly all the country's only natural resources, phosphates and potash, are exported through here.

not brassy

Unlike the Israeli town a few kilometres to the west, Aqaba has remained an essentially quiet place. Looking across to the Israeli resort you see a town of high-rise buildings, mainly hotels, reaching right down to the beach, almost obliterating the landscape behind them. Aqaba has remained — and I for one hope it will remain — a largely low rise resort. The hotels that do border the shore are no more than two storeys, and the whole town has a peaceful air about it. Although there is not too much to see here, Aqaba has a rich and important history, which I shall take you through now.

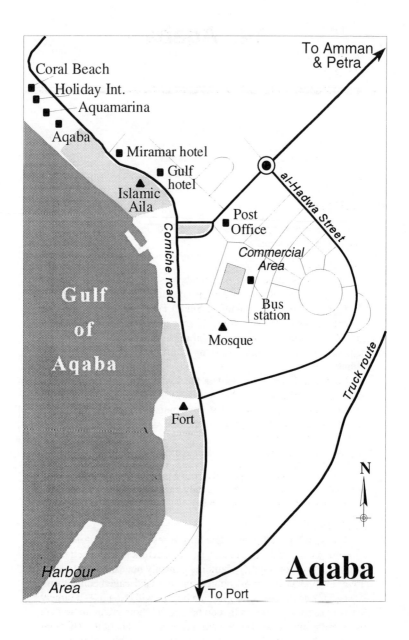

HISTORY

In the Bible, settlements in the Aqaba vicinity have variously been called Etzion-Geber, Elath and Eloth, but it is generally considered that these were one and the same place, (though this seems to contradict the biblical narrative in I Kings 9:26 quoted below).

Israelite camp

Its first mention in the Bible occurs in Numbers 33:35-36 as a place where the Israelites camped during their post-Exodus wanderings. Both Etzion-Geber and Elath are referred to in Deuteronomy 2:8. In Solomonic times the area belonged to Israel and was already a port. As copper is to be found in the vicinity, it was also an industrial centre for the manufacture of copper tools.

Solomon's ships

The names are repeated again in an account about King Solomon's ships: *"King Solomon also built a fleet of ships in Ezion-Geber which is near Eloth on the shore of the Red Sea..." (I Kings 9:26).* The town at this time was a centre for the importation of gold and other precious materials from such distant places as Ophir.

It appears that after Solomon the town changed hands between the Jews and the Edomites (or Syrians) a couple of times. It is called Elath when, in the reign of Ahaz, the Syrians cleared the Judeans "out of Elath", and they (the Syrians or Edomites) retained it (II Kings 16:6). This is the last biblical reference to the town.

one town

The site of the biblical town is most likely a spot called **Tell al-Khalayfa** half a kilometre north of the shoreline and between Aqaba and modern Eilat. Discovered in 1934, it was excavated by Nelson Glueck in 1938, who came to the conclusion that Etzion-Geber and Elath were one and the same place as there was no room at that site for two towns. Several strata of occupation were unearthed in the dig, the best being the Solomonic one.

windy city

The town had an important copper smelting industry, the raw ore being obtained from local mines. (There is a location named "King Solomon's Mines", just north of Eilat, and copper was mined at nearby Timna on the Israeli side until about 1970). It appears that the furnaces were placed on the northern side of the town in order to catch the strong winds that blew down the Arava, enabling them to reach an extreme temperature.

shoreline dilemma

If this site was indeed the port of Ezion-Geber, it has yet to be answered conclusively why it is some distance from today's shore. But this is a puzzle for the archaeologists to answer and on which, no doubt, many pages can be written!

As Tell al-Khalayfa straddles the 1948 Jordan-Israel cease fire line it has been unapproachable for the past 50 years. Perhaps now with the advent of peace further exploration work can be carried out.

goods from China

After the arrival of the Nabateans in the area they built a new town and port on roughly the site of today's Aqaba. It was called Aila and served the Nabateans and subsequently the Romans as a port to which all manner of goodies from lands as distant as India and China were imported. From Aila, trade routes led via Petra to Gaza and to Damascus. When the area was annexed by the Romans in AD 105, Trajan built his great road, the *Via Nova Traiana* which connected Damascus and Petra with Aila (or Aelana as they called it).

the bishop and the caliph

In the third century the Romans transferred a legion to the town and it became an important point of defence throughout the Byzantine era. Some churches were constructed there and the remains of one dedicated to Saints Theodore and Longinius have been discovered. At the time of the Muslim conquest there was a Bishop of Aila, and Caliph Omar lodged with him while on a visit.

discovery of Islamic Aila

In 1986, on a site just off the shore and facing the Aqaba Gulf Hotel, remains of the Islamic port of Aila were uncovered. With traces going back to the pre-Islamic period and continuing into the Fatimid and Crusader eras, this has proved a significant find for the history of the region.

Arab geographers of the 9th and 10th centuries have described the commercial prosperity of Aila on the shores of the "salt sea". One geographer called it a city on a branch of the China sea, such were its links with that country! He added that it had great prosperity with its fish and palms.

pilgrim route

In the medieval era, Aila was a harbour of Palestine and a storehouse of the Hejaz. Being on the *haj* route, roads from North Africa, Egypt and Syria all passed through the thoroughly Muslim port. Typically, the medieval city was enclosed by a stone wall and towers. Two of these towers flanked the main gate and were 4.5 metres high. Above the gate was a Kufic inscription of a well-known verse from the Koran.

Ming vases?

Among artefacts discovered at the site were many items imported from Iraq such as blue-green glazed stone jars, and celadons and porcelains imported from China. Also unearthed were architectural elements from a church and pieces from a Latin inscription. These are possibly relics of an earlier Byzantine occupation of the site but could indicate that Christians lived here alongside the Muslims. A Jewish community also resided in Aila until at least the middle of the tenth century, and perhaps beyond.

island fort

In 1116 Baldwin, the Crusader King of Jerusalem, captured the port and proceeded to build a fort on the island of Jazirat Faroun which they called *Isle de Graye,* about 10 kilometres south of Aila and just off the Sinai coast.

The Crusader presence was eventually brought to an end by the great Muslim warrior, Salah al-Din. From then the town was just a stopping place on the road to Mecca. The Mamelukes constructed a fort for the protection of the pilgrims, and the Ottomans continued to station troops there.

cannon folly

In the First World War the Turks strengthened this garrison expecting an invasion by the British from the sea. The fort's cannon were anchored in that direction (south), and were unable to turn inland. When, in 1917, the Arab army attacked from the north, the fixed guns were useless, and being heavily outnumbered the place quickly fell.

It was the first major victory of the Arab Revolt. Sharif Husayn then used the fort as a headquarters.

advent of Eilat

During the Arab-Israeli war of 1948-9 Israeli soldiers reached the Red Sea and hoisted their flag over the former British Police post of Umm Rashrash. A settlement was established, and from this the town of Eilat has grown. Although the Israelis have chosen something akin to the biblical name for their town, no ancient settlements are known to have existed on the site of modern Eilat.

THE VISIT

beach paradise

Assuming that you have not arrived in the heat of summer when temperatures can soar to over $40°C$, a very enjoyable couple of days or so can be spent here. There will not be much to do except enjoy the beach, the water sports and the crystal clear water, but then who minds that!

In the 1960s Aqaba was still no more than a largish village. The French Hachette Guide *(Guide Bleu)* of that period describes it as "a small port with about 9000 inhabitants". It lists only 2 hotels as being available for tourists. That has now changed; the population has flourished and the choice of hotels is vast.

busy port

The actual port lies a few kilometres further south, on the road to

Saudi Arabia and, as Jordan's only sea outlet, it is busy. The majority of Jordan's imports and exports pass through it. Before the Gulf War, and especially during the conflict between Iraq and Iran, the former imported much of its supplies through Aqaba, and there was a constant stream of very heavy trucks plying the route to the Iraqi frontier. This has ceased for the time being, although there are still many heavy vehicles on the route north.

freight train

The port is also serviced by a freight only railway that was originally part of the famous Hejaz Railway which ran from Damascus to Mecca. After the line went out of operation the trains terminated at Ma'an and the freight was transported to and from there by truck. In the 1970s a branch line was laid from Ma'an to Aqaba, and this extension was opened in 1975. Most of the freight carried is phosphates and potash.

planes and ferries too

There is an airport in Aqaba with daily flights to and from Amman; in addition, a shipping line runs a car and passenger ferry to Nuweiba in Sinai (Egypt). Now that there is peace between Jordan and Israel it is possible to cross the border into that country. Details of all these are given in Part III of this book.

tropical fish and deep sea diving

One great attraction of Aqaba is the rich marine life. You can see this either by snorkelling, or by renting a glass bottom boat. If you choose the former you should do so under the auspices of one of the diving clubs in the town, as there is an element of danger attached to it, particularly from some marine species who are not too pleasant to come into contact with! The boats can be found almost anywhere along the shore.

► Aqaba fort

There are really only two places of historical interest to visit. The first is the **Fort of Aqaba** which can be found just past the commercial area on the way to the port. Over the main gateway is the Hashemite coat of arms. Inside there is nothing of notable interest. A further section, the part where Sharif Husayn had his HQ now doubles as a museum and tourist office.

► Aila

The other site is the **archaeological site of Aila** facing the Aqaba Gulf Hotel (see history above). The site consists of diggings and a few reconstructed walls. There are blue signs with explanations but, as in many similar places, the history is more interesting than the viewing.

► Jazirat Faroun (Isle de Graye)

sail to Coral Island

An excursion that is worthwhile making if you have the time, is to the Egyptian island of **Jazirat Faroun,** the Crusader stronghold known as **Isle de Graye** (see history above). No special formalities are required for this visit. Captured by the Israelis in the 1967 war, who called it Coral Island because it is surrounded by a coral reef, it was returned to Egypt in the 1980s, and the castle has now been restored.

The incredibly beautiful coral formations make snorkelling and undersea swimming great here.

15. The Dead Sea

INTRODUCTION

A visit to Jordan would not be complete without a visit to the Dead Sea *(al-Bayer al-Mayit)*, that strange body of lifeless water in the Great Rift Valley at the southern end of the River Jordan. Its western shore is bounded by the inhospitable mountains of the Judean Desert, while to the east rise the precipitous sides of Jordan's cultivated plateau. From the sea's southern end the mainly arid Arava Valley extends away towards the Red Sea.

lowest point on earth

At nearly 400 metres below sea level, the Dead Sea is the lowest reachable place on earth; and if you go there between the end of May and the beginning of October it will feel like it, with temperatures reaching 40 degrees or more!

Lake of Sodom

This, the most unusual of lakes, has been called by many names. The Romans named it *lacus asphalitis,* sea of asphalt and the Muslims knew it either as the Lake of Sodom, after the infamous biblical city of that name which is presumed to lie near its southwestern shore, or *al-Bahr Lut*, the Sea of Lot, for the same reason. It was the Crusaders who named it the Dead Sea, the appellation most used today, although the Israelis still use its biblical name, *yam ha-melakh*, the Salt Sea.

plenty of fresh water

The Dead Sea, actually an inland lake, gets its water mainly from the River Jordan which empties whatever water it has left into the northern end. Many of the seasonable water courses from both the eastern and western mountains empty their torrents there as well. In a wet winter this can amount to a very substantial quantity of water. There are also a number of fresh water springs along both sides of the sea.

deep and shallow

About 75 kilometres long and 16 wide at its broadest point, the salt lake covers an area of just over 900 square kilometres. Its average depth in the north east section is almost 400 metres, whilst in the south, near the Lisan (from the word for tongue) peninsular that almost cuts the lake in half, it is barely a couple of metres.

There is no outflow, but there is a huge amount of evaporation.

saltier than the ocean

The salinity of the lake is its main claim to fame; over 25 per cent as compared with about 5 per cent for the oceans.

Chemical extraction is the industry down here, although tourism is also achieving importance. Both Jordan and Israel extract potash, and this is a very prominent foreign currency earner for the Kingdom. Other chemicals that are obtained from the waters include common salt, bromide and asphaltite.

taking the cure

Since biblical times the water and the mud from this lake have been known for their therapeutic qualities. Herod the Great, for one, found they helped to relieve his many aches and pains. The practice continues today, either by the local people who plaster mud all over their bodies themselves or in special treatment centres where "specialists" control (and charge!) for every aspect. Jordan still has much to do in order to develop tourism in this area, and this is ongoing.

experience the unsinkable

Most people want to bathe in the water and experience the sensation of floating on it. Because of the high salinity, the water is very buoyant, and you really do just float on top. Start to lie back and you'll find your feet floating up in front of you. Even a non-swimmer can do it! (This so fascinated the Roman Emperor Vespasian that he would have prisoners thrown in with their hands tied!)

Before taking the plunge you should know that the chemical-laden water stings excruciatingly if you have a cut or open wound. As it also leaves an unpleasant slimy coating on the skin, it's preferable to choose a spot to bathe where you can wash when you get out.

fresh water showers

The best place for a brief visit is the **Rest House** at the northern end of the sea, at Suweima. Here, for an entrance fee of one dinar, you can use the fresh water swimming pool and shower down after your dip in the sulphurous sea. You also have access to the restaurant and other facilities. If you feel inclined to spend more than one day, the Rest House has a newly-opened area of comfortable air-conditioned bungalows (for details of these see the Amenities chapter). Further south there is a new hotel, the Dead Sea Spa Hotel, a four star affair. This is mainly a treatment centre for skin diseases.

How to get there

From Amman: Take road number 40 out of Amman signposted to Suweima and the Dead Sea. When you reach the valley other signs point to the Rest House.

By bus: Suweima can be reached from Amman by a direct minibus that departs from Jerusalem Street. The last bus back to Amman leaves around 1600, but check first to be sure.

drive along the shore

There is now a road which runs along the entire shore of the east side of the Dead Sea and there are one or two places along it worth visiting. You could do this when returning from the south of the country by descending via the road **from al-Karak** and driving up to Amman from Suweima. You will then avoid having to retrace your journey or travel back on the dull Desert Road. (Our tour is described in this direction, that is south to north, below.)

wadi's end

Travelling from the south (you turn right when you reach the Dead Sea from al-Karak), the first place you come to is the **Mujib Bridge,** c50 km north of where the Karak road reaches the valley. As its name implies, this is where Wadi Mujib (the huge canyon on the King's Highway) empties into the Dead Sea. You will notice this is a very new bridge, as indeed is most of the road before it. To stop here you will first have to cross the bridge to the checkpoint and then make a U turn, driving back across it; just where the bridge begins, a track leads off to the right (W) (towards the lake). Drive down it and find a place to park.

You can then walk under the low concrete structure to get a magnificent view of the final stretch of this deep and sheer-sided wadi, the second longest watercourse between the Mediterranean and the desert, as it plunges down. On Fridays and Muslim holidays many Jordanian families come here to picnic or wash their cars. In the summer and fall the water is shallow, but in winter and early spring it can be quite deep. It is definitely a sight worth stopping for.

the pools of Callirhoe?

Some 30 km further north is another, but far less noticeable, bridge (in reality a conduit under the road) which crosses the mouth of **Wadi Zarka Ma'in** and this is where the waters of the hot springs of Hammamat Ma'in flow into the Dead Sea. This is **Ain Zara,** and either Hammamat Ma'in (see Madaba chapter) or Ain Zara is the **Callirhoe** of the classical period, where Herod used to venture from his palace at Machaerus in order to treat his many illnesses.

Park on the shoulder of the road. To the east is a pool where you can bathe. You can get to the water on either side of the bridge, but the part on the western side is more dramatic. There is quite easy access to the sea shore and from there it is possible to walk back up the stream for a few metres.

dressed up for a swim

The water is hot and therefore less than refreshing on an equally broiling day; but if you want to get a thorough soaking or wash off after a dip in the salt lake, stand under the weir just where the water comes out from under the bridge. You will notice that it is mainly the male sex that participates in these water sports. Females who choose to join in do so fully clothed!

A road from Hammamat Ma'in down to the Dead Sea is under construction, and will end up nearby. At the end of 1995 this road was still not finished.

The Rest House at the northern end mentioned above is a further c30 kilometres. On the way there are many places where you can get down to the water for a float, but you will have no fresh water to rinse with.

PART III
INFORMATION FOR TRAVELLERS

16. GENERAL INFORMATION

1. Travelling to and from Jordan
2. Currency and costs
3. Getting around
4. What to take
5. Health
6. Things to know
7. Etiquette
8. Accommodation
9. Food and drink
10. Border crossings

17. AMENITIES

Services, hotels and restaurants listed
A-Z by town

16. General Information

WHEN TO GO

The ideal time to visit Jordan is spring or autumn, the former being the preferred season. Unfortunately this is not a big secret, and at these times tourism is busy. (You could try late winter/early spring, but then you do run a risk of some inclement weather; this may be better than crowds!) In spring the countryside bursts with new life; myriads of wild flowers are strewn among the fresh grass and even some desert hills sprout a down of green. The air is clear, temperatures just right, and if you want to bake on a beach for a couple of days, you can just go down to Aqaba. From mid April to mid October the risk of rain is slight. Even if you do catch a bad day, by tomorrow it will be fine again.

Late June through to mid September is too hot for serious touring especially in the south and Jordan Valley, and if you have to choose these months bear in mind that from about noon till three you will have to rest. Good weather frequently continues after late October to the end of November and there are less crowds. Winter is out, as it can be very cold and wet.

HOW TO GET THERE

♦ By air

If you are only visiting Jordan then you will come by air. Most national airlines fly into Amman, and the prices vary. The cheapest is Tarom, Romanian Airlines, who fly via Bucharest but arrive after midnight, but they may not be too reliable. Tarom's current fare is GBP 240.00. Other airlines offer excursions at favourable rates depending on the time of year. Turkish Airlines sometimes offers a special from London via Istanbul for GBP 250.00, but it involves much waiting about at Istanbul airport.

A more normal fare for a direct flight by BA or Royal Jordanian is between GBP 330.00-350.00. Royal Jordanian offer an excellent service and arrive at a good time of day. Shop around, and if your budget is limited check on all possibilities.

♦ By land

From Syria: You can cross into Jordan from Syria's southern border. The only purely overland route from Europe is through Syria, which is reached after a long train journey from Istanbul. For additional information on this route see the section on border crossings into neighbouring countries below.

From Israel: You can now enter Jordan from Israel or from the West Bank. Flights from London to Tel Aviv start from as little as GBP 190.00 for a return charter (about GBP 100 one way), but you will incur additional expenses on this route (see the section on border crossings below).

From Egypt: A ferry service operates between Aqaba and Nuweiba in Sinai.

♦ Bringing your own vehicle

You can bring your own car or camper into Jordan. From Europe the drive will be through Bulgaria to Istanbul, then onwards through Anatolia and Syria. You will have to buy Syrian and Jordanian insurance at the respective borders. Driving direct from the UK, not counting any touring you may want to do en route, this journey requires about 9 days, covering a distance of around 4000 km.

You can drive into Jordan from Israel, using the Arava or Jordan Valley crossing points (see section on border crossings below). You can get to Israel by car ferry (3 days) from Piraeus (Athens) to Haifa. (Israeli insurance has to be purchased at Haifa.) If you do not want to drive to Greece there is a good ferry service between the Italian ports of Ancona or Brindisi and Greece. It takes between one and two days to drive from London to Ancona.

Whichever route you choose, taking your own vehicle is very expensive and requires a great deal of time, but it is a splendid journey if you are planning a long trip of this type.

♦ Organised Tours

Do-it-yourself tours can be more exciting and flexible, but are not suitable for everyone. A number of UK companies offer organised and escorted tours of Jordan. Operators include Jasmine Tours, The Imaginative Traveller, Explorer Tours and Voyages Jules Verne.

ENTRY FORMALITIES AND VISAS

A Jordanian visa is required for entry into the Kingdom. These are available from the Jordanian Consulate in your country, or on arrival at Queen Alia Airport, or at the Jordan-Syrian frontier. Please note that at the time of writing visas are **not** available in Israel, and are not issued at the border crossings with Israel or controlled by Israel (King Hussein (Allenby) Bridge). So if you are entering Jordan by these routes make sure you acquire a visa before leaving home.

considering every angle

Another point to bear in mind is that certain Arab countries, Syria among them, will not give you entry if there is evidence on your passport that you have been in Israel. Although Israel will, at your request, refrain from stamping your passport, the Jordanians will not. Therefore the point of entry into Jordan will be on your passport, making it clear that you came via Israel. The Syrians may refuse you entry in such a case even though you have a visa. A second passport may be accepted, but this is not 100% certain. If you plan to leave Jordan for other Arab states which have not yet made peace with Israel, check first with the appropriate consulate in your country.

♦ Consular addresses

Some Jordanian Consulate addresses are:

UK 6, Upper Phillimore Gardens, London, W8 7HB
Phone 0171 937 3685 Fax 0171 937 8795

USA 3504, International Drive, NW, Washington DC 20008
Phone 202 265 1606 Fax 202 667 0777

Canada Suite 701, 100 Bronson Ave Ottawa, Ottowa, Ontario
KIR 6C8 Phone 238 8091

Australia: 20 Roebuck Street, Redhill, (ACT 2603) Canberra, Phone
295 9951

♦ Air Arrival and departure

Queen Alia International Airport is about 30 kilometres south of Amman, and connected to the city by a good highway. Bus and taxi services are available. If you are getting your entry visa at the airport, change money at the airport bank first as you can only pay in JD. The visa charge varies according to nationality and is currently JD25 for British nationals.

There is a **departure tax** of JD 10 per person. The duty free facilities at the airport are not very good.

2. CURRENCY AND COSTS

♦ Money in use

The local currency is the Jordanian dinar or JD. It is divided into 1000 fils, or 100 girsh. Both these subdivisions are used, but as the

235

denomination is rarely specified, it is up to you to determine whether you are quoted fils or girsh (it's usually the former). These subdivisions of the JD are coins. Notes are issued in JD 0.5, 1, 5, 10 and 20. Always try to carry enough half, one and 5 dinar notes, as larger ones can be difficult to change. Ten dinars is a lot of money to the average Jordanian.

♦ Changing money

Cash can be changed in banks or with money changers, who are authorised. You may get a slightly better rate from a money changer. Some hotels will also change or take USD and GBP, but the rate will be unfavourable. It is best if all your money changing is transacted in Amman or Aqaba. Remember, banks are closed on Friday, although *some* money changers may be open PM.

♦ Credit cards

Credit cards are accepted by most hotels of two stars and over, but not all accept all cards. Visa is the most commonly honoured. Visa and Amex will do nicely. Don't rely on a cash advance with your plastic.

At the end of 1995, the exchange rate was JD 1.10 to GBP 1.00, and JD 0.65 to 1 USD.

♦ Budgeting

prices fall

Until 1988 Jordan was a very expensive country to visit, in fact one of the most expensive in the Middle East. After the devaluation and currency exchange control relaxation of that year, the Jordanian dinar lost nearly 40 per cent of its value, and for a short time Jordan became very inexpensive for the traveller.

prices rise

Those heady days are now past; although still cheaper than it was in pre-devaluation days, prices are creeping up and I would now consider prices to be medium. Restaurants offer very good value for money, while hotels definitely tend to be overpriced for what you get.

Budgeting, like everything else, depends on personal tastes and how much you want to spend. The item which will most affect how much you spend is the type of hotel you stay in. A guide (double room per night) is as follows:

Cheapest budget hotel	- JD 8 to 12 JD (in these you can sometimes bargain).
Medium budget hotel	- one star JD 14-18;
	- 2 star JD 22-40.
Three star hotel	- JD 60-70.

If you want something better then budgeting will not be your problem!

Food and drink is inexpensive; at local type restaurants, where you get delicious Jordanian specialities, a sum of JD 5-6 per couple will be adequate. You will, however, be in and out fairly quickly – these busy non-stop eateries are not places to linger. If your preference is for upmarket places where the surroundings may be more congenial (but the food no better), you will spend at least JD 16, perhaps more, per couple.

---

3. GETTING AROUND

The choice is chiefly between either self-drive or a combination of bus, service taxi and hitch-hiking. (Bus travellers will need to hitch hike if they want to get to some of the more off-road destinations.) But in order to see the country properly in a reasonable time a vehicle is almost a necessity, at least for part of your stay. All the options are discussed below.

CAR HIRE

Rent-a-car, dearly

Car hire is costly; too costly for a country where the only satisfactory way of seeing it all is by car, but this can be mitigated slightly by choosing the rental firm carefully, plus a bit of bargaining. Sharing with a second couple helps. An international name in car hire will cost about JD 260 or more for seven days (more if you book from abroad). An average local firm will charge a minimum of JD 180.00 for seven days for a small car. However, there are one or two rental companies that are cheaper.

By way of compensation, petrol prices are far lower than in Europe. In 1995, 4 litres cost less than JD 1.00!

♦ Car Rental Agencies

do it yourself

Amman is full of rental agencies, but many are not serious affairs. Often an "agency" will just be an intermediary for a real firm. Many hotel receptionists will also offer to arrange a vehicle for you. In many such cases this adds to the price as they expect commission from the company. Far better to deal directly with the firm, and better still to arrange it before you arrive in Jordan. That way you'll save a lot of running about, and ensure that you get one of the better cars. Booking in advance through a local firm is not too much trouble; Saturday and Sunday are normal working days in Jordan so you can make use of off-peak charges for phone calls and faxes.

All the major international agencies are represented in Jordan, and you can of course book a car through their offices in you own country.

As mentioned, this is the most expensive way of doing it, but it will save you the direct communications with Jordan.

don't damage!

In Jordan you cannot waive all damage liability. The driver is responsible for the first JD 100.00 for all damage which cannot be put down to the other party. Payment is made in advance, and some security is required, usually an open signed credit card slip. If you do not have a credit card then the rental firm may accept your return airline ticket as surety. Although many national driving licences can be shown, an international one makes matters easier.

Nearly all renters will deliver your car to Amman airport, and a few of them will even meet you at the King Hussein Bridge terminal - another advantage of booking ahead.

Some international agencies in Jordan are:
Avis Tel: 6 699420 Fax: 6 699430; **Hertz** Tel: 6 668958 Fax: 6 688406; **Budget** Tel: 6 698131 Fax: 6 673312; **Europcar (Inter-Rent)** Tel: 6 639197 Fax: 6 642401.

Local firms:
Reliable Rent a Car Tel: 6 819676 Fax: 6 819675. This is a local company offering quite good prices. A Daihatsu Charade with air-conditioning costs JD 182 per week with unlimited kms and insurance. A more substantial Nissan Sunny with A/C costs JD 210 per week, also including unlimited kms and insurance. Reservations have to made at least 3 days prior to your arrival, and the car will meet you at the airport at any reasonable time.
Al-Safeer Rent a Car Tel :6 691505 Fax: 6 602329. This firm offers a non A/C Hyundai for JD 210 per week, unlimited kms and including insurance.
Safari Rent a Car Tel: 6 605080 Fax: 6 690993. Safari specialises in 4 wheel drive vehicles that start from JD 50 per day.
Dinar Rent a Car Tel/Fax 6 610520. Cars from Dinar start at JD 30 per day including 200 kms and insurance.
Star Rent a Car Tel/Fax 6 604904. On Fridays and holidays phone the owner at home Tel: 6 6835954. The best deal is obtained from here and this is where I rent from. The owner, Taisir Zayed, is a very pleasant man to do business with, and he is admirably assisted by his two young sons. All speak good English.

Star rents out both new air-conditioned cars and some two or three years old, and these older ones come at a very good price. What I like about Star is the willingness to go out of the way to satisfy you. The car will be brought to the airport at any time of day or night, and if you are leaving Jordan late at night or early in the morning Mr Zayed will make sure you get there without using a taxi. He will even meet you at the King Hussein Bridge if you are entering the country that way. A new 1500cc A/C car with power steering will cost you around

JD 182 per week, while an older one still in good driving condition could be had as low as JD 145. You can bargain, but beware — Mr Zayed knows more about this Middle Eastern business activity than you! Within reason he will do everything he can to accommodate you.

To get the best deal book as long in advance as you can. If you can't book until you get to Amman, Star is situated quite far from the city centre, but a phone call will have someone calling for you. This may not be the slickest operation in Amman, but it is among the friendliest.

♦ Driving in Jordan

Anyone who has driven in the Middle East will know that driving manners (and methods) fall short of what we find on the roads in most (but not all) Western countries, and often such driving can be a nightmare! Jordan, however, is not as bad as most of its neighbours, and a strong traffic police presence on the streets of Amman brings a good sense of order. Traffic drives on the right.

Check your spare tire, especially before travelling along desert roads. Don't drive on tracks unless you have a four wheel drive vehicle.

fast road to Petra

Outside town the roads are quite empty. From Amman north there is a new motorway that reaches Jerash and the Syrian border. An older motorway, the Desert Highway goes all the way to Aqaba, and is also the fastest route to Petra. The Desert Highway is flat and monotonous so try and stop a few times to eliminate boredom. The official speed limit on this highway is 120 km/hour.

slow road to Petra

Other roads are, for the most part, in variable condition, so keep an eye out for unexpected potholes. The King's Highway is particularly winding in many places and passes through numerous small towns and villages, making progress quite slow. Note that the European sign for a motorway is used to signify any dual carriageway road, especially those through a town! These signs do not give you motorway "rights".

watch your tank!

On the Desert Palaces loop or the Dead Sea-Aqaba road, make sure you have sufficient fuel, as filling stations are rare. Phone numbers for emergency are given in the section **Useful Telephone Numbers** (page 245).

driving in Amman

As Amman is the only really large city, it's the only town where you will encounter traffic jams and the like. Brilliant new roads and underpasses alleviate most of these, and except in the downtown area the traffic keeps moving. The one-way system in the downtown sector is a nuisance, as is finding a place to park. There are parking penalties, and in some cases the police will tow away a vehicle parked in a restricted zone. If your hotel is not downtown, try to visit without the car; taxis are cheap.

◆ Public transport

tourist special

The main company providing services for visitors is JETT, the Jordanian Enterprise for Tourism and Transport. They operate out of their own station just north of the Abdali bus station in Amman. JETT run services to Aqaba (5 times a day), Petra (once a day), Jerash (3 times a day), and the King Hussein Bridge terminal (once a day). Schedules often change, especially with the seasons.

cheap and cheerful

Other (extremely low priced) buses and minibuses can be found at the Abdali bus station for destinations north of Amman, and at the Wahadat Station for destinations south of the capital. Abdali is situated on King Hussein Street about 3 kilometres north of downtown. Wahadat is in south Amman near the circle called *Duwaar sharq al-Awsat*, Middle East Circle. A *servees* connects the two.

unscheduled start

From Abdali buses run to Irbid, Jerash, al-Salt, Deir Allah, Suweileh, and other points north. There is no real schedule, the buses departing when full, or nearly so. For those travelling to Irbid there are luxury buses run by the Hijazi company.

From Wahadat buses leave for al-Karak, Wadi Musa (Petra), Madaba, and Ma'an. Luxury buses leave for Aqaba.

Local buses or minibuses also run from place to place and details of these are to be found in the touring text. In Amman they leave from a number of points including the Abdali bus station. These local services are cheap. If you need any information on bus services, you should be able to obtain it from that location.

all share

Besides buses there is that marvellous Mid-East form of transport, the shared taxi, or *servees*, service taxi. These often ply similar routes to the buses, but are more speedy. The interurban ones depart from the same bus stations as the appropriate buses. Servees taxis are slightly more expensive than buses.

◆ Transport to Syria

JETT and the Syrian company Karnak run a daily service to Damascus, costing about JD 4.00. These leave from JETT's terminal north of Abdali. Service taxis also make this run and leave from the east side of the Abdali Bus Station. I have found it better to travel by bus as the border controls are more orderly for buses.

There is also a once a week train on the Hejaz Railway. As this takes almost forever I can see no point in using it, especially as the two stations, Amman and Damascus, are very far from the city centres.

4. WHAT TO TAKE

♦ Clothing etc

When planning your clothing needs (particularly women), remember that you will be travelling in a Muslim country, albeit a not very traditional one. Too much body should not be displayed. Whilst men can wear shorts (see below), they look out of place in the towns, and in any case you will not be allowed into mosques etc wearing them. Women should not wear shorts at all, it is really insensitive to do so. Likewise, miniskirts should be avoided. It's also best not to wear completely sleeveless tops (other than perhaps in Aqaba) – short sleeves are generally OK, but when visiting mosques it's better if the arms are covered, at least as far as the elbow. By following the above guidelines, not only will you feel more relaxed in a conservative environment, but you will keep cooler – as any Arab knows less clothing does not always mean less hot.

Take the clothing, according to season, that you would take on a visit to, say, Greece or southern Italy. Between April and mid October you should not require a rainjacket.

keeping cool

Shorts on men are OK in Aqaba, Petra and Wadi Rumm but experience has shown me that very lightweight loose trousers are more comfortable as the sun is kept off your legs. Likewise, if you are the type who sunburns easily, think about very lightweight long-sleeved shirts. Take clothes that wash and dry easily and quickly.

from shoes to shampoo

Make sure your shoes are stout and easy on your feet. Trainers may be suitable if they are sturdy. Sites like Petra are very dusty and after a day walking about your shoes will show it! You might prefer a light rambling type boot. Take a good pair of sunglasses and a hat (the latter can be purchased locally).

Take with all the bathroom supplies (toothpaste, shampoo etc) you will need. You can of course buy these items in Jordan, but you may not find what you are used to and may waste time looking around. For washing your clothes, one of the readily available tubes of specially formulated travel detergent is ideal.

♦ Travel Insurance

Take out proper travel insurance! Most companies put Jordan in the Europe price band. If yours does not then apply to TIA, Suite 2, Percy Mews, 775b High Rd, North Finchley, London, N12 8JY. Tel: 0181 446 5414, Fax: 0181 446 5417.

♦ Useful items

My indispensables are a small travel iron and an electric "dipper" element for boiling water in a cup, plus tea and instant coffee. If you take these items don't forget the cup and a teaspoon!

Don't forget a pocket compass. The guide is written with the use of this in mind!

♦ Electricity

Jordan's voltage is 220 volts. Most hotels have 2-pin electrical sockets which use the thin pin plug, although some of the new ones use the British three pin type. A mains testing screwdriver comes in very handy to make sure an outlet works.

♦ Photography

Jordan is a splendid country for photography. Because of the bright light 100 ASA film is adequate. If you generally like to carry much equipment, remember that in a hot climate this can be tiresome. From my own experience, the less you carry the more you are inclined to use it. One zoom lens of about 35 to 85mm should do for most situations. A polarising filter for darkening the blue sky and for use as an ND filter is useful.

Keep your camera out of the sun as much as possible, and do not leave it in a hot car. Likewise your film should be kept as cool as possible. Only carry what you think you'll require for the day.

If you have to buy film locally, and you are particular, buy it from a shop, and not a peddlar. Check the expiry date!

5. HEALTH

You do not require any special inoculations for Jordan, but it is sensible to have up-to-date tetanus protection. In case of emergency the hospitals in the Kingdom are of a good standard, especially the King Hussein Hospital in Amman. For non serious ailments pharmacies are happy to recommend a suitable remedy.

A supply of aspirin or paracetamol may come in handy, as would some wound plaster and antiseptic ointment (also obtainable in any Jordanian pharmacy). Don't forget any medications you usually take.

stomach upsets

Unfortunately, those of us who live in a generally sanitised society have lost a lot of natural immunity to even mild stomach infections. The change of diet etc and different ways of preparing food can easily bring on stomach upsets, especially in hot climates. Thankfully these unpleasant infections don't usually last more than a couple of days.

abstinence the best remedy

I have found the best way to deal with the problem is to abstain from food totally for a day or two. Drink plenty of fizzy sweet drinks. The sugar will sustain you. After the runs have stopped continue for another day or so eating "safe" food such as yoghurt and hard-boiled eggs. Avoid fresh salad and fruit.

If you have never taken diarrhoea blockers such as Imodium or Lomotil, consult your doctor before buying them. With some people they cause very severe stomach cramps, worse than the infection!

dehydration

In the hot summer months it is very important to drink a lot. Never walk around without a bottle of water! Drink as a matter of course; not only when you feel thirsty. The first signs of dehydration are tiredness, headache and a sick feeling. A good swig of even lukewarm water will alleviate all these like magic!

---

6. THINGS TO KNOW

◆ Time

GMT+2; GMT+3 from April to September.

Day of rest:
Friday is the Muslim day of rest. Many shops, car rental establishments and all banks and government offices will be closed on that day. Some Christian owned places may be closed on Sunday.

Opening times:
From Saturday to Thursday.
Government offices 8.00-14.00
Banks 8.30-12.30; some reopen from 16.00-17.30
Travel agencies & airline offices 9.00-13.00 and 16.00-17.00
Shops 8.00/9.00 to 20.00 or even later. Many shops, especially those in downtown Amman are open on Fridays from about midday.

◆ Holidays

There are two types of holidays in Jordan: civil, according to a fixed

243

calendar, and religious that move in relationship to our Gregorian calendar.

The **civil holidays** are as follows. (Businesses, especially those tourism related, do not necessarily close on these days).

Arbour Day (new year for trees) January 15th
Arab League Day March 22nd
Labour Day May 1st
Independence Day May 25th
Arab Revolt Day June 10th
Accession of King Hussein August 11th
King Hussein's Birthday November 14th

The precise date for **Muslim holidays** cannot be given because of the different calendars, and these 1996 dates may vary by a day. For subsequent years subtract 11 days.

Eid al-Fitr (3 day holiday) February 22nd
Eid al-Adha (3 day holiday) April 29th
Muslim New Year March 20th
Prophets Birthday July 20th
Leilat al-Meiraj December 9th

During Muslim holidays shops, restaurants and all tourist services usually operate as normal, however some disruption cannot be discounted.

Eid al-Fitr comes at the end of the Muslim month of Ramadan when many fast during daylight hours (see Geography chapter under **Islam**). During that time many ethnic restaurants are closed during the day, but those that cater to tourists should remain open. Food shops are open. During Ramadan you should not eat, drink or smoke in a public place before sunset.

Christian holidays are celebrated by the Christian community, the most important ones being, of course, Christmas and Easter. Although mainly Orthodox, Christmas is observed on December 25th, but Easter is celebrated in accordance with the Orthodox calendar, which can vary between two weeks before or after the western one. New Year's day is also celebrated. For Orthodox Christians Easter is the main Christian festival.

♦ Telephone communications

You can make international phone calls from the phone offices in Amman and Aqaba, or from your hotel, but this will cost you more. You cannot make a reverse (collect) charge call from Jordan. For local calls the dialling code prefixes are:

Amman - 6; Karak, Petra, Aqaba - 3; Irbid - 2; Jerash - 4

The international code for Jordan is 962.

Faxes: Facsimile communication is much used in Jordan, and nearly all hotels and car rental offices have them. It is the ideal way to make your bookings.

♦ Visa extensions

Your visa is valid for one month. You can renew it, free of charge, at the Directorate of Foreigners in al-Nabulsi Street, Amman, near the new (blue) King Abdullah Mosque, not far from the Abdali bus station.

♦ Tourist Offices

Jordan does not have tourist information offices as such. However important sites like Petra and Jerash have "Visitors' Centres" which are really the same thing. In Amman the only source of information is the Ministry of Tourism in Jabal Amman, just off the Third Circle.

♦ Personal safety

Jordan is a very safe country to visit. Traditional Arab hospitality sees to that. Having said that, you should still take the usual precautions with your valuables etc. You will not be accosted or molested even if you walk the streets at night. Obviously in a male dominated society, women should dress sensibly and not invite unwanted attentions.

♦ Newspapers

An English language newspaper, the Jordan Times, is published daily. Overseas papers are available about a day late, mainly from hotel bookstalls.

♦ Radio and television

Jordan has an English language radio station, and its second TV channel broadcasts in English and French. Additionally you can pick up the BBC World Service on 1323 khz (MW) from Cyprus. Israel radio and television can also be received. Many of Israel's TV programmes are English language films or soaps. Israel Radio also has English language newscasts at xxam and xxpm. These can be heard on these frequencies xx.

♦ Maps

Road maps of the country are obtainable from hotel book stalls, or the Jordanian Tourist Office in your home country. More up-to-date maps are available outside Jordan! In London they can be bought from Stanford's, 12 Long Acre, WC2E 9LP. Tel: 0171 836 1321.

♦ Useful Telephone Numbers

Police	192
First Aid, and Ambulance	193

Highway Police	6 843402
Traffic Accidents	6 896390
Airport Enquiries	8 53200
Tourist Police	6 642311
JETT	6 664146

Consulates:

United Kingdom	6 832100
USA	6 820101
Australia	6 673246
Canada	6 666124
Syria	6 641076
Egypt	6 605202
Israel	6 696511

7. ETIQUETTE

Most Jordanian men, certainly in Amman, dress western style. In fact dress formality is often more pronounced than in Europe. A businessman is expected to wear a suit and tie, even in the hottest summer temperatures. Women tend to dress more traditionally, at least outside the home, although in Amman you will see plenty of women in western dress. If you follow the guidelines under **Clothing** in **WHAT TO TAKE** above, your own dress should not be offensive to Muslim sensibilities.

code of hospitality

Arab hospitality is legend, especially among the Bedouin peoples. The heritage of their desert ancestry, often reflected in the Koran (and also the Bible), prescribes a pattern of behaviour still very much evident today. One only has to recall how guests were treated in biblical narratives to appreciate this. A classic example is the story of Abraham who, while sitting at his tent door, saw three strangers standing opposite him:

> *"He ran from the tent door to meet them, and bowed himself to the earth, and said, '... Please let a little water be brought and wash your feet and rest yourself...and I will bring a piece of bread that you may refresh yourselves; after that you may go on...' "* (Genesis 18:2-5)

The offer of hospitality by way of food and drink, even to strangers, is part of the Arab way of life.

polite curiosity

Despite their formality in many areas of life, Arabs are not shy about asking you personal questions – especially about a guest's family, profession etc – even if you have only just met. You should do likewise and show an interest. You may be invited to a Jordanian home for tea or a meal. If so, you will be amazed at the attention lavished upon you.

hugs and kisses

At a meeting between family or very good friends, there is much hugging and kissing, Mediterranean style, with each person kissing both cheeks. Handshaking is commonplace in Arab society. Even the most casual meeting between men will be preceded by handshakes. In traditional Arab society men do not shake hands with women, although this may not be so among the more westernised Arabs. A woman should not proffer her hand, but wait until the man does so.

eating habits

Many Bedouin eat their food traditionally – by hand. If you are invited to a Bedouin meal, the custom is to use the right hand only. (The left hand is considered unclean as it is reserved for sanitary chores!) Make sure you stick to this if the meal is a *mensaf* communal feast, where everybody helps themselves from a central dish.

ancient custom

You will find that Jordanian men preserve the ancient custom of standing to offer their seats to a woman on a crowded bus.

Jordanian welcome

If you can, take the trouble to learn some simple Arabic greetings and phrases. The exchange of pleasantries is part of everyday life.

8. ACCOMMODATION

Hotels in Jordan are rated with stars. However, in practice there can be a lot of difference between hotels with the same number of stars, both in quality and price, especially in Amman. My recommendations in the **Amenities** chapter will help you with this. It is quite acceptable to view the room first before deciding. Always find out if the quoted price includes breakfast and taxes.

◆ Budget hotels

For those on a limited budget there are unclassified hotels where after a bit of negotiation a double can be had for 8 to 10 JD. These are found in Amman in the downtown area or near the Abdali bus station. This type of place may be very tatty, if not worse, though they do vary.

You can find single star affairs costing around 14 to 16 JD in the same areas. These will be rather spartan, but kept in a reasonable condition. Always examine the room at such establishments first, particularly the bathroom. Make sure to ask about the availability of hot water.

◆ Two star comfort

I travel a great deal and, while wanting comfort, strive to keep my costs down. I have found most Jordanian hotels in the two star category to be adequate, even if they do lack certain facilities, (especially some of Amman's older establishments). Amman is full of such places and they cost from 22 to 35 JD. Breakfast is nearly always included. Some are better or newer than others and this is reflected in the price.

Three star will cost over 50 JD and some may not be much better than a good two star affair, although they will sport a fancier lobby.

◆ many stars, many dollars

There is, of course, a full array of four and five star hotels, some with international names. Expect to pay the prices you are familiar with if this type of establishment is your norm.

Names and addresses of specific hotels are listed in the Amenities chapter which follows this (A-Z by town).

9. FOOD AND DRINK

Reasonable eats

Eating out is the one thing in Jordan that remains cheap, especially if you stick with the ethnic eateries. In fact once you leave the tourist sector, in most things prices tumble down, reflecting the real cost of living in the country. A satisfying meal for two in a downtown Amman restaurant should not cost you more than JD 5.00, and perhaps less. You will certainly come away with a full stomach! If you go to the upmarket places in Jabal Amman you'll pay much more, and the food will be no better.

Diet:

Jordan's cuisine, like that of all countries that were once part of the Ottoman Empire, has absorbed many facets of the Turkish diet. In the main its cuisine is typically Middle Eastern, although there are a few very distinctive local dishes.

One point you should note: pork is not served. Like Judaism, Islam proscribes the consumption of the pig. However, there the dietary constraints of the two faiths part. Milk and meat can be consumed together (and often are), and all types of seafood are permitted.

Bread:

The staple bread of Jordan *(khubz)* is the flat bread we often call by its Greek name "pita". The type used in Jordan is round, rather than the oval Greek variety. There is also a much larger and thinner kind which is sometimes used to "wrap" sandwiches. Both are used for mopping up the plate. Another distinctive and very tasty bread which I have only found in Amman (although it is common on the West Bank) is a large bread ring covered with sesame seeds. These are often sold on carts in the street accompanied by a dried herb, *zarta*, a kind of wild thyme, wrapped in a screw of newspaper. Rolls are available in grocery shops, and are sometimes served in hotels.

Meat:

Lamb or mutton is the standard meat of the Arab countries. It does not have quite the same taste as lamb eaten in Europe, as it is a fat-tailed sheep which has a far stronger flavour. Lamb or mutton is served in a variety of tasty ways:

Muloukhia: An Egyptian dish also popular in Jordan. It's a stew made of mutton and a type of Middle Eastern spinach.

Shawarma: Comprises of thin layers of lamb, with alternating layers of fat piled onto a vertical spit, and roasted in front of a grill. As the outer layers are cooked they are sliced off, exposing the underneath layers to the grill. Shawarma is usually eaten rolled in flat bread and garnished with raw onion, parsley, and tomatoes.

Daoud Pasha: A stew of meat balls, tomatoes, onions, and pine nuts.

Mensaf: Perhaps Jordan's national dish, this is primarily a Bedouin meal, and meant to be eaten with the (right) hand. It consists of boiled pieces of mutton placed on a bed of rice. It is accompanied by a soup of the mutton broth, yogurt and lemon which is used as a sauce. In the Bedouin tradition everyone eats from a communal plate taking meat and rice together between the fingers. This dish is also sometimes made with chicken instead of mutton.

Chicken:

Jordanians eat a lot of chicken, and the price is very cheap. You will see many eateries with gas fired spits outside. The chicken is always fresh, and a portion is half a chicken, since they are smallish birds and not always accompanied by vegetables, though some establishments may serve chips. Among the more distinctive chicken dishes are:

Circassian chicken: In this ethnic dish from the Circassian community the chicken is simmered in water until tender and then dressed in a sauce made from garlic, nuts and vegetables, and served on a bed of burghul (cracked wheat).

Musakhan: This may be the finest of all Jordanian dishes, and something that I never miss. The chicken is steamed in olive oil, plenty of onion, and crushed sumak (a hard, red berry with a distinctive lemony taste). When almost cooked, the chicken is placed on a piece of flat bread which has first been smothered with the onions and sumak, and topped with another piece of bread. It is then baked in the oven until both bread and chicken are crisp on the outside and moist on the inside. Lightly fried pine kernels are sprinkled on top just before serving. Most English menus list this dish as "chicken and onions". I urge you to try it; you will only find it in Jordan or the West Bank.

Salads etc:
The usual Mid-East selection of salads are common:

Hummus, a ground chick pea paste, *tahina*, sesame paste that is usually mixed with plenty of parsley, *salat mashwi* mixed vegetable salad, often dressed with tahina, and for me the best of the lot, *baba ghanoush,* roasted and mashed eggplant, mixed with tahina, and served with a topping of olive oil.

Sweets:
Naturally, Arab pastries *(baklawa)* dominate; these are made from well-buttered layers of filo pastry, filled with nuts and dried fruit. The pastries packed with pistachios are particularly delicious. There are patisseries everywhere specialising in baklawa. Some of the good ones are very good indeed (see recommendations in **Amenities** chapter), while others less so.

Another purely Arab pastry is *knaafeh*, and this must rank as my favourite. The calories I consume every time I stay in an Arab country just devouring this confection! It is a sweet made of burghul and a stretchy chewy cheese, served hot with honeyed syrup, prepared in a huge round pan, nearly a metre in diameter, and kept warm over a gas burner. Pieces are cut off for each customer and it is normally eaten in the shop. It is also made with a shredded wheat type pastry.

Drink:

Water
There is no reason not to drink tap water in Jordan, except perhaps in small villages. Certainly the water in any hotel or restaurant is perfectly potable. However the usual bottled spring water is available everywhere. If you buy this from a kiosk or such like, make sure the factory seal is still intact.

Tea and coffee
Tea, *shai*, is the everyday, all day drink. It is served in small glasses, usually already heavily sweetened. Unless you like your tea syrupy, always specifically request it without sugar and add this yourself. If

you thought the British were *the* tea drinking nation you were wrong! The Arabs (and Turks) win hands down! Office workers, shopkeepers and most others drink it constantly. The Bedouin often serve it flavoured with sage or mint.

Coffee is brewed in the manner preferred from the Balkans to the Persian Gulf: the coffee and sugar are brought to the boil in a small long-handled pot and then decanted into small cups, grounds and all. Sometimes it is flavoured with cardamon (*hel*) pods. Generally referred to outside the region as Turkish coffee, every nation which takes its coffee this way claims it as their own: Greek coffee in Greece, Cypriot coffee in Cyprus, and Arab coffee in Arab countries. It is very strong and bitter and, as coffee originated in Yemen, should be ground only from Arabica beans. Coffee is always served with a glass of cold water.

Soft drink
The usual array of soft drinks is available. Most of the big internationals bottle their brew in Jordan, and there are a number of local ones.

Alcohol
Islam of course forbids the consumption of alcohol, and consequently it is not broadly available throughout the Kingdom. In Amman, ordinary restaurants certainly do not serve it, although the higher class ones should. All the top hotels will, but very few of the others. A lot will depend on the sensibilities or religion of the owner. Some supermarkets in the better areas of Amman stock it and even one or two downtown stores. The Safeway supermarket, which is open 24 hours a day, has a small liquor store. In Aqaba, alcoholic drinks are sold more widely.

There is one brewery in Jordan and they bottle, under licence, Carlsberg lager. This comes in thirst quenching 650ml bottles, but its alcohol content appears to be low. Wines are mainly from the West Bank where two monasteries, Latroun and Cremisan, have wineries, the former being the better of the two.

10. BORDER CROSSINGS

◆ EGYPT

There is a car ferry service from Aqaba to Nuweiba, in Sinai. This is a twice daily service, and takes about 3½ hours. As sailing times vary it is advisable to check these on the spot. Visas are required for Egypt, and are available from the consulate in Aqaba.

You can also enter Egypt by land from Israel. This involves crossing over to Eilat, and then exiting Israel at the nearby border post at Taba. Although you might expect this route to be cheap, it is not — you must pay border dues at both the Jordanian and Israeli frontiers, and then a whopping USD 22 (about GBP 15) exit tax at the Israeli frontier with Egypt plus a further more modest payment to the Egyptians. Land crossings in this part of the world are expensive, besides the costs of visas!

◆ SYRIA

The only frontier post between Jordan and Syria is at Ramatha. Buses and shared taxis ply the route from Amman to Damascus daily. Although Jordanian visas are available at the frontier for travellers from Syria, Syrian visas **are not** available at the border for those travelling *to* that country and should be acquired, if possible, in your home country. If you intend to enter and leave Jordan by this route you will need a multiple entry Syrian visa at twice the cost.

If you want to visit Syria from Jordan and do not have a visa, you'll need to get one from the Syrian Consulate in Amman. To obtain this you need one photograph, JD 35 and a letter of recommendation from your own country's consulate, a procedure that may cost you money. Far better to have obtained the visa before you left home.

◆ ISRAEL AND THE WEST BANK

King Hussein (or Allenby) Bridge
The most convenient crossing point for Israel and the West Bank is the King Hussein Bridge, or Allenby Bridge, as the British named it and the Israelis call it. This is actually a crossing between Jordan and the occupied West Bank, and although it is right by the town of Jericho in the Palestinian entity, it is controlled by the Israelis, and they designate it as crossing to or from Israel.

From Israel: If you are on your way to Jordan you get there by taking a shared taxi from East Jerusalem (about GBP 7.00 or USD 10.00). These depart from the Damascus Gate taxi station. In spite of what you may be told, there is no convenient bus service there.

The crossing is open Sunday to Thursday, 08.00 to 20.00; on Fridays, and the eve of Jewish holidays from 08.00 to 13.00. It is closed on Saturdays, Jewish holidays and Israel Independence Day.

There is a burdensome exit tax of about USD 28 (GBP 18) for each person. From the terminal a Jordanian bus ferries you to the Jordanian terminal. The bus charge is JD 1.50. After formalities (remember you must have a visa as they are not available at the terminal) you can take a shared taxi to Amman which takes about 30 minutes and costs around JD 3.00. (You can calculate that from Jerusalem to Amman will cost about GBP 33.00 per person)..

To Israel: For those leaving Jordan by this route the procedure is as follows. Take a Jett bus (JD 6) or shared taxi (JD 3-4) from the Jett station near Abdali bus station to the bridge terminal. After formalities, and paying an exit tax of JD 5 a Jett bus will ferry you to the terminal on the West Bank for JD 1.50. There you pass through Israeli formalities. From there you can get a shared taxi to Jerusalem (about 35 minutes) at a cost of about 10 US dollars (GBP 7). (Thus the journey from Amman to Jerusalem will cost about GBP 18.50 making the round trip — if you intend to do this — a grossly inflated GBP 50.00+!)

Arava Crossing

From Israel: You can also enter Jordan from Eilat. A bus service, No.16, runs every hour from the bus station in Eilat to the frontier. The border is open Sunday to Thursday 06.30 to 20.00, and on Friday and Saturday from 08.00 to 18.00. It is closed on the Jewish festival of Yom Kippur, and the Muslim new year. Exit tax is about USD 14 (GBP 9) per person. From the Jordan terminal you can take a taxi to Aqaba.

To Israel: If you are leaving Jordan by this route just reverse the procedure. Bear in mind that if you wish to return to Jordan a new visa will be required.

Third country cars are allowed to cross, subject to prevailing regulations.

Jordan Valley

The Jordan valley crossing point is not really suitable for tourists unless they have their own cars. There is no regular transport to or from the Jordanian or Israeli terminals, although there may be on an *ad hoc* basis. It is open the same hours as the Arava crossing.

Please note the above information is correct as of January 1996, but as normalisation of relations between Jordan and Israel proceed, regulations may change. However, any changes are bound to be for the better.

17. Amenities

Services and hotels
A-Z by town

Ajlun

HOTELS

There are two comfortable hotels in Ajlun, both on the road from Ajlun to the Castle.

** **Ar-Rabad Castle** Tel: 4 462202. This is the preferred of the two, having a fine view of the castle. Its 18 rooms are well appointed and have TV. The hotel has a restaurant. The fine air of this location brings many visitors, and the Ar-Rabad is often full, so try and book in advance.

** **Ajlun Hotel**. Tel: 4 462524 Smaller than the Ar-Rabad Castle; also has a restaurant.

Amman

Amman is a sprawling city, and not too easy to find your way around. Built on hills, you are almost always going uphill or down. Though there are commercial areas all over, the one of most importance for travellers will be the downtown area of "old" Amman.

SERVICES

Post:
The main downtown post office is on Prince Muhammad St.

Money changing:
Banks will change travellers' cheques and cash. However it is easier (and quicker) to change cash in an authorised money changer's office. These are plentiful in the downtown area.

254

Tourist Office:
There is no proper state tourist office in Amman. If you need some information you can go to the Ministry of Tourism situated near the 3rd Circle in Jabal Amman. You can also phone them on 642311.

Bus stations:
The two main ones for public buses are: Abdali (half way up al-Malak al-Hussein St) for buses going north of Amman, and Wahadat (near Duwaar Sharq al-Awsat), for buses going south. JETT buses leave from the JETT offices on al-Malak al-Hussein St just north of Abdali.

Public transport:
What is difficult, especially for travellers without a vehicle, is transport around the city. This is mainly provided by *servees* taxis and often long queues form for these. The main routes are as follows:

No 6 – from the al-Hussein cinema, downtown, via Abdali Bus Station, the JETT office, to the Ministry of the Interior Circle.

No 7 – this also departs from the al-Hussein cinema and runs past the Abdali bus station, then to the King Abdullah Mosque, and along al-Nabulsi Street.

No 26 – from the Church of the Saviour, downtown, to Jabal al-Ashrafiyyeh, and the Abu Dawish Mosque.

No 2 – this route is from the post office on Basman Street, downtown, to the first and second circles on Jabal Amman.

No 3 – as above but to the third and fourth circles.

There are a few **buses**, or more correctly **minibuses**, but these are infrequent and crowded. Often when a bus arrives at a stop there are so many people waiting to get on that it is almost impossible to get off in the fight to board. Once I was nearly crushed in such an incident!

Ordinary **taxis** are quite easy to stop, and the fare is low. Make sure the meter is activated and don't accept a fixed rate – it will always be against you!

Car Hire:
See preceding chapter, General Information, under **3. Getting Around**.

HOTELS

Hotels in Amman tend to be expensive for what you get, although there are some exceptions. Hotels are given a star classification by the Ministry of Tourism, but this classification is not uniform. Especially in the two and three star category standards vary greatly, with some three star establishments being no better than two star, and some two star being more like one star.

In general the two star hotels tend to be old and in need of modernisation and renovation, although they are still comfortable and adequate by Middle Eastern standards. The same applies to some of the three star places, but in this range there are a few that are newer and offer a better standard of comfort and amenities. Budget hotels are just that. They are situated in the downtown area, often in rather dilapidated buildings. These also vary and the lower the price the more unpleasant they may be. Of course there are the usual array of first class hotels as well, including some internationals, and these have everything you would expect from such establishments.

Prices below are for a double room and include breakfast unless otherwise stated.

*****5 and ****4 Star
Amman Marriot Tel: 6 660100 Fax: 6 670100
Amman Plaza Tel: 6 674111 Fax: 6 674261
Jordan Intercontinental Tel: 6 641361 Fax: 6 616791
Philadelphia International Tel: 6 663100 Fax: 6 665160

***3 Star
Carlton, Jabal Amman, Third Circle. Tel: 6 654200 Fax: 6 655833. P.O.Box 811666, Amman. Situated opposite the Intercontinental, it's new, and offers a high standard of comfort and amenities, but it costs. JD55+20% service and tax. (Visa, AMEX, MC)
City Hotel, Jabal Amman, Nr.Third Circle. Tel: 6 6342251 Fax: 6 652634 P.O.Box 2734 Amman. Formerly a two star hotel, and at the bottom end of the 3 star range. Centrally situated with a small swimming pool. Not too bad at JD 35+20% service and tax. (Visa)
Crown Hotel, Radio and TV Street. Tel/Fax: 6 758180 P.O.Box 1318, Amman. A largish hotel but has seen better days. Passable. JD40+20% service and tax. (Visa, AMEX, MC)
Ramada, Jabal Amman, 7th Circle. Tel: 6 817622 Fax: 6 823061 P.O.Box 183494 Amman. What you would expect from a hotel with the Ramada name. Rather far from the centre. (Visa, MC)
Ambassador Hotel, Shmeisani Qtr. Tel: 6 605161-686161-671261 Fax: 6 681101 P.O.Box 925390 Amman. Well situated large hotel with plenty of amenities. (Visa, AMEX, Diners, MC)
Other hotels in this category include:
Commodore, Shmeisani Qtr. Tel: 6 607185 Fax: 6 668187
Middle East, Shmeisani Qtr. Tel: 6 607150 Fax: 6 667422

**2 Star
Merryland Hotel, off al-Malak al-Hussein St. Abdali. Tel: 6 615441 P.O.Box 9122 Amman. This is an oldish hotel, but a new wing has just been built. The new rooms, with their modern bathrooms are fine and well furnished. Somehow lacks a warm atmosphere. At JD 25 plus the usual 20%, about the lowest you'll get for a reasonable place. Very near Abdali bus station. (Visa, AMEX, Diners)

Canary Hotel, Jabal Alwehdeh, Opposite the Terra Sancta College. Tel: 6 638353 Fax: 6 674676 P.O.Box 9062 Amman. This is a small hotel that has seen better days. The bathrooms, while clean, are old and could do with modernisation. Still, this place is popular and has a nice veranda where you can take breakfast. The rooms vary in size and comfort so you can look at a couple. What it lacks in amenities is made up for in warmth and a touch of old world charm. My hotel when in Amman. JD 25+20%. (Visa and AMEX)

Caravan Hotel, Abdali. Tel: 6 661195 Fax: 6 66196. P.O.Box 9062, Amman. A small, oldish hotel not far from Abdali bus station. Average for this class. No breakfast. At JD 22+20%, I see no reason for using this establishment unless others are full. (AMEX, Diners)

Ramallah Hotel, Prince Muhammad St. Tel: 6 636122 Fax: 6 639551 P.O.Box 182157, Amman. Situated downtown, and very average. Parking may be a problem. At JD 22-25.50 plus 20%, there are better deals around. (AMEX, Visa)

Cameo Hotel, Jabal Amman, 4th Circle. Tel: 6 644515. Fax: 6 644579 P.O.Box 5058, Amman. A medium-sized hotel much the same as others in this category. Quite a good location. The price of JD28+20% is slightly more than others. (AMEX, Visa, MC, Diners)

Pasha Palace, Shabsoah Street opposite the Roman Theatre. Tel: 6 639181/645290 Fax: 6 645313 P.O.Box 1 Amman 11118. In a side street facing the Roman theatre this downtown hotel is well placed if you want to stay in this lively area. The building is quite new, and the rooms and bathrooms above average for a two star in Amman. Also has an oriental restaurant. JD 25 plus the usual 20%. Good value in spite of a noisy and traffic clogged area.

Safeer Motel, facing the Marriot. Tel: 6 602312 Fax :6 602339 P.O.Box 20188, Amman. Large rooms complete with a small fridge and simple cooking facilities. Suitable for a long stay. The building is new, and there is a car park at the rear. JD 30 plus 20%. Better value than many three stars. (AMEX, Diners)

Others in this category include:

Dove, Qurtubah, Tel: 6 697601/2 Fax: 6 674676, JD 30+20%

Manar, Shmeisani, Tel: 6 662186 Fax: 6 684329 JD 36+20%

Rum Continental, Basman St, downtown Tel: 6 611962

*1 Star

There are not too many of these, and the only one I can recommend is the **Jerusalem Jewel**, Abdali Bus Station. Tel: 6 613970/649482 Fax: 6 619933 P.O.Box 7334, Amman. Situated at the top of a modern office tower. There is an underground car park, and a lift from it to the hotel. The rooms are quite large but spartan, and the floors are bare. No breakfast is served, but at JD 15+20% it will suit a tight budget.

Budget Hotels

Downtown Amman is full of them, and the quality really does vary. Don't always go for the outside appearance! It's a case of inspecting and deciding for yourself. As you don't usually have to add tax and service in this range, if you find a decent one, it can work out very inexpensive compared to a two star, for not much less comfort, though the locations may not suit some, especially if you have a vehicle to park.

One in particular stands out but it is not the cheapest: The **Palace Hotel**, al-Malak al-Feisal Street, down an alley called the Suk Manko. Tel: 6 624326/650602   Fax: 6 650602   P.O.Box 6916 Amman. Looks a dump from the outside, but the rooms have been refurnished and decorated. It's not bad for this type of hotel. A double is JD 13, and you should not have to pay tax or service. Not including breakfast, but there is a restaurant. There is nowhere to park anywhere near this hotel!

For the young and fearless, the very basic **Lords Hotel** on al-Malak al-Hussein Street charges JD 9-10 nett for a double. There are plenty more like it along the same and adjoining streets.

RESTAURANTS

Most travellers will want to try the local fare during their visit to Jordan. The best local food is served downtown, and the cost is very low. Those who enjoy a leisurely dinner may find the pace too quick — you generally eat up and leave as soon as you've finished — but for an authentic taste of Jordan they can't be bettered. Although there are Chinese, Korean, Italian, Spanish, etc restaurants in the city, these are expensive, and will often be inferior to those you are perhaps used to.

Al-Kuds Restaurant. Al-Kuds is the Arabic name for Jerusalem, and the walls of this busy eatery are covered with pictures of that city. From the outside the restaurant looks like a *baklawa* patisserie, but the restaurant is at the rear and upstairs. Locals will tell you that this is the best restaurant in town, and if the quantity of clients is any guide, it must be! Typical Middle Eastern food is served together with Jordanian specialities such as *mensaf.* For some reason the wonderful Jordanian/Palestinian chicken dish *musakhan* is not served. The *baklawa* and *knaafeh* is also very good, although I eat this next door (see under). Pleasant if utilitarian service. A meal for two here will not cost more than JD 5-6. No alcoholic drinks served. Situated right at the downtown end of al-Malak al-Hussein St. Don't confuse it with the other *baklawa* places nearby; they are not restaurants.

Al-Salaam Restaurant. This eatery is also located inside a *baklawa* shop, the restaurant being upstairs. Not as big or bright as al-Kuds, al-Salaam serves mainly chicken, including a passable *musakhan.* All meals include a salad such as *houmus, tahina,* or *baba ghanosh* (eggplant), and chips. Very good pickled cucumbers are included in unfinishable quantities. No alcohol served. A meal for two will set you back the princely sum of JD5. You'll find it on the west side of al-Malak-al Feisal Street, just at the point where the street forks into one way arms. There is a grill with chickens turning outside.

There are plenty of similar places to eat downtown, but none as good as the aforementioned two. For a more upmarket meal in stylish surroundings try —

Nouroz Restaurant. On the 3rd Circle, Jabal Amman. Serves everything from steaks to pizza. Wine is also available. A meal for two here will cost anything from JD12 upwards.

Carlton Hotel. Opposite the Intercontinental off the 3rd Circle, this hotel offers a "help yourself" buffet, composed mainly of local delights. The price here is JD9 + service per head. Although the surroundings are plush, the food in al-Kuds is better.

Many uptown restaurants are apt to charge far more than they are worth. All the big hotels have first class restaurants, and if you want to splurge try eating at one of these. In particular the **Marriot** offers a different buffet on each night of the week. These can be very good, but cost from JD13 per person. To find out the menu phone 670100 and ask for the al-Mansaf restaurant.

Cafes and cake shops
If, like me, you love *baklawa* and other Arab sweets, there are a number of downtown shops that have a really delicious selection (in addition to those in the restaurants mentioned above). The one I like best is just a few metres south of the al-Kuds restaurant, called **Habiba.** Ground level is the take away section where you can see all the goodies that are on offer. Watch the server as he cuts off each portion with a deft movement of his hand; it will always be within a few grams of the standard measure. Upstairs is where you eat in. Try their *knaafeh* a typical sweet beloved by Jordanians, Syrians and Palestinians. It's quite the best I've ever eaten! When I'm in this part of the world rarely a day will pass without me eating this treat! A large portion, about a quarter of a kilo, costs 400 fils. In the "better" parts of the city you'll pay double for a smaller portion and it will not be as good. Habiba's *atayif* (puff pastry, cheese-filled pancakes drenched in melted butter and syrup) are also delectable. You can also order soft drinks, tea or coffee.

If you want to take some *baklawa* home they have a 1.5 kilo selection well packed in a plastic container. It costs JD 6.5 and is worth every fil.

The Jordanians who frequent the downtown area are generally more traditional, and it is uncommon for unmarried men and women to go out in public together. You will therefore often see groups of young men in cafes, coming especially to eat these sweets in much the same way as their counterparts elsewhere would pop into a pub!

To cool down and take the weight off your feet while touring Amman, there is no better place than in one of the *al fresco* café-restaurants overlooking the Roman theatre. They serve a whole range of fresh fruit juices and ice creams as well as full meals.

Aqaba

SERVICES

All the main services, post, banks and money changers are found in the commercial centre of the town.

Tourist Office:
This is located in the Aqaba Visitors' Centre at the seaward end of Aqaba Fort.

Watersports etc.
Aqaba is a perfect place for all kinds of watersports, the diving being especially good. The Aquamarina hotel has it's own diving centre and you do not have to stay at the hotel to use it – just pay! The Alcazar hotel has similar facilities, but be warned this is an expensive pastime!

JETT Office:
This is located just west of the Aqaba Gulf Hotel, facing the sea.

Air Travel:
Royal Jordanian has a daily flight to and from Amman. Their offices are at the southern end of the commercial centre.

Ferry boats:
For details of the ferry service to Egypt, and the Arava crossing point into Israel see the previous chapter, General Information, on **border crossings**.

HOTELS

****4 Star
Aqaba Gulf Hotel, Tel: 3 316636 Fax: 3 318246. This is Aqaba's largest hotel. Fully air-conditioned, it has a swimming pool, and all the comforts you would expect from a high class establishment. However, it is not on the shore, and therefore does not have its own beach. (Visa, AMEX)
Coral Beach Hotel, Tel: 3 313521 Fax: 3 313614. This is the most westerly of Aqaba's hotels and is situated on the shore. The hotel has its own pool, beach and tennis court. A double room at this hostelry will set you back about JD 100. (Visa, AMEX)

260

The Holiday International, Tel: 3 312426 Fax: 3 313426. A large hotel on the shore with pool and beach. A double room here is JD 95+20% service and tax. (Visa)

Alcazar Hotel, Tel: 3 314131 Fax: 3 314333. A large beachfront hotel boasting a scuba diving centre, with a professional instructor. Equipment is available for renting. (Visa, AMEX, MC)

***3 Star

Aquamarina Hotel, Tel: 3 316250 Fax: 3 314271. Private beach and pool. This hotel has a watersports centre. (Visa, MC)

Aqaba Hotel, Tel: 312056 Fax: 3 314089. One of the town's oldest hotels, situated on the shore with its own beach. (Visa, MC)

Miramar Hotel, Tel: 3 314340 Fax: 3 314339. Not on the shore, but has a pool. The reasonable price is JD 49 for a double including breakfast. Twenty per cent service and tax is added. (Visa)

Medium price hotels

There is a plethora of two and one star hotels. Many are very comfortable, quite new, and will satisfy most visitors. Prices for doubles vary from JD 18 to JD 30, including breakfast. Most of these are situated in and around the commercial centre. They may or may not add extra for tax. If they do not mention it when enquiring, it is probably included, but make sure. Ask first re credit cards. Prices below are for a double with breakfast. A partial list includes:

Amira Hotel, Tel: 3 318840 Fax: 3 312559. This is a new hotel, with bright, pleasant rooms. About JD 20.

Nairoukh Hotel, Tel: 3 319284 Fax: 3 312980. Also a very pleasant place to stay. Slightly more expensive at JD 25.

Aqaba Star Hotel, Tel: 3 316480. JD 24.

Budget hotels

If you want to spend the very minimum, you can find hotels with doubles as low as JD 10. Expect to get what you pay for. Examples:

The Petra Hotel Tel:3 313746. Located to the south of the commercial centre.

Hotel Qasr al-Nil. A very low price establishment situated on the north side of the square park.

Al-Quds. Tel:3 314815. Slightly dearer than the two above. In southern part of the commercial centre.

RESTAURANTS

Ali Baba Restaurant. Perhaps the most expensive non-hotel restaurant in Aqaba. Here you'll find not only fish, which can be viewed first in a glass-fronted refrigerator, but steaks and other pricey items. You can either sit inside or out on the streetside veranda. A pleasant place to eat, but I prefer the more down-to-earth eateries in the commercial area that serve the traditional Jordanian fare. Ali Baba is situated on the corner of the main street just by the commercial centre. You'll spend between JD 5 and JD10 per person here. By the way, they also serve wine and beer. (Visa, MC)

For the more traditional places just wander around the commercial centre; there are many of them, all at very reasonable prices.

To placate your sweet tooth, the best *baklawa* and *knaafeh* in town are served in the Ata Alui cafe just past the Alui Baba restaurant. You can either sit outside or upstairs where there is a balcony.

Azraq

Should you wish to spend a night in the dry warm air of Azraq there is the **Azraq Resthouse** which will cost you JD 32 + 20% for a double room with breakfast. They have a swimming pool.

Dead Sea

HOTELS

Dead Sea Resthouse. Tel/Fax 5 572901. Fully air-conditioned two room bungalows (one is a lounge) with a fridge. A bungalow for two is JD 47 including breakfast, for four JD 72. Dinner is JD 6 per person. All prices exclude 20% service and tax. (Visa, MC)

Irbid

HOTELS

**** Hijazi Palace Hotel. Tel: 2 247267 Fax: 2 279520. Typical four star style with prices to match. (Visa)

*** Ar-Razi Hotel. Tel: 2 275515 Fax: 2 275517. Near the Yarmuk University, and although fairly comfortable does not warrant its three stars. (Visa)

* Omayed Hotel Tel/Fax 2 245955 On Palestine Street, the second floor above the Jordan Investment Bank. My choice. A pleasant hotel with adequate rooms. The owners are friendly, and you'll get a good breakfast in the 3rd floor restaurant. JD 18-20 for a double room with breakfast (don't pay more!) (no plastic).

RESTAURANTS

Either in the **Omayed Hotel's** restaurant or preferably across the road in the **al-Saadi** restaurant. If you do choose this place order *musakhan*, the wonderful Palestinian/Jordanian dish of chicken baked with loads of onions and sumak, and served on flat bread (called "chicken with onions" on the menu). It is so good here that often back home in England I wish I could fly there for the evening just to have dinner! Don't get a shock when you get the bill of about JD 4 assuming you both had salads! Further up the road (westwards) are some *baklawa* shops.

Karak (Kerak)

In case you find yourself spending the night here the only good place is the **Karak Resthouse**. Tel:3 351148 Fax:3 353148. Sited right by the castle you will not have any complaints about this hostelry. JD 26 for a double plus JD 2.200 each for breakfast. All plus 20% service and tax. (Visa, MC)

Nearby is a budget hotel which some may find passable. It is clean although the rooms are shabby: **Towers Hotel** Tel/Fax 3 354293. They charge according to your face! JD 14-16 would be about right.

Wadi Musa (Petra)

SERVICES

All the facilities, post office, bank, buses etc are found in the tourist commercial area near the Petra Rest House and site entrance.

HOTELS

A few years ago Petra's hostelries could be counted on the fingers of one hand, and that hand did not have to be complete; now there are too many to list them all here, and the number is growing. It is common practice in Petra to offer rooms on a half board basis. If you do not want this, you won't save much on price and, as there are no decent restaurants apart from those in the big hotels, half board is not a bad idea. You may in any case be so tired after a day trekking around Petra you'll be grateful to "eat in"!

Tight budget travellers can find plenty of decent places to stay where a bed costs JD 5. These are usually in shared rooms with four or more beds in each. (Some are listed below.) As most hotels in Petra are recently built, these are generally much better than the Amman equivalent.

Top of the range:
Petra Forum Hotel, Tel: 3 634200 Fax: 3 634201. This was the first of the luxury hotels in Wadi Musa, and boasts all the conveniences you could wish for, including a swimming pool. It is situated very near the site entrance.
King's Way Inn, Tel: 3 336797 Fax: 3 336796. A new luxury hotel situated high up at the very entrance to the township of Wadi Musa. Transport to and from the site entrance is provided.
Taybet Zaman Tel: (Amman) 6 668606 Fax: (Amman) 6 669905. About 10 kms from Petra, this hotel is actually in an old village. The old site has been completely modernised and converted into an unusual and luxurious place to stay. In addition to the comforts one would expect from a superior hotel, the view is truly marvellous. Regular, first class transport is provided to and from the Petra site. Recommended if you can afford the JD 100+ price.

Lower price hotels:
Unless otherwise stated all prices are for a double room including breakfast and dinner. Service and tax may or may not be included. When checking the exact price, if nothing to the contrary is said, assume that these are included by stating, "That's with the service and tax, of course." It might work!

Petra Rest House, Tel: 3 336011 Fax: 3 336686. This is the ideal hotel to stay in, as it is adjacent to the site entrance. Unfortunately it is also the most difficult to get a room in. You will have to book weeks, if not months, in advance. As soon as you know you are going, try to book; you can always cancel later. The rooms are spacious, and the bathrooms have really big baths. After a day trekking in the sand and heat it is marvellous to lay back and soak in a bath. Breakfast is buffet style and substantial. Dinner will not be the best in your life, but you'll enjoy it. This hotel serves alcohol and when you're really thirsty knock back a cold 650ml Carlsberg; not too strong, but very thirst quenching! JD 44 and 20% will be added. Good value. Recommended. (Visa, MC)
Edom Hotel, Tel: 3 336995 Fax: 3 336994, P.O.Box 18, Wadi Musa. This is a brand new hotel with finely appointed rooms. It's about 7-10 minutes from the site entrance. It has an elevated situation so the front rooms have a fine view over Petra. A good alternative to the Rest House. JD 50 (Visa)
Al-Rashid Hotel, Tel: 3 336800 Fax: 3 336801 P.O.Box 96, Wadi Musa. On the first and second floor in the centre of Wadi Musa. It is used a lot by groups. As it is some way from the site a car is a must if you stay here. The rooms on the second floor are on the small side,

but room numbers 101-2 & 3 on the first floor are very spacious. The food is quite good, and the hotel has a pleasant atmosphere. The price is JD 40 (Visa, Diners)

Petra Palace Hotel, Tel/Fax: 3 602460. This newish hotel is about 5 minutes from the site. The rooms are fine, if a bit small. JD 35.

Elgee Hotel, Tel/Fax:3 336701 P.O.Box 121, Wadi Musa. A comfortable hotel situated about 10-15 minutes walk from the site. According to the management, films are available in all rooms. JD 35. Also offers beds in a shared room for JD 5 each, not including food.

Candles Hotel, Tel: 3 336779 Fax: 3 336954 P.O.Box 181, Wadi Musa. About 250 metres from the site, but up quite a steep hill. A new hotel with very nice rooms. The front ones have a terrific view. JD30 (triples JD42).

Rose City, Tel: 3 336440 Fax: 3 336448 P.O.Box 61, Wadi Musa. An adequate hotel facing the Elgee, JD 25 with breakfast only.

Petra Gate Hotel, Tel/Fax: 3 336963 P.O.Box 85, Wadi Musa. This small hotel is some way from the site so if you do not have a car it's a bit of a walk. Rooms are very average. The price is "about" JD 18 with breakfast only. The hotel has a restaurant with a menu.

Sunset Hotel About five minutes from the site, this hotel has "flexible" prices. They may ask JD 30, but will settle for less if rooms are vacant. Also have student rooms where a bed only costs JD 5.

Al-Anbat Hotel, Tel: 3 336265 Fax: 3 336888 P.O.Box 43, Wadi Musa. This is the first hotel you will see as you enter the township. It is on the right, a couple of hundred metres past the Spring of Moses. Its high position means it has a marvellous view, and even if you do not stay here, go there for a drink and watch the magnificent sunset. A very pleasant place with a Bedouin owner who treats his guests with the hospitality of his people. The hotel offers a buffet breakfast and dinner you are sure to enjoy. (You don't have to stay there to eat there.) Often used by groups. It is a long way from the site, but has an hourly free minibus service to and from. Very worthwhile at JD 30. Students and young people can have a bed in a shared room for JD 5 not including food. The "eat as much as you like" buffet dinner will not break even the tightest budget at JD 4.

RESTAURANTS

As nearly all the hotels quote prices that include dinner, finding a place to eat will not be a problem. This is fortunate, as there are no restaurants worthy of the name outside of the hotels.

For lunch, during your visit to the Petra site, you can either take something from your hotel, or eat at one of the Bedouin tent eateries around the Rest Area. The **Forum Hotel** has a smart air-conditioned restaurant there, and they offer a self service, fixed price hot and cold buffet. However the price is JD 6 per person.

Wadi Rumm

Although there is no hotel as such in Wadi Rumm, the **Government Rest House** has hostel facilities. You will require your own sleeping bag or similar. The facilities comprise mainly of large tents where you can lay your bag. Showers and toilets are in the main building as are cooking facilities, but you will need your own food. Otherwise you can eat in the Rest House restaurant which is not too expensive and not too good!

PART IV

REFERENCE SECTION

LANGUAGE

    - About Arabic
    - Getting by in Arabic
    - Vocabulary

GLOSSARY

BIBLIOGRAPHY

INDEX TO BIBLICAL REFERENCES

TOURING INDEX

Language

ABOUT ARABIC

To most westerners Arabic appears a daunting language. This is mainly because it is written in a different script, which to the unaccustomed eye may appear more like scribble than identifiable letters, and also because it is written from right to left. While it is true that to master Arabic can take years, the colloquial, or conversational, language is surprisingly simple to learn. Transliteration into the Latin alphabet helps speed the process!

three versions

It can be said that there are three forms of the Arabic language: the Arabic of the Koran, Modern Standard Arabic, often called MSA, and colloquial Arabic.

The first, Koranic or literary Arabic, is the most difficult. Fortunately this is no longer in everyday use. Modern Standard Arabic is the language that unites Arabs from the Gulf to the Atlantic. With MSA a newspaper published in Oman can be readily understood in Morocco. A news broadcast from Jordan will be understood in Algiers. Colloquial Arabic, on the other hand, differs from region to region. It is difficult for example, for Arabs from the Maghreb to comprehend Yemenis or Saudis or for Egyptians to understand Kuwaitis.

diverse dialects

Colloquial Arabic has no written form, and any written material will revert to MSA. The version spoken in Jordan is similar to that spoken in Syria, but different to that of Cairo. However it is close enough so that if you have any knowledge of the Egyptian, you will be understood in Jordan.

ahlan wa-sahlan!

Besides being polite to be able to speak a few words of your host's language, Jordanians will be very pleased if you know the familiar greetings in their language. Arabic is full of pleasantries and they are used in profusion, even to people you meet casually.

There are many ways to greet somebody, but whatever the greeting it is always accompanied by handshaking, or in the case of friends hugging and kissing. Each person kisses the other on each cheek. Never ask a question of anyone without first greeting them. Even if you ask in English, try to express the greeting in Arabic.

Getting by in Arabic

A good idea is to copy on a small piece of card some of the most common words you may need, keeping this in your shirt pocket. It will always be handy for quick reference. A useful addition to this is a list of the numbers used in Arabic for figuring out shop prices, bus numbers etc. (I hesitate to call them Arabic numerals because the ones we use are titled just that — though most likely they are derived from elsewhere and were simply introduced to the west by Arab scholars.)

Pronunciation

A word on pronunciation. Some sounds may be difficult to produce as we do not have them in English. In the vocabulary they are given as follows.

gh	this is like the French "r".
kh	similar to ch in Scottish "loch"
	a glottal stop similar to how butter may be pronounced by those who drop the t's, bu`er, but farther back in the throat.
H	this is a very aspirated 'h'. When making it you should feel a slight grating in your throat.
h	is almost identical to the English and always sounded with the normal "h" exhaling breath sound.

VOCABULARY

Greetings

An initial greeting and one that is frequently used is *salaam alaikum* meaning "peace be to you" the reply is made by reversing the order of words, *alaikum salaam* "to you [also] be peace".

Other common greetings are:

hello!	*marhaba* or *ahlan wa sahlan* or just *ahlan*
hello as reply	*marhabtein* or *ahlan beek* (*beeki* f)
how are you?	*kayf haalak* (*kayf haalik* f)

fine	*kwayyis* (*kwayyisa* f). (A useful word which covers fine, nice or even beautiful, eg *"Urdan kwayyisa"* – "Jordan is fine/ nice/beautiful?")
thanks be to God	*ilHamdu lillaah* is often the reply to "how are you?"
God willing	*inshallah*, an answer to everything!
goodbye	*ma'a salaama*
good morning	*sabah ilkheer*
good morning (reply)	*sabah innur* (ie "morning of light")
good evening	*masa ilkheer*

Common words and phrases

yes	*na'am* or *aiwa*
no	*la*
thank you	*shukran*
for nothing *or* you are welcome	*afwan*
please (request)	*min fadlak* (*fadlik* f)
I'm sorry	*ana `assif* (`*aaifa* f)
what is your name?	*shu ismak* (*ismik* f)
my name is...	*ismi...*
where are you from?	*min wain inta?* (*inti* f)
I am from...	*ana min...*
do you speak English?	*bititkalim* (*btitkalimi* f) *inglisi?*
I speak...	*ana bititkalim...*
how much (does it cost?)	*bikaam* or *adaish*
expensive	*ghaali*
cheap	*rakhees*
very	`*awi*
something	*Haaga*
something cheaper	*Haaga 'arkhas*
may I?, is it possible?	*mumkin*
impossible, you can't	*mish mumkin*
how many?	*kam?*
how many kms?	*kam kilometer?*
is there (any)?	**fi...?**
there is not (any)	*ma fish...*
open	*maftuuh*
closed	*musakkar*
what is this?	*shu hadha?*
big	*kabeer*
small	*sagheer*

Getting around

aeroplane	*al-tayara*
airport	*al-mataar*
bank	*bank*
bus station	*mahattat al-bas*
bus	*bas*
car	*sayyara*
church	*kaneesa*
gate	*bab*
hospital	*mustashfa*
left (direction)	*shimaal*
mosque	*jami*
petrol (gas)	*benzeen*
pharmacy	*saydaliyya*
police	*shurta*
post office	*maktab bareed*
railway station	*mahattat al-qitaar*
right	*yameen*
ruins (historical)	*khirbet*
site (historical)	*ataar*
square	*midaan*
straight on	*duughri*
street	*shari'a*

Where is King Hussein St? *wain shari'a al-Malak al-Hussein?*

tourist office	**maktab al-siyaha**
train	**qitaar**

At the hotel

breakfast	*fitar*
clean	*nardif*
dirty	*wishikh*
full	*malyaan*
hot water	*mayya sukhna*
hotel	*otel, funduq*
night	*leela*
room	*ghurfa*
shower	*doosh*
soap	*sabun*
the bill	*al-hissab*
towel	***futa, manshafa***

Food and drink

apple	*tuffaaH*
apricots	*mishmish*
bananas	*mooz*
bread	*khubz, aish*

butter	*zibda*
carrot	*gazar*
cheese	*gibneh*
coffee	*'ahwa*
egg	*beid*
fish	*samak*
fruit	*fawakeh*
juice	*'asir*
meat	*lahma*
milk	*halab*
mineral water	*mayya ma'daniyeh*
orange juice	*'asir burtu`aan*
orange	*burtu`aan*
restaurant	*mat'am*
tea	*shay*
vegetables	*khudra*
water	*mayya*
yogurt	**laban**

Time

day	*yom*
hour	*sa'a*
today	*al-yom*
tomorrow	*bukra*
week	*usbu'a*
year	*sana*
What time is it?	*assa'a kam?*
It is 3 o'clock	*assa'a talata*

Days of the week:

In Arabic the days from Sunday through Thursday are simply called "the first" through to "the fifth". Saturday is called the sabbath even though Friday is the Muslim day of rest

Sunday, *ilhadd;* Monday, *iltneen;* Tuesday, *ittalaat;* Wednesday, *ilarba';* Thursday, *ilkhamees;* Friday, *ilgum'a;* Saturday, *isabat.*

Numerals

The number always comes after the noun except in the case of "one" e.g. one night, *wahad leela;* three nights, *leela talata.*

Numbers 1-10: *wahad, itneen, talata, arba'a, khamsa, sitta, saba'a, tamanya, tisa'a, ashara.*

Numbers 11-20: *hadashar, itnaashar, talattaashar, arba'taashar, khamastaashar, sitaashar, sab'ataashar, tamantaashar, tisa'taashar, ishreen.*

273

Some fractions:

half *nuss;* quarter *ruba;* threequarters *talata ruba.*

The Arabic numerals are written as follows:

• = 0	٦ = 6
١ = 1	٧ = 7
٢ = 2	٨ = 8
٣ = 3	٩ = 9
٤ = 4	١• =10
٥ = 5	٢٥ = 25

Postscript

Gesticulations are an important part of person to person communication in the Arab world. Two of the most common:

"No" is quite often indicated by the slight throwing back of the head and lifting of the eyebrows. Such a "no" can be taken as final!
"What do you want?" is queried by an outstretched hand and a flick of the wrist. Taxi drivers often do this in the expectation that you may want to hire them, as do shopkeepers standing by their shop fronts if they think you are out shopping.

Glossary

The glossary explains the following —

♦ Architectural terms used.
♦ The various nations, dynasties, and groups of people referred to.
♦ Non-English words normally rendered in the original.

Abbreviations: **L** Latin; **Fr** Medieval French; **Gr** Greek
                     I Italian; **A** Arabic; **R** Russian

Abbasids (A)   Caliphate dynasty (750-968) centred on
                            Baghdad which succeeded the Omayyads.

Achaemenid Persians   Ancient Persian dynasty which lasted
                            from 559-330 BC. Their empire stretched
                            at one time as far west as Macedonia and
                            Libya.   Rulers included Cyrus II and
                            Xerxes.   It came to an end in 330 BC
                            when Darius III was defeated by
                            Alexander at Issus.

acropolis (Gr)   Elevated part of a Greek city.

agora (Gr)   Market and public meeting place.

aisle   The part of a basilica that lies either side
                            of the nave.

apse (L)   Curved and vaulted end of the nave in a
                            church.

aqueduct (L)   Elevated bridge-like structure for carrying
                            water.

aquifer (L)   Underground rock strata which carries
                            water.

Ayyubids (A)   The dynasty (1176-1260) founded by
                            Salah al-Din or his father.

bab (A)   Gate

basalt (L)	Hard, black volcanic rock.
basilica (L,Gr)	Building, usually a church with a central nave and an aisle each side.
bastion (Fr)	Strongpoint usually, but not necessarily, in a castle.
Bedouin (A)	Desert-dwelling Arab. In the past they were all nomadic. Now many are settled.
Byzantine (L)	That part of the Roman Empire which was ruled from Byzantium (Constantinople).
caliph (A)	Head of Islam after Muhammad. From the Arabic word *Khalifa,* meaning successor. Caliphs eventually became dynastic with no relationship to religious knowledge, and the first four were not accepted by all Muslims.
capitals (on columns)	The head of a column often decorated.
cardo maximus (L)	Main street of Roman city, usually running from north to south.
cella (L)	Sacred chamber of a temple.
citadel (It)	Fortified part of a city, often elevated.
colonnade (L)	Area flanked by columns and roofed.
corbelling	A way of laying stone and brick in which each layer projects beyond the one beneath.
Corinthian (capital) (Gr)	Column capital decorated with acanthus leaves.
cupola (L)	Dome.
decumanus (L)	Major east/west street in a Roman city.
diwan (T)	Arched reception area at one end of courtyard in Ottoman house.
Eastern Orthodox	That part of the Byzantine rite which has as its head the Byzantine Patriarch of Antioch. Often called Greek Orthodox, they use Arabic as their prayer language.

exedra (L)	Semi-circular area with seats, usually by a nymphaeum.
Fatimids (A)	A Shi'ite dynasty (970-1055) of caliphs centred on Cairo.
Franks	Name often used for the Crusaders.
frieze (Fr)	Horizontal band of decoration around a building, door or gate.
Ghassanids	An Arab Christian tribe in the Byzantine era.
Ghor	Arabic name for the Jordan Valley
glacis (Fr)	Sloping surface in front of a castle wall or tower (or even city wall) that makes it difficult to scale.
Greek Orthodox	General term for followers of the Byzantine rite of Christianity, but correctly only applies to the Orthodox Church of Greece.
hammam (T)	Turkish or Arab bath.
haremlek (T)	Family area in Ottoman house
Hasmoneans	Jewish dynasty which followed the Seleucid rule in Palestine 152-37 BC
Hospitallers, Knights of St. John	Order of (Christian) Knights who once had responsibility for taking care of pilgrims in Jerusalem. In Crusader times they became a military order.
iwan (T)	See **diwan**.
jabal (jebel) (A)	Mountain or mountain range
khan (T,A)	Inn where travellers and merchants could stay and trade in a city. Also called caravanserai but the latter term is more correctly used for inns outside cities.
khirbet (A)	Ancient ruins
Kufic (A)	Stylish Arabic script used in the early Muslim era.

lintel (Fr)   Horizontal beam (of stone) above a door.

madrasa (A)   Islamic theological school.

Mamelukes   Slave soldiers of Turkic origin who took power in 1250 in Cairo and controlled most of the region from 1260 to 1516.

mihrab (A)   Niche in wall of a mosque's prayer hall to orient worshippers towards Mecca.

minbar (A)   Pulpit in a mosque.

Mongols   Central Asian warrior people.

muhaafaza (A)   Governorate or province.

Nabateans   People from Arabia who established themselves in what is today Jordan. As they lived on the caravan routes from the east and the Red Sea they were prosperous. With the decline of the Seleucids they took control of much of southern Syria, including Bosra and Damascus. Eventually incorporated into Roman Empire. Their capital was the rock city of Petra (in southern Jordan).

narthex (Gr)   Entrance hall in an (early) church.

noria (A)   Wooden water-wheel used to lift water from a river.

nymphaeum (L)   Public water fountain, dedicated to nymphs.

Omayyads (A)   Caliphate dynasty (661-750) founded by Mu'awiya, centred on Damascus.

Ottomans   Turkish tribe centred on Anatolia. Took Constantinople in 1453 and in early 16th C all the Middle East and parts of Europe. The Ottoman Empire lasted until 1918.

portcullis (Fr,L)   Grille that can be lowered across a castle gateway to prevent entry.

portico (L,It)   Porch, or area confined within columns.

propylaeum   Monumental entranceway to a temenos.

qala'a (qala'at) (A)	Fort or castle
qasr (A)	Palace, often a fortified one.
Sasanian Persians	Persian dynasty from 224-650 AD founded by Ardashir 1. They constantly harassed the power of Rome and Byzantium. Destroyed by the Arabs in 650.
Shi'ite (A)	Muslims who supported the right of Ali, Muhammad's son-in-law, to succeed him. From the word *shia* which means faction, i.e. faction of Ali.
souk (A)	Market street or area.
stele (Gr)	Upright slab of stone with an inscription
Sunni (A)	Orthodox Muslim, i.e. not a Shi'ite.
tell (Aramaic)	Hill, usually an artificial one, made up of layers of succeeding civilisations.
temenos	Broad area in front of a temple building.
tetrapylon (Gr)	Pattern of columns marking a major street junction in a Roman/Greek city.
thermae (L)	Roman baths
Thumud (A)	Very literate and ancient Arab tribe, mentioned in the Koran.
via sacra (L)	Sacred way for pilgrims to a shrine.
vomitorium (L)	Exit and entranceway to a Roman theatre.
wadi (A)	Seasonable water course.

Bibliography

The following is a list of some interesting reading for before or after your travels. Some of the books are hard to find, but your local library should be able to help.

Seven Pillars of Wisdom, T.E. Lawrence, London, 1926 (Republished by Penguin in 1976)

Hussein of Jordan, James Lunt, Macmillan, 1989

Deities and Dolphins The Story of the Nabateans), Nelson Glueck. Cassell, 1966

Travels in Syria and the Holy Land, J.L. Burckhardt 1822. Republished by Darf, London.

East of the Jordan, Selah Merill 1881, republished by Darf London 1986.

A Crackle of Thorns, Alec Kirkbride, John Murray 1956

Treks and Climbs in the Mountains of Petra, Tony Howard. Jordan distribution Agency, Amman

Walks and Scrambles in Wadi Rum. Tony Howard and Diana Taylor, Al Kutba, Amman

The Modern History of Jordan, Kamal Salibi. B. Taurus 1993

The Story of the Arab Legion, John Bagot Glubb. London 1948

My Memoirs Completed, King Abdullah Ibn Husayn, Longman 1978

A Soldier with the Arabs, John Bagot Glubb. Hodder & Stroughton 1957

The Arab Israeli Wars, Haim Herzog, London 1982

From Abdullah to Hussein, Robert B. Satloff. Oxford Univ. Press 1994.

The Jordan Valley, Life Below Sea Level. Rami G. Khouri. Longman 1981.

Azraq — a Desert Oasis, Ryan Nelson, London 1973.

Uneasy Lies the Head, King Hussein Ibn Talal, London 1972

Herod the Great, Michael Grant, Weidenfeld and Nicolson 1971.

Search for Peace, Crown Prince Hassan Ibn Talal. Macmillan 1984

The Hashemite Kings, James Morris. Pantheon 1959

The Blood of Abraham, Jimmy Carter. Sedgwick & Jackson 1985

The World of Josephus, G.A. Williamson, Secker and Warburg 1964

The Jordanians and *The People of Jordan*, Amman 1980

Petra, Iain Browning, Chatto & Windus

Jerash, Iain Browning, Chatto & Windus

The Land of The Bible — A Historical Geography, Yohanan Aharoni, London 1974

History of the Arabs, P K Hitti, Macmillan 1970

Allah's Commonwealth A History of Islam, F E Peters, Simon & Schuster, 1973

Children of Abraham—Jews, Christians and Moslems F E Peters, Princeton University Press, 1983

Oxford Bible Atlas, H G May, Oxford University Press 1984

Index to Biblical References

Biblical quotations used in this book are from the New American Standard Bible (NASB)

Touring Index

Index to Part II (touring section). Names in capitals are main cities or sites.

NOTES